# HUMAN RESOURCE INFORMATION SYSTEMS: DEVELOPMENT AND APPLICATION

## Michael J. Kavanagh, Hal G. Gueutal, and Scott I. Tannenbaum

*State University of New York*
*at Albany*

---

### Kent Human Resource Management Series

---

Series Consulting Editor: Richard W. Beatty
*Institute of Management and Labor Relations*
*at Rutgers University*

**PWS-KENT Publishing Company**
*Boston, Massachusetts*

# PWS-KENT
## Publishing Company

20 Park Plaza
Boston, Massachusetts 02116

*Dedication*

To my wife Barbara and my sons Sean, Colin, and Timothy     M.J.K

To Meg and my parents Gretchen and Gordon     H.G.G.

To Becky and my parents Shirley and Norman     S.I.T.

*Sponsoring Editor:* Rolf A. Janke
*Assistant Editor:* Kathleen M. Tibbetts
*Production Editor:* S. London
*Interior Designer:* DeNee Reiton Skipper/Leslie Baker
*Cover Designer:* Linda Belamarich
*Manufacturing Coordinator:* Peter D. Leatherwood
*Printer and Binder:* Alpine Press, Inc./A Courier Book Company
*Cover Printer:* New England Book Components

PWS-KENT Publishing Company is a division of Wadsworth, Inc.
Printed in the United States of America
1   2   3   4   5   6   7   8   9   10—94   93   92   91   90

**Library of Congress Cataloging-in-Publication Data**
Kavanagh, Michael J.
   Human resource information systems: development and application/by Michael J. Kavanagh, Hal G. Gueutal, Scott I. Tannenbaum

   p.   cm. — (Kent human resource management series)
Includes bibliographies and index.
1. Development and application.     2. Human resource information systems.
I. Gueutal, Hal G., Tannenbaum, Scott I.   II. Title.   III. Series
HF5549.5.C67K38     1990     658.4'5dc19     89–6098

# Series Preface

I t is with considerable pride that we offer an expanded Kent Human Resource Management Series from PWS-KENT Publishing Company. The original four books on federal regulation, human resource costing, compensation, and performance appraisal were a great success, as evidenced by both academic and trade sales. We thank you for your support of this series.

The first revision of the series offered significant updating and expansion of the four original texts. We also added two new books to the series, in benefits and human resource information systems. We are currently developing new series entries in recruitment and human resource planning, and we plan to add titles in areas such as executive development, human resource strategy, and collective bargaining.

As organizations face the new competition created by global markets, deregulation, and advancing technology, they are beginning to "resize," and they are looking at human resources as a source of competitive advantage. Preparing to gain, sustain, or regain competitive advantage raises concerns over the fact that human resources are indeed an organization's most expensive and least well-managed resource. Certainly, organizations have designed and engineered systems that include specific planning and control methods and tools for material resources, financial resources, information systems, and time management. The new competition, however, recognizes the need for better utilization of human resources. Ultimately, this series is designed to have an impact on the practice of human resources in the contemporary economic environment. Implementing these approaches to solving human resource problems will be the ultimate proof of its success.

Many people have helped in the development of this important series. I would like to thank Keith O. Nave for the original idea and Wayne Barcomb for his faith to expand it; and Rolf Janke, Diane Miliotes, and Kathleen Tibbetts for their enthusiastic support of the continued revision.

*Richard W. Beatty*

# Preface

A mong the most significant changes in the field of human resources
management in the past decade has been the use of computers to develop what have become known as human resource information systems
(HRISs). This book is about that major change. With the increasing record
keeping in human resources (HR) required by statutes and laws and the
decreased cost of computer technology, HRISs are becoming an integral
part of the HR management system. However, HRISs have only begun to
appear as a topic in some human resources textbooks, and there are no texts
currently available that are devoted soley to this topic. Further, specific
training in HRISs has only recently begun for professionals in the HR field.
The major purpose of this book is to fill the void in the professional literature
regarding the topic of HRISs. As the title indicates, this book is concerned
with the development, use, and application of computer technology to the
human resources management system.

In creating this book, we really struggled—with the material, with the
field, and with each other. The important word in the previous sentence is
*we*. This book was truly an equal effort on the part of the authors. We feel
this book could not have been done without our combined efforts.

It is our strong opinion that professional education and training in
human resources management should include an understanding of the use
of computer technology in the field. We have attempted to make this book
relevant for the novice as well as the more experienced professional. Thus,
it is intended for both the traditional academic student as well as the HR

practitioner. In an academic setting, it could be used as the primary textbook in an HRIS class or as a supplement to a general HR text at either the graduate or undergraduate level. For example, we will be using this book to supplement our survey courses in HR at both the graduate and undergraduate level and as a primary text for our advanced courses in HRIS. Naturally, this book could be used in combination with the other texts in this PWS-KENT series.

We feel this book can also be used within a variety of organizational and training settings, and much of the orientation of the book is to this audience. This book could be used, for example, as part of an in-house training program or in conjunction with a professional training seminar. It could also serve as the primer for the specialist in human resources, payroll, or compensation who is involved in the development, implementation, or use of an HRIS. We hope it will help professionals in these jobs sort through the variety of vendor claims to make HR functions computer-based and result in the effective implementation and use of an HRIS.

In order to fully appreciate this book, the reader must have some knowledge of the HR field in general. It is useful, but not necessary, to have had some exposure to computer systems before reading this book. Since it is difficult to keep track of all the special jargon and terms in both the computer and HR fields, a glossary has been included at the back of the book.

The topics are arranged in a sequence that we find effective when teaching about HRISs. Thus, the novice in this field should begin with the first chapter and proceed through the book in order. The more knowledgeable reader may want to skip some of the introductory chapters and go to the later chapters on specific topics.

The style for all chapters is quite similar. The introduction to each chapter describes the topics to be covered within it, allowing the reader to find materials quickly. This also allows the more knowledgeable reader to skip chapters. Each chapter concludes with a summary and discussion questions. The discussion questions are meant to build and extend the chapter material. Finally, the notes provide a fairly comprehensive source of additional readings. This material can be used in a variety of ways. For example, the course instructor may want to assign specific additional readings from the notes or assign specific discussion questions in combination with additional readings. For in-house training programs, the notes should provide the additional sources professionals need to make their HRIS function effectively.

Throughout this book, we refer to incidents that have actually occurred in organizations in both the private and public sectors. These incidents are based on our work in the HRIS field for the past ten years. Some incidents are from formal consulting contracts, some are from field projects with our graduate students, and a large number are simply from personal interaction with other professionals in this field. Since in some cases the confidentiality of this information must be maintained, the name of the organization is not always mentioned. Obviously, when we have permission to do so, the firm is identified. The first chapter begins with three incidents drawn from our personal experiences. We try to identify real examples throughout the book to aid the reader in realizing that an HRIS can work!

Many individuals contributed in a variety of ways to provide assistance in the completion of this book, and we would like to thank them. A number of HR and systems professionals gave freely of their time and shared their insights and expertise. Our thanks to Hank Johnson, formerly with Key-Corp and currently with Deloitte, Haskins, and Sells (who also reviewed parts of the manuscript for us); Kathleen Westbrook and Pat Robinson of KeyCorp; Ellen Silberstein, Mary Ellen O'Connor, Yolanda Chard, and John Alsdorf of Pfizer; Randy Velez of McGraw-Hill; Doug Harders of The Chase Manhattan Bank; Judeth Fiala and Karen Jurman of Metropolitan Life Insurance Co.; Lynn DeLeo of the Depository Trust Company; Jack Schonhaut of American Express; Martha Glantz and Mark Howe of Matthew Bender; Cynthia Diers, past president of HRSP, Inc.; and Neil Reddington of Exxon. In addition, special thanks to Mike Mitchell, Michelle Tenzyk, Bonnie Piper, Donna Misrok, and Steve James of The Swiss Bank, who shared with us their ongoing experiences in developing their HRIS. All these people are actively involved in working with HRISs—we hope we have reflected some of their practical expertise in the book.

Richard Beatty, consulting editor for this series, provided the early encouragement for this book and stayed with us through the lengthy writing process. Others at PWS-KENT who deserve thanks are Rolf Janke and Kathy Tibbetts. Rolf provided much encouragement and guidance in the early stages of the book, and Kathy completed the awesome task of motivating and guiding us to complete it. In addition, Charles H. Fay of Rutgers University provided valuable suggestion throughout the editing and revision process. We also wish to thank Mark Rosen, Bentley College; Randall S. Schuler, New York University; Albert L. Lederer, University of Pittsburgh; Jeffrey S. Kane, University of Massachusetts-Amherst, and Carl A. Venable, the Squibb Corporation for their comments and reviews.

We would also like to thank our MBA students in our HRIS specialization, who, over the past six years, have been the sounding board for our ideas; and, most of the time, our best critics. In addition, we would like to thank Liz Berg and her project team for their excellent work on the human resource planning DSS shown in Chapter 8, the vendors and practitioners who provided sample screens and reports, and Gary Yukl, chairman of our department, for his support throughout the project.

Finally, we would like to thank our families, who provided the kind of warmth and support needed when writer's block crept in!

Michael J. Kavanagh, Hal G. Gueutal, and Scott I. Tannenbaum

# Contents

**10**   **Applications III: Payroll Systems and HRISs**   **294**

## Part IV   Future of HRISs   313

**11**   **Future Directions**   **315**

# I
# Foundations
# of HRIS

# 1

# Introduction
# and Overview

In this introductory chapter, three real-life incidents are presented to illustrate why a human resources information system (HRIS) can be useful in meeting an organization's human resources (HR) needs. Next, the history of the HR field is examined, showing how it has changed and why using an HRIS is critical to any modern organization. This provides an introduction to Chapter 3, which discusses how the necessity for an HRIS has been a function of environmental factors. Following this, the reasons HR has been one of the last functions within the organization to begin using computers in its operation are examined. The different types of computer-based HR systems that can exist within an organization and still be called an HRIS are then covered. A systems model for the operation of an organization, showing the place of the HR management system and the HRIS in relation to the larger organization and its environment, is then presented. Finally, an overview of the entire book using this model, which indicates how the various chapters relate to the model, is provided.

## Real-Life Incidents

The three incidents described below actually occurred. Rather than creating hypothetical events to illustrate points throughout this book, real-life situations are used to emphasize that HR professionals have experienced, in some cases painfully so, all the issues discussed in the development, implementation, and use of an HRIS. Thus, this book begins with three incidents drawn from personal experiences that show both the need for and value of an HRIS.

## Incident 1

The newly appointed personnel director of a health services organization employing 1,200 people got a phone call early one morning from the executive vice president. The executive vice president chairs the company's Strategic Planning Task Force. He wanted to know the current gender composition of the work force, the number of males and females currently employed by the company by job title, for use in strategic forecasting of needed personnel in the next five years. After two hours and numerous phone calls, the personnel director could not find this information. The HR department still used a manual file system for employee records, and the best information he could obtain was "guesses." Getting better figures from the payroll department or his own department would take about five days. Needless to say, the executive vice president wanted the information for his committee's meeting at 11:00 A.M. that morning and was not happy that it was unavailable. This one incident led this company to investigate and eventually purchase and implement an HRIS.

## Incident 2

The personnel director of a small manufacturing company employing 375 people had been on the job six months. The personnel department consisted of her, one assistant, and a secretary. Their annual Equal Employment Opportunity (EEO) report, required by law, was due by February 1. She began the report at the beginning of January with manual personnel records and finished the report in time; however, she estimated that it took about 80 percent of her time for the full month to complete the report. After installing an HRIS on a microcomputer, the same report took about three hours.

## Incident 3

In a strategic planning session concerned with adopting a new product line, the vice president of marketing wanted to know how many new employees, and in what departments, would be required if the company increased sales by 12 percent. He also wanted to know if the company would have to hire all new people or if they could train and transfer existing employees to higher-level jobs. In general, he was asking the kinds of questions that are handled by the HR department in their human resources forecasting program. The personnel director was unable to answer the questions and indicated that the only information they had was on the local labor market—information provided by the Chamber of Commerce. However, the personnel director assured the vice president of marketing that he could search his manual personnel files and give him an answer in about two to three weeks.

These three incidents illustrate two of the more serious problems that have historically plagued the operation of personnel offices that have only manual files on employees: no easy access to important employee information and unnecessary time spent on required reports. In the first situation, the information needed required a manual search of 1,200 employee files and was complicated by subjective determinations, such as whether the first name "Jackie" indicated a male or a female. In the second situation, one of the effects of the dramatic increase during the 1970s of the legislation requiring personnel reports, additional record-keeping and reporting responsibilities for the personnel department, is illustrated. With only manual employee records, long hours were necessary to meet the reporting requirements. In the third incident, the changed nature of the personnel function is reflected; that is, it is now tied to the strategic planning process. Increasing market share may not be possible if the additional employees needed are not available in the labor market. And, because of the manual system, the personnel director could not provide the needed information for strategic decision making in a timely fashion.

These incidents demonstrate the need for an automated or computer-based personnel system, called here a human resources information system (HRIS). Why hadn't these companies implemented an HRIS? What did the companies really need an HRIS for? How could they best develop and implement it? What are some of the problems they will encounter? What are some of the best uses for an HRIS? Where is more information on HRISs available? How is the best HRIS for the particular organization and human resources department chosen? This book is aimed at answering these and other questions. Its purpose is to aid both the novice and the professional in personnel/human resources in planning, developing, and implementing an HRIS.

The prospect of performing jobs faster is not the only motivation for developing and implementing an HRIS. Getting information and reports faster or in a more timely manner is indeed a goal of an HRIS, but not the only goal. Another major objective is improved accuracy of the information. Timely information is useless if it is inaccurate. A properly implemented and maintained HRIS will provide both more timely and more accurate HR information than a manual system. This point is stressed throughout the book because of its importance.

Because some of the systems and HR terminology used in this book will be unfamiliar to the reader, whether student or professional, a glossary of terms is included at the back of the book. Although many of these terms are defined and discussed throughout the book, the glossary will be useful as a quick reference.

In order to explain why an HRIS is appropriate for the HR function within an organization, the next two sections of this chapter cover some background material. First, to understand more clearly the recent explosion of interest in computer-based HR systems and to put these new developments in perspective, the history of the field of personnel/human resources is examined, with specific attention paid to the impact of computer technology. Then the problems HR has had in implementing computer technology are discussed.

## History of the Personnel/Human Resources Field

In this section, the coverage of the history of the development of the field of human resources in industrialized societies is not comprehensive. A detailed history is best left to other authors and texts.[1] Here, the examination of history has a more scientific and practical purpose. You must know where you have been, particularly in the HRIS field, to know better where you are going. For example, in the early stages of HRIS development, it is comforting to know that the terrible "glitches" you may have discovered in your files also exist in the files of almost every other company. The following description of the history of the HR field, particularly as it relates to computer-based systems, will help reassure you that you can do battle with the computer and win.

The history of human resources, at least in the United States, involves the evolution of the role of the personnel department from "paper pushers" to partners in the strategic planning process. A quick examination of the social and political factors over the history of industrialized society, from approximately 1915 to the present, illustrates why the various roles for the personnel function were appropriate for the time. The four historical eras depicted in Exhibit 1.1 caused important changes in the operation of the personnel function. Within each era, the HR function is described to show how the current demand for HRIS has developed.

**Exhibit 1.1**   Historical Eras in HR

| Era | Emphasis in HR |
| --- | --- |
| Pre–World War II | Reactive, caretaker activity; not part of the mainstream of business; record keeping and caretaker of employees. |
| Postwar: 1945–1960 | Importance of employee morale; personnel part of operating costs but not yet in mainstream of operations; research and development (R&D) in selection of employees; payroll automation; early applications of mainframe computers for personnel use in defense industry. |
| Social issues era: 1963–1980 | Social issues legislation changes HR; increased paperwork and reporting requirements; protector of employees; advent of MIS in computer world; introduction of IBM/360; HR now more in mainstream of operations. |
| Cost–effectiveness era: the 1980s | HR expected to cost justify activities; the increased government regulation of the 1980s increases HR role and paperwork; advent of microcomputer and HR software explosion; HRIS capabilities lower in cost, thus affordable by smaller firms; HR becomes part of the business strategy process; increased emphasis on the R&D for HR, particularly utility analysis. |

## Pre–World War II

Prior to the mid-1940s, the personnel function was primarily a reactive, caretaker activity that involved little more than "paper pushing." Personnel was not part of the mainstream of business activity for the firm, and its main concern was keeping accurate employee records, particularly for payroll. Because the major emphasis in management was on the increased efficiency/productivity of employees, much of the applied personnel research involved pay plans and industrial engineering projects. Personnel was the "caretaker" of employees and, thus, the office for employee complaints and problems. This caretaker activity of Personnel, particularly in terms of employee records, continues to the present. There was no significant automation of either the personnel or payroll functions, simply because the technology did not exist.

## Postwar: 1945–1960

The lessons from the war experience, both in personnel classification and the importance of individual morale, impacted both research and practice in the personnel field. The recognition that an effective personnel administration could impact the operating efficiency and profitability of the firm led to an enlarged role for the personnel department. There was an increased awareness that the costs of human resources were a significant part of a company's operating cost; and by controlling these costs, the company could be more competitive in the marketplace. Further, the importance of employee morale and, consequently, the increased use of employee attitude and opinion polls, added another responsibility to the personnel department. The lessons from the wartime experience in personnel selection and placement also led to an increased emphasis in this area. Thus, programs of personnel research and development (R&D) began to appear within many organizations.

Personnel continued to be the caretaker of employee records. In fact, the records were now increasing in size due to the introduction of employee selection and classification systems, attitude surveys, and R&D efforts, particularly in larger firms. Thus, the role of Personnel changed and expanded. Management began to be aware that personnel programs could affect the operating efficiency of the firm and began to request specific personnel programs. At this point Personnel was not yet in the mainstream of the company's operation but, rather, still in a service function, responding to requests from management. Personnel, despite its increased role and the increased amount of record keeping it was responsible for, still primarily reacted to management. However, rather than having only the limited caretaker and bookkeeping functions that Personnel performed prior to the war, the personnel department now had multiple functions—taking care of employee records, conducting employee attitude surveys, and doing research on better selection and placement of employees. This trend toward increased responsibilities for the human resources function has continued.

Alfred Walker, in his historical account of the use of computers in the field of personnel, describes the immediate period after World War II as primarily concerned with payroll automation.[2] The personnel information kept was limited to items needed to support the payroll function. These automated records were little more than name, salary, date of birth, and other personal information. However, with the tremendous growth of the computer industry in the late 1950s and early 1960s, some organizations began to apply the power of computer systems to the personnel function. Because of the large number of employees within the defense industry, there was a compelling need to use new computer technology to help keep track of them all more efficiently than was possible with manual systems. Also, firms (contractors) that did business with the Department of Defense found the new computer technology useful. Using computer-based skills inventories on employees proved quite useful in submitting competitive bids for government contracts. The firm's proposal would identify the people skills necessary for a given project, and the computer could be used to search for employees of the firm that possessed the required skills. These employees would then be identified as the project team for the proposed work.

Within the military R&D laboratories, computer technology opened the possibility for large-scale job analysis and classification. Perhaps the largest and most significant of these efforts in terms of occupational surveys of enlisted positions was within the U.S. Air Force at the **Air Force Human Resources Laboratory (AFHRL)**.[3] These scientific efforts at describing jobs within the Air Force not only established the most effective and comprehensive approach to job analysis yet attempted but clearly identified the tremendous power and impact that the use of computers could have in personnel. The AFHRL distributed thousands of task inventories to airmen in all the enlisted jobs in the Air Force. Through the use of computers and statistical software, called the Comprehensive Occupational Data Analysis Programs (CODAP), these data were analyzed to identify different jobs within the U.S. Air Force. This led to a comprehensive occupational structure. These task inventories and

CODAP are still used annually for selected jobs to update them or to identify new jobs. Before the AFHRL survey, occupational classification was done manually, and, thus, most job descriptions were out-of-date and inaccurate. The use of computers in occupational analysis in the Air Force showed the power of computers to identify clusters of tasks and form them into jobs. This task inventory and clustering approach using computer analyses is a major methodology still used for job analysis in both the public and private sectors.

As Walker notes, personnel departments outside the defense industry had little use for computers at this time.[4] Most of the computer programmers were in departments outside Personnel. Data processing resources were used in accounts receivable, order processing, inventory control, and other areas of business that dealt directly with cost data. Remember that computer technology was in its infant stage at this time and was very difficult and costly to use. Professional programmers were a scarce commodity and, unlike today, little commercial software was available. This meant that all computer-based analyses had to be tailored to specific problems, and specific programs (and computer system code) had to be developed for each problem. Given these facts, it is no wonder that most firms did not use computers in Personnel other than in the payroll function. This avoidance of computer-based systems within Personnel has had long-term effects on the HR function, such as a reluctance of personnel departments to adopt new computer technology as it became cheaper and easier to use.

Of greater importance for HRISs in today's firms was the early development of a computer-based payroll function. Considering the early computer technology, it is apparent why payroll was the first personnel program to be automated. First, remember that payroll was part of the personnel function; in many firms today it still is. Second, early computer technology was crude by today's standards; however, it operated best with numbers, and payroll is primarily numbers. Third, and most important, the payroll function provided the cost information on people in the firm's operation. These payroll costs were critical in determining the price of goods or services provided by the firm and impacted directly on profit. It is not surprising that top management wanted payroll to be computer based. In calculating crucial dollar-based indices for stockholders, a computer-based system in payroll to calculate employee costs was critical.

For the human resources function, the introduction of the computer first in payroll had both positive and negative effects. On the positive side, it began the introduction of computers to account for the people costs in organizations, a trend that has become a reality in most firms today. It also recognized that people, as well as fiscal and material resources, are important in the operating efficiency of any organization. On the negative side, the computer systems developed for payroll were not concerned with the other needs of the personnel department. In fact, many companies separated payroll from Personnel. Computer-based systems for payroll were made part of the operations department or put in the data processing (DP) department. Thus, most subsequent attempts to build an HRIS have had to deal with an established computer-based payroll system. This has led to interdepartmental conflicts (HR versus Operations/DP/MIS), a problem that remains even today.

In sum, personnel departments at this point in history were getting increased responsibilities, but the computer was not being widely used outside the payroll function. The exception to the use of the computer in personnel was in the defense industry, and that was primarily in terms of job analysis only.

### Social Issues Era: 1963–1980

This time frame, in terms of its importance to the human resources function, is difficult to describe in a single phrase. So much was going on in the field of personnel, the world, and computer technology that impacted the state of today's HR departments that simplistic phrases cannot adequately describe this time. However, for simplicity's sake, the dominant theme of this era is conveyed using the term *social issues*. The reasons for this choice will become apparent as this historical era is discussed.

Perhaps the most important aspect of this era that affected human resources was the volume of legislation aimed at social issues in the workplace. The major thrust of legislation in the 1960s was aimed at prohibiting unfair discrimination in all HR practices through Title VII of the Civil Rights Act of 1964 and other regulations and laws. The regulatory influence of federal legislation increased in the 1970s with the Occupational Safety and Health Act (OSHA), the Age Discrimination in Employment Act (ADEA), the Employee Retirement Income Security Act (ERISA), and tax regulation. In addition to legislation, there were numerous executive orders that had to be followed by any firms with government contracts. And, most important, court cases were being decided, with punitive damages in terms of fines, that further defined the provisions of the laws.[5]

The net result of these government influences was that Personnel was given the task of compliance with all regulations. As the early court cases revealed, the most serious deficiency in most firms was a lack of records. The immediate response was that in order to comply with government regulations, the record-keeping function of Personnel had to be greatly increased. The legislation and executive orders all had required reports, most of which were extremely time-consuming, particularly for personnel departments with manual systems only. Recall the personnel director's dilemma with the EEO report described in Incident 2 at the beginning of this chapter. Keep in mind that all the legislation had similar reporting requirements.

In addition to the increased paperwork requirements, the role of Personnel changed in other ways during this time. Instead of being concerned with limited employment functions within a caretaker model, Personnel's responsibilities expanded to include multiple functions. Because the regulations regarding unfair discrimination applied to all employment functions, Personnel had to be actively involved in areas in which it had previously held only a minor role, such as promotions, pay equity, and terminations. This led Personnel to take a more active role in protecting employees' welfare. Naturally, this increased the cost of the personnel function and caused firms to pay more attention to their human assets, since the costs of litigation were affecting the "bottom line" of operating costs. As a result, the term *human resources* began to be introduced, and many personnel departments were renamed Human Resources. This greater awareness of the costs of human resources led to increased research activities, further expanding the role and functions of the traditional personnel department.

Things were also happening in the computer world at this time that would impact HR. The rigid, stand-alone computer programs and systems developed during the 1950s and early 1960s resulted in redundant data collection and information storage. The notion of better storage and uses of information led to the advent of management information system (MIS) thinking. This coincided with the introduction of the IBM/360 line and, subsequently, other large-scale commercial machines. No longer were informational needs and data processing hindered by limited computer processing. Unfortunately, as Walker notes, most personnel departments were slow to adopt the progress made in the computer field.[6] As he notes, early computers and computer software for Personnel were quite costly. Further, projects to include Personnel in an all-encompassing MIS were simply too large for most companies. However, as paperwork requirements grew and computer costs started falling in the late 1970s, more firms began to investigate and adopt HRISs.

## Cost-Effectiveness Era: The 1980s

The trend toward lower costs for computer-based HR systems in the late 1970s continued into the 1980s. More important, the microcomputer explosion began. At the same time, HR departments were coming under increasing pressure to process employee records more efficiently, and government regulations continued to increase paperwork and information requirements [e.g., the advent of 401(k) retirement plans and the passage of the Comprehensive Omnibus Budget Reconciliation Act (COBRA) and Section 89 of the Tax Reform Act of 1986].[7] Of course, this additional legislation, added to that from the previous era, only increased the pressure from the external environment on the HR management system. (This environmental pressure is discussed in detail in Chapter 3.) Furthermore, during this era advances in HR research, such as utility analysis applied to selection,[8] and techniques to estimate the costs of human resources,[9] provided the tools to attach dollar values to HR programs.

The net effect of these developments was an emphasis on cost-effectiveness in the HR function of the firm. With the advent of the microcomputer and the software explosion for HR total computer-based systems and specific applications, the costs of technology acquisition dramatically decreased—a trend that continues today. Meanwhile, HR costs have continued to increase. The joint effect of decreasing costs of computer technology for the HR function with increasing costs of employee salary and benefits from 1950 to 2000 is shown in Exhibit 1.2. As indicated in Exhibit 1.2, computer technology in the 1950s and 1960s was quite expensive compared to personnel costs. With the increased demand on HR for required government reports in the 1970s and 1980s, as well as increasing salary and benefits, the acquisition of computer technology, with lower costs, became extremely cost-effective.

There have been three major implications for the HR function during the cost-effectiveness era. The first is the availability of computer-based HR systems for smaller companies. In the 1970s, HRIS software existed primarily for mainframe environments and required professional computer expertise to implement and maintain. Companies could either acquire this software for their mainframe or build their own HRIS. In either case, the costs were high. These high costs meant that only larger companies could afford investing in an HRIS. With software that requires very little programming knowledge now available for the microcomputer, developing and implementing an HRIS is feasible for smaller companies. For example, it is

**Exhibit 1.2**   Relation of Computer and Human Costs from 1950 to 2000

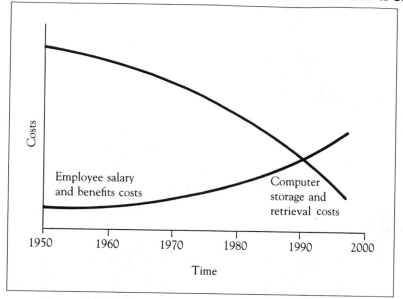

*Source:* Adapted from the Association of Human Resource Systems Professionals, HRSP 101–Introduction to Human Resource Information Systems Seminar. Reproduced by permission.

now possible to purchase a software-hardware configuration for a company of 500 employees for approximately $15,000 to $25,000, as contrasted with $250,000 to $500,000 in the 1970s.

The second major implication for HR during this cost-effectiveness era has been the involvement of HR in strategic planning for the firm. As seen in recent publications, HR professionals have become equal partners in an attempt to integrate business and human resources planning.[10] This is not the only function of a modern HR department, however. It still retains the many functions discussed in conjunction with the earlier historical eras, such as record keeping, caretaker, and employee protector.

The third major implication has been an increase in funding of research efforts, particularly in costing human resources. Firms have realized the value of their human resources and have become aware of the applied research on establishing cost-effectiveness in the HR function.[11] This has caused HR to shift from a reactive to a more proactive stance. Thus, HR has begun to be involved as a new-program developer. By focusing on cost-effectiveness, HR departments have been able to convince management of the feasibility and profitability of developing and implementing new programs. Again, HR is still involved in reactive activities, particularly compliance with new legislation and court decisions.

## HRIS Development: Why the Delay?

Given the increased record-keeping requirements and reduced costs of computer technology relative to increased human resources costs, the obvious question is, Why have HR departments been so slow in developing and implementing HRISs? Although recent surveys have shown an increase in the use of computer-based HR systems, this increase has only occurred in the past few years.[12] Further, from these surveys it is obvious that a large number of companies and public agencies, particularly those of medium size, have not yet installed HR computer systems.

There are several reasons for the slowness of HR departments to install an HRIS, and they are similar to the reasons Fitz-enz gives for the reluctance HR departments exhibit in conducting cost-benefit analyses for their activities.[13] Namely, HR professionals are poorly trained to use the HRIS and many, in fact, resist computerization because they are defensive about their operations. The lack of training in HRIS for HR professionals is one of the reasons for this book. The latter reason, defensiveness, unfortunately has led HR operations to become a secret to most operational managers; and, as a result, it is simple for these managers to blame most of their "people problems" on the HR department, whether deserving or not.

Considering the history of human resources just reviewed, there is no reason for HR professionals to be ashamed of their lack of progress, since their management objectives have usually been set by people outside the HR function. Thus, in examining the reason for the slowness of HR departments in adopting computer-based systems, keep in mind these contextual forces. The current ease of using many computers should be an incentive for HR professionals to overcome their fears of computers, if they have any, and make the effort to learn to use them as tools. A major theme of this book for HR professionals is, Why leave the whole arena and advantages of computer-based systems to people outside the HR department?

Given the current ease of using many computers, the question still remains, Why are HR departments still so slow in adopting the technology?

The primary reasons for the slowness of HR departments to adopt computer-based systems follow:

1. *Lack of support by top management.* Often cited as a reason for slowness in implementing new HR programs, this is probably the major organizational reason that HR departments do not implement an HRIS. Since top management cannot see an immediate and direct relationship between HR functions and profit (profit margin), as they can with capital and fiscal resources, they find investing in an HRIS a low priority. As a major lesson from this book, HR managers should remember this initial problem; and, when a proposal for an HRIS is presented, make sure a cost-benefit analysis, as discussed in Chapters 5 and 6, is completed.

2. *Satisfaction with the status quo.* When offered the opportunity to have a computer-based human resources system, many HR managers respond that it is not needed since they are doing just fine with their current manual system. This is one of the strongest arguments against computerizing the HR function within an organization. The question is clear: "Why bother? We are already meeting the needs of management." Further, the development of an HRIS involves a great deal of tedious work, frequently with no additional staff to handle it. However, the payoffs for the additional effort required to develop and implement an HRIS are worth it. It is the responsibility of the HR manager to recognize these payoffs and help overcome the resistance to change.

3. *Defensiveness about revealing HR operations.* Some HR managers are defensive about revealing their operations, and a computer-based system can indeed make their operations more public. Tied to this defensiveness is a real fear of losing ownership of the HR function by distributing HR products to line managers. If line managers have these products and the capability to request ad hoc reports from the HRIS, then there is a fear that HR will become unnecessary. Although this type of HR manager is probably becoming obsolete, a semblance of these feelings still remains, which increases the initial resistance to the development of an HRIS. By a careful needs analysis and cost justification, these defensive feelings should be assuaged. HR managers will learn how they can become better partners with line managers in the management of the firm's human resources.

4. *Lack of HRIS knowledge and skills.* In terms of individual training and preparation, most HR managers and professionals are poorly prepared to develop and implement an HRIS. With a few exceptions, to be discussed

later in this chapter, professional education and training in human resources does not include an HRIS component. HRIS as a topic has only recently begun to appear in textbooks, and training programs in HRIS began only in 1980.

# Types of HRISs and Terminology

Before turning to the model of an organization that integrates business strategy, human resources, and HRISs within its environmental context, some basic information systems terminology will be covered to assist in future chapters. As depicted in Exhibit 1.3, there are three major types of computer-based HR systems—EDP, MIS, and DSS.[14] These three types are located on a continuum of relative activity by users, ranging from storage files at one end to interactive decision systems at the other. This activity continuum has two attributes: level and ease of use. Computer-based HR systems on the left side typically have lower levels of activity and are more difficult to use; those on the right side have the opposite characteristics.

**Exhibit 1.3    Types of Computer-Based HR Systems**

### User Activity Continuum

*Inactive* ←——————————————→ *Active*

| **EDP** | **MIS** | **DSS** |
|---|---|---|
| Data and files storage | Information retrieval | Interactive for user |
| Transaction processing | Analyzing data | "What if" analyses |
| Summary reports transactions | Inquiry and report generation | Generation of decision alternatives |

*Note:*  EDP—electronic data processing; MIS—management information system; DSS—decision support system.

This continuum does *not* imply differences in importance. An electronic data processing (EDP) payroll file can be as important as a decision support system (DSS). Although three discrete types of systems are shown in Exhibit 1.3, combinations of these particular types can occur within a single firm. Further, there may be types within a company that can be classified between the types listed in Exhibit 1.3 in terms of activity levels. Exhibit 1.3 is meant to provide a starting point for understanding the various configurations of computer-based HR systems, not an absolute classification scheme. Chapter 2 defines an HRIS in much greater detail.

The three types in Exhibit 1.3 are based on the distinctions made among information systems for organizations by Sprague and Carlson.[15] Their definitions of the three types of information systems are reviewed as a way of understanding the systems' applications to computer-based HR systems.

## EDP Level

Sprague and Carlson define **electronic data processing (EDP)** as the automated processing of routine information. Its first application is to automate paperwork at the lower operational level of the organization. Its focus is on data, storage, processing, and flows at the operational level. An EDP system for Human Resources performs similar functions. However, because the EDP system for HR normally resides on a mainframe computer and is controlled by another department, such as a computer center, it may not be accessible or appropriate for the demands of all HR department users. The most common files found in an EDP system are payroll and basic personnel information on employees. These tend to be the first manual or paper files to be automated since employees must be paid accurately and on time. Unfortunately, as discussed in Chapters 5 and 10, this creates problems for the HR department, since computer files created for other organizational functions and departments do not usually meet the needs of the HR department.

## MIS Level

The second type of information system defined by Sprague and Carlson is the **management information system (MIS)**, which changed the focus of information system activities from the EDP level to emphasis on the integration and planning of the information systems function.[16] They further define MIS as having an information focus, being aimed at middle managers, and having inquiry and report-generation capabilities. As shown in Exhibit 1.3, an MIS for Human Resources performs similar functions, except that its focus is on HR information. Typical uses of this type of a system would be EEO and other government reports as well as time and attendance and turnover reports. It can also support ad hoc reports such as age and gender distributions of employees.

In this book a distinction between "dead end" reports that are simply filed and reports used as aids in decision making is made. These latter types of reports focus on analyses against expected values. They provide managers with reports on variances, particularly negative ones, from expected operations. An example of this for line managers would be an overtime report that shows variances from projected overtime to meet operating costs. In the HR area, an example would be the EEO compliance report, both in terms of initial hires and promotion rates of protected minorities. These reports use mathematical and statistical models to determine compliance with expected operational directions. They can be used to alert decision makers of the need for some action, thus the term *decision aids*. This distinction between reports is discussed in more detail in Chapter 2.

## DSS Level

The third type of information system described by Sprague and Carlson is the **decision support system (DSS)**.[17] It focuses on decisions made at a higher level in the organization, usually by top managers and executives. It is an interactive system, capable of analysis through the use of models and able to answer "what if" questions concerning decision alternatives. A DSS for Human Resources, as shown in Exhibit 1.3, performs these same functions, again being concerned with HR information. An example of this type of system would be in human resources planning (HRP), with a computer-based system capable of examining future scenarios regarding how an organization can continue to attract and recruit effective employees from the labor market. The DSS in HRP would be able to answer "what if" questions about the future staffing of the firm and the availability of human resources. These were the kind of questions being raised in Incident 3 at the beginning of this chapter. A specific application is covered in Chapter 8.

## Combinations

One final note concerning the types of computer-based HR systems shown in Exhibit 1.3. As indicated earlier, all types could exist within a single organization. In fact, this is a desirable goal for HR departments. However, an effective HRIS cannot be built without a complete and accurate EDP system in HR. Likewise, it would be difficult to build an effective DSS without having developed the other two types. The reasons for this should be obvious. In order to have an accurate DSS, the EDP system and MIS must also be accurate. The MIS develops the summarization, called aggregation, rules of data to apply to the EDP system to produce reports.

# Systems Model
# of Organizational Functioning

In order to understand the need for and the value of an HRIS in an organization, it is important to recognize the interrelatedness of the various parts that comprise the functioning of an organization. Exhibit 1.4 depicts a model of organization functioning that, as will be apparent, is consistent with both the managerial literature and the chapters of this book. This exhibit illustrates the interrelatedness of the activities among the HR management system, the strategic management system, the HRIS, the external environment, and the goals of the organization. Several features of Exhibit 1.4 make it appealing for both better understanding the HR function and as a basis for developing an HRIS.

## HR Management System

Exhibit 1.4 shows the HR management system, which is covered more fully in Chapter 2, as comprised of the integration between the various HR subfunctions and the HRIS. Although most authors of HR texts have their own classification scheme for the entire HR field, the six **HR subfunctions** in Exhibit 1.4 were chosen for this book for two reasons: (1) they represent the breadth of human resources in both the literature and practice, and (2) these six subfunctions are used to categorize the HRIS applications in Chapters 8 and 9.

**Exhibit 1.4**   Systems Model of Organizational Functioning

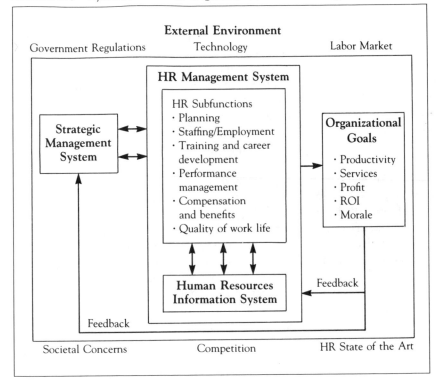

## *Relationship to Strategic Management System*

The second important feature of Exhibit 1.4 is the relationship of the HR management system to the strategic management system. The strategic management system integrates the information from various functional departments of the organization, such as Human Resources, Marketing, Finance, R&D, and Production, into a corporate or business strategy. This process and the resultant strategy, though beyond the purposes of this book, have received considerable attention in the managerial literature.[18] What is important, as noted in the discussion of HR in the 1980s earlier in this chapter, is that HR has become an important player in the strategic management process.[19]

## Organizational Goals

The third aspect of Exhibit 1.4 that is relevant to the effective function-ing of the organization is the role of organizational goals. The selection of various goals such as productivity, services, profit, return on investment (ROI), and morale recognizes the importance of managing *all* the organiza-tion's resources—human, fiscal, and material. More important, the feedback loops show that organizational performance drives the total system for both strategic and HR systems. In terms of the strategic management process, this means that feedback indicating a failure to meet expected goals, as defined by the overall strategy, will result in adjustments to either make the strategy work or revise it.

In like manner, this happens with the HR management system. This is an important perspective not just for using an HRIS but for the opera-tion of any HR department. This perspective means the various personnel programs must be judged in terms of their impact on some measure of orga-nizational performance. Thus, when an expected level of performance based on expectations from HR activities is not attained, this feedback indicates that the HR programs, the HRIS, or both need reexamination. For exam-ple, if a supervisory training program is designed to improve performance in a selected activity, such as completing performance appraisals on time, the actual performance of supervisors after the training program would determine the effectiveness of the training program.

This focus on performance as the criterion also means that all changes to the HR management system must be evaluated in terms of their impact on performance. For example, the introduction and use of a new recruiting program must be evaluated by the improvement in performance of new hires. Similarly, the implementation of a new HRIS must eventually meet the test of improved performance, a topic covered in Chapter 7.

## Environmental Envelope

The fourth important aspect of Exhibit 1.4 is that organizations func-tion within an environmental envelope. The factors in this envelope—government regulations, technology, the labor market, societal concerns, competition, and the HR state of the art—are discussed in Chapter 3 as they relate to the influence of the external environment on the develop-ment of an HRIS. However, these factors can also impact the HR man-agement system, the strategic management system, and the organizational goals. Although other environmental factors such as international competition, currency exchange rates, and forecasting economic trends may also affect the strategic management process, they are not the focus of this book.

## System Theory Parameters

The final important feature of Exhibit 1.4 is its configuration as a *system* of information flow within an organization, as indicated by the arrows. This means that the HR management system has general system theory properties or parameters, which are useful in determining its effectiveness.[20] These parameters can be used to analyze an existing HR system as well as design a new HR system. For the development and implementation of an HRIS, the following four general parameters are important: (1) structure, (2) process, (3) boundary, and (4) human.

**Structure**   Perhaps the best description of the structure parameter comes from the work of Lawrence and Lorsch on differentiation and integration.[21] The amount of differentiation in the structure of an organization, or of a department such as Human Resources, is a function of the number of environmental and internal demands on the organization. Thus, a department with a diverse and large number of demands would require considerable differentiation or diversity. However, this required differentiation must be controlled, and this is accomplished by the integration or connectedness among the parts.

The HR management system depicted in Exhibit 1.4 requires a considerable amount of both differentiation and integration. In terms of HRIS design, this means that the various HR programs must exist as separate units or, in systems terms, modules. This allows the HR management system to serve diverse and specialized needs. However, the requirement for integration means there must be computer-based systems to interconnect the HR programs. This provides consistency of information, prevents duplication of effort, and helps avoid conflicts between modules. This aspect of the HRIS is covered in more detail in Chapters 4, 5, 6, 8, and 9.

**Process**   The process parameter means that the HR management system in Exhibit 1.4 operates on input to produce output. Several aspects of the process parameter have a potential impact on an HRIS. The first is termed *self-reflexivity*, which refers to the capability of a system to provide feedback and direction for correcting problems. This is a critical design feature of an HRIS. Computer-based messages that indicate to the user when incorrect entries or data are being entered or used in a HR report must be included. The HRIS should alert the user and provide directions for correcting the errors. For example, only certain entries should be valid for basic personal information on each employee. Assuming the ages 16 to 65 are allowable for hourly employees, an operator who tried to enter an age of an employee outside this range would receive an error message with instructions to recheck the entry.

The second aspect of the process parameter for HRIS design is *innovativeness*. This means that the system must allow innovative solutions to problems. As most HR professionals recognize, the most frequently requested HR report is usually an ad hoc one. This type of report is one for which a standard report does not exist within the software of the HRIS. Most HRIS software contains a number of standard reports, for example, the EEO report. An example of an ad hoc report would be a request for the number of male and female employees with a certain level of job experience at a given salary level. The HRIS must be capable of handling these ad hoc reports, that is, be high on innovativeness. This design feature is discussed again in Chapters 8 and 9.

**Boundary**   The third system parameter is boundary. This system parameter defines the system's linkages and sensitivity to systems outside itself. Part of this is the linkage between the HR management system, the strategic management system, and organizational goal performance within the organization. As discussed earlier in the chapter, this linkage has become increasingly important as organizations seek to tie staffing and development plans to long-range strategic planning. The second aspect of this boundary parameter relates to the environment external to the total organization, as discussed earlier.

**Human**   The final system parameter, human, means that the system will be operated by humans. In terms of HRIS design, this means human factors must be included in its development and implementation. This refers not just to the traditional "user friendly" factors of computer-based design, such as ease of use, documentation, and physical characteristics of the system, but also to the human issues raised by the introduction and implementation of a major technological change. For example, are employees going to resist the temptation of the new system for fear of losing their jobs, of being replaced by machines? The human issues for HRIS design are covered in Chapter 7.

# Needed Skills for HRIS Work and Plan of the Book

Our experience in the design and delivery of an HRIS specialization within an MBA curriculum has helped clarify for us the knowledge and skills that are needed by HR professionals in HRIS.[22] In addition to being current on recent developments in human resources, the professional working in an HRIS function must have skills and knowledge in the following areas: (1) a systems view of HR and its relation to its environment; (2) systems concepts as they apply within an HR context; (3) management skills in designing and justifying an HRIS; (4) computer skills in understanding the interface between computer technology and HR functions; and (5) an understanding of the future of the HRIS field. The structure of this book generally follows these skills and knowledges.

## Section I: Chapters 1–3

The first section of the book, Chapters 1, 2, and 3, lays the foundation for understanding the changes that have led to the development and importance of HRISs in human resources. The internal aspects of a systems and strategic view for the HR function were covered earlier in this chapter. Chapter 2 describes the basics of an HRIS. Chapter 3 details the important relationships between the internal system and the external environment.

## Section II: Chapters 4–7

The second part of this book introduces systems and management skills needed to develop an HRIS. Chapter 4 borrows systems ideas and concepts from the MIS literature and applies them within an HR context to describe the systems development process for an HRIS. Chapters 5, 6, and 7 extend the discussion of systems ideas in more detail relative to designing and implementing an HRIS. The importance of involving all the users and stakeholders of the HRIS in the various stages of the system needs, design and development, and implementation and evaluation is highlighted in these chapters.

### Section III: Chapters 8–10

The third section, on human resources management applications, emphasizes the interfaces between computer technology and the HR function.

This is done in Chapters 8 and 9 by discussing and demonstrating specific computer-based application uses within the HR subfunctions listed in Exhibit 1.4. Commercially available software for HRIS use is also covered. Chapter 10 concludes this section by covering the important interface between the HRIS and payroll systems.

### Section IV: Chapter 11

The final section of this book discusses future directions in the HRIS field. Chapter 11 discusses some of the crucial applied research issues as well as the technological and practical developments that are now emerging that will significantly impact the HRIS field.

## Summary

This chapter has provided an introduction to the field of HRIS. Through an examination of the history of the HR field in relation to that of computer technology, the importance of the development of an HRIS in current personnel departments was emphasized. The reasons for the reluctance of personnel departments to develop and use an HRIS were highlighted to help explain why these departments have been so slow, compared to other departments such as payroll, in adopting computer technology. The different types of computer-based HR systems were discussed as an introduction to Chapter 2. Finally, a systems model for the operation of an organization was examined in Exhibit 1.4, and this model provided a structure for the overview of the entire book.

## Discussion Questions

1. What were the major periods of HR development? How was the computer involved in each stage?
2. What do you believe was the most important reason that HR was slow to adopt HRISs?

3. What are the major subfunctions of HR management?
4. Why might some HR professionals resist automating the HR function?
5. What are some practical examples of the four systems parameters in terms of the HR function in an organization?

## Notes

1. For example, see Chapter 2 in W. F. Cascio, *Managing Human Resources: Productivity, Quality of Work Life, Profits,* 2nd ed. (New York: McGraw-Hill, 1989).
2. A. J. Walker, "A Brief History of the Computer in Personnel," *Personnel Journal* 16 (1980): 33–36; A. J. Walker, *HRIS Development: A Project Team Guide to Building an Effective Personnel Information System* (New York: Van Nostrand Reinhold, 1982), 5.
3. R. E. Christal, *The United States Air Force Occupational Research Project* (Lackland Air Force Base, TX: AFHRL-TR-73-75, AD-774 574, Air Force Human Resources Laboratory, 1974); R. E. Christal and J. J. Weissmuller, *New CODAP Programs for Analyzing Task Factor Information* (Lackland Air Force Base, TX: AFHRL-TR-76-3, AD-A026 121, Air Force Human Resources Laboratory, 1976).
4. Walker, *HRIS Development,* 5.
5. J. Ledvinka, *Federal Regulation of Personnel and Human Resource Management* (Boston: PWS-Kent, 1982); D. P. Twomey, *Equal Employment Law,* 2nd ed. (Cincinnati: South-Western, 1990).
6. Walker, *HRIS Development,* 7.
7. For further information on the impact of these laws on compensation and benefits, see R. M. McCaffery, *Employee Benefits Programs: A Total Compensation Perspective* (Boston: PWS-Kent, 1988), and M. J. Wallace, Jr. and C. H. Fay, *Compensation Theory and Practice* (Boston: PSW-KENT, 1988).
8. F. L. Schmidt, J. E. Hunter, and K. Pearlman, "Assessing the Economic Impact of Personnel Programs on Workforce Productivity," *Personnel Psychology* 35 (1982): 333–347.
9. W. F. Cascio, *Costing Human Resources: The Financial Impact of Behavior in Organizations,* 2nd ed. (Boston: PWS-KENT, 1987).
10. L. Dyer, "Studying Strategy in Human Resource Management: An Approach and an Agenda," *Industrial Relations* 23 (1984): 156–169; A. O. Manzini and J. D. Gridley, *Integrating Human Resources and Strategic Business Planning* (New York: AMACOM, 1986).
11. Cascio, *Costing Human Resources.*
12. M. J. Kavanagh, H. G. Gueutal, and S. I. Tannenbaum, "Government: Who Needs an HRIS?" *Computers in Personnel* 2 (Fall 1987): 40–43; M. Magnus

and M. Grossman, "Computers and the Personnel Department," *Personnel Journal* 58 (April 1985): 42–48; J. A. Verdin, "Up and Down the HRIS Career Ladder," *Computers in Personnel* (Spring 1987): 35–39.

13. J. Fitz-enz, *How to Measure Human Resources Management* (New York: McGraw-Hill, 1984).
14. R. H. Sprague and E. D. Carlson, *Building Effective Decision Support Systems* (Englewood Cliffs, NJ: Prentice-Hall, 1984), 16–20.
15. Ibid., 4–10.
16. Ibid., 6–10.
17. Ibid., 7.
18. For example, see W. F. Glueck, *Business Policy and Strategic Management* (New York: McGraw-Hill, 1980); R. E. Miles and C. C. Snow, *Organizational Strategy, Structure and Processes* (New York: McGraw-Hill, 1978), 7–10.
19. See note 10 above.
20. For a discussion of general system theory in terms of a HR model, see M. A. Von Glinow, M. J. Driver, K. Brousseau, and J. B. Prince, "The Design of a Career Oriented Human Resource System," *The Academy of Management Review* 8 (1983): 23–32.
21. P. R. Lawrence and J. W. Lorsch, *Organization and Environment* (Cambridge, MA: Graduate School of Business Administration, Harvard University, 1967).
22. H. G. Gueutal, S. I. Tannenbaum, and M. J. Kavanagh, "Where to Go for an HRIS Education," *Computers in Personnel* 2(3) (1988): 22–25.

# 2

# What Is an HRIS?

What is an HRIS? Does a computer and "some good software" constitute an HRIS? What does a typical HRIS do? Who uses an HRIS? In this chapter these questions are addressed. A human resources information system is defined, and its interfaces with other systems are considered. The reporting and analysis capabilities of an HRIS are then examined. Next, an overview of the modules of a typical HRIS is given. The chapter concludes with a discussion of the user groups that may rely on the HRIS for information and decision-making support.

## Defining an HRIS

A **human resources information system (HRIS)** is the system used to acquire, store, manipulate, analyze, retrieve, and distribute pertinent information regarding an organization's human resources. An HRIS is not simply computer hardware and associated HR-related software. Although an HRIS includes hardware and software, it also includes people, forms, policies and procedures, and data. The purpose of the HRIS is to provide service, in the form of information, to the "clients," or users, of the system. Because there are a variety of potential users, the focus of that information may be to facilitate or support strategic, tactical, and operational decision making (e.g., to compare compensation strategy alternatives), to avoid litigation (e.g., to identify discrimination patterns), to evaluate programs, policies, or practices (e.g., to monitor the cost of sick leave policy), and/or to support daily operations (e.g., to remind of pay increases and to make sure that people are paid on time). Regardless of the purpose of the information, the data must be accurate and timely and the user needs must be understood. This theme is emphasized throughout the book and covered in detail in Chapter 7.

In a computerized HRIS, manually completed forms or a computerized entry screen may be used to acquire data, a data base management system is used to store data, a query language or HRIS report writer (e.g., FOCUS) is used to retrieve, manipulate, and analyze data, and the resulting reports and screen outputs are used to distribute data. In addition, a variety of software packages or programs may be used (e.g., a spreadsheet package such as LOTUS 1-2-3) to further analyze the data. The focus in this book is on automated or computerized functioning, and the term *system* is used to refer to that automated functioning. However, remember that the system is more than just the hardware and the software. One HR practitioner continually reminds us that his manual information system is still an information system even though he does not use a computer.

A state-of-the-art computer supported by poor procedures and ill-trained users will certainly be an ineffective HRIS. It is the effective integration of the computer, people, policies and procedures, and information flow that yields an effective HRIS.

## Interfaces with Other Systems

Another way to understand the HRIS is to examine its interfaces with other systems—to explore its boundaries or linkages. The HRIS, as defined above, interfaces with several other systems (as seen in Exhibit 2.1). These interfaces can be categorized into five types: (1) the HR subfunctions, (2) other information systems within the company, (3) the strategic management system, (4) information systems outside the company, and (5) the environment in general.

**Exhibit 2.1**   Interfaces with Other Systems

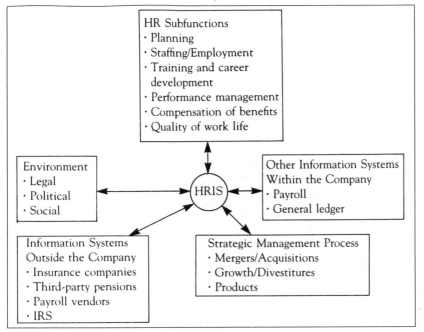

## Interface with HR Subfunctions

The HRIS is an integral part of the overall **human resources management system (HRMS)** and interfaces with each of the major HR subfunctions listed in Exhibit 1.4. In fact, the HRIS and the HR subfunctions share certain people and information. To use an analogy, if the HR function is the human body, the organs would constitute the various subfunctions and the HRIS would serve as the neural system or the circulatory system connecting the organs within the body.

## Interfaces with Other Information Systems within the Company

The HRIS may also interface with other information systems within the company. A typical link is between the HRIS, the payroll system, and the

**general ledger** or accounting system. The link with the payroll system is covered in Chapter 10.

### Interface with the Strategic Management System

The HRIS may also interface with the strategic management system. The **strategic mangement system** is not a computer system but is the process by which upper management determines the strategic direction of the firm. A company's senior management could consider their future acquisition strategy and request information about projected head counts and payroll costs to assess the feasibility and cost of different strategies. In this case, there is an interface between the strategic management system and the HRIS. The interface can occur in two ways. HRIS data may be used to influence company strategy (e.g., Do we have the appropriate personnel to support a possible acquisition? If not, we may change strategies or hire additional personnel.) or company strategy may influence the HRIS (e.g., Our planned growth will require us to change hardware or add modules.).

### Interfaces with Information Systems outside the Company

In some companies, the HRIS interfaces with external systems. For example, the HRIS may send benefits information to insurance companies, actuarial data to third-party pension plan administrators, payroll information to outside payroll vendors, or tax-related information to the IRS. Sometimes the information is passed via computer links; sometimes the interface is via magnetic tape or manual transfer. In addition, some companies bring labor market data and information about competitors' human resources into their HRIS from commercial data bases.

### Interfaces with the Environment

The environment refers to events occurring outside the organization. Changes in the marketplace or the legal environment can and should influence the HRIS. For example, recent and pending changes in benefits legislation (e.g., COBRA, Section 89 of the Tax Reform Act of 1986) will force many companies to change their HRIS. New modules may need to be developed, new data elements collected and retained, and new analyses (e.g., benefits compliance testing) conducted. This interface is discussed in detail in Chapter 3.

Below is a hypothetical case based on the HRIS at several companies. It illustrates how the HRIS interfaces with some of the HR subfunctions as well as with other systems within the company and demonstrates some of the acquisition, storage, manipulation, analysis, retrieval, and distribution functions of the HRIS.

## The Case of John Donson

John Donson reads about an ad for a job opening in the local paper. He comes to RLB International (2,500 + employees), fills out an application, takes a test, gets interviewed, and eventually is hired. He is evaluated three times during his probationary period (30, 60, and 90 days) and annually thereafter. He attends some training courses and receives periodic raises and promotions. Five years later he leaves RLB to work for another company. During John's entry into, progression through, and exit from RLB International, what has happened from an HRIS perspective?

When an opening occurred in the marketing department the marketing manager sent a requisition form to the employment office to initiate hiring procedures for a "marketing representative II." This requisition identified the requirements for the job (e.g., a college degree, one to three years of experience, etc.) and included a position control number. The position control number is used to track and control head count (it also facilitates interface with the general ledger system).

After the position was approved for hiring (the HRIS generates a report monthly that identifies variances—positions requested and filled versus positions budgeted) the employment office advertised the job internally. Ten working days later, after no internally acceptable candidates had applied (company policy is that current employees have the first right to apply for the job), three newspaper ads were sent out. Many applications were received, including John's, and data from the applicants (e.g., educational background, languages spoken, how the applicant heard about the job) were keyed into the system. As part of the staffing process, the employment manager checked a historical data base of recent applicants and generated a list of two additional candidates that were qualified for the new position. The two potential candidates were contacted to see if they wished to be considered for the marketing II position.

John's qualifications met the general job requirements and he was invited in for testing and interviews. His test and interview results were entered into an applicant-tracking system. A list of the top candidates was generated and John was offered the job. Actually, Jill Michaels was offered the job first but turned it down. Both John's acceptance and Jill's rejection were recorded into the computer (for subsequent EEO analyses). Upon acceptance, John's data were electronically transferred from the applicant file into the employee file. Then, additional data (e.g., benefits options) were collected (manually, using standard company forms), and passed to the Human Resources Information Center (HRIC), where the data were also entered into his computerized record. To this point the HRIS has mainly been involved in the acquisition and storage of HR data. Where does the HRIS get involved in the manipulation, analysis, retrieval, and distribution of information?

The recruiting staff accesses the system to determine the effectiveness of the company's recruiting efforts and to target future recruiting dollars more effectively. They use the HRIS to produce a report that shows which recruiting sources (e.g., postings, local paper, walk-ins, referrals) lead to the most hires. A computerized recruiting-source analysis computes the ratio of the number of hires per recruiting dollar, broken down by job type and company division. They also analyze which colleges have provided the best hires on the basis of performance evaluation and turnover data from new employees.

The Equal Employment Opportunity/Affirmative Action (EEO/AA) staff uses the system to evaluate the company's compliance with equal employment law. They need to retrieve, manipulate (e.g., sort, categorize), and analyze information from the applicant files and compare this information with local labor market statistics to determine if the company is in compliance with EEO guidelines. Each unit's EEO compliance data are distributed to each unit head. The EEO/AA subfunction also analyzed data from the Domestic Division to assess the effectiveness of their new minority recruitment program and will use the results to decide whether to recommend expanding that program to other divisions.

The personnel research group downloaded historical hiring data from the HRIS and, using a statistical package on a microcomputer, validated the company's selection tests. This validation described how well the test scores and interview results predicted future job performance. The results of the analysis help determine which tests and interview questions the company should use in the future to select the best applicants.

The payroll subfunction uses data from the system to generate paychecks, calculate deductions, and feed the accounting systems. Built-in error checking helps ensure that payroll checks are accurate and reflect employee benefit decisions. Revisions to the tax laws required changes in the payroll module several times during John's tenure.

Non-HR users also rely on the HRIS. John's boss and all other line managers receive "tickler" reports reminding them which employees are scheduled for performance evaluations next month. All division heads receive a report on a monthly basis that compares their division's actual head count and payroll expenses to budgeted head count and payroll expenses. John's manager also received an attendance and vacation record on his employees quarterly.

Four years after John was hired, senior management contemplated opening an office in Italy. To support this effort they wanted to know which employees, if any, (1) had assignments where they were responsible for profit and loss, (2) spoke Italian, and (3) were willing to relocate. The HRIC generated a list that included John Donson.

Finally, the HRIC examined turnover data across RLB International (by job type, division, years of experience, etc.) and informed senior management that there was a turnover problem in the International Division. Data from exit interviews, including John's, revealed that many employees left the company for higher-paying jobs. As a result, the research unit and the compensation department were asked to conduct a salary survey study to see if company compensation practices were competitive in the marketplace.

This scenario illustrates how an HRIS interfaces with the other HR subfunctions and with others outside the HR system. Consider any of the activities performed using the HRIS: How could they be performed with a manual system? For example, how long would it take to tally EEO information from each employee's file? To go through a year's worth of employment applications to compare the effectiveness of newspaper advertisements? To identify all acceptable candidates for the new position in Italy? A manual information system might allow you to perform some of these tasks. However, the time and expense of generating the information would be greater and the accuracy of the data lower than with a computerized HRIS. And some tasks, such as administering a flexible benefits program, are virtually impossible to perform using a manual system. The John Donson case illustrates how a computerized HRIS can provide valuable services to an organization—if the HRIS is well conceived, well developed, and effectively implemented.

In the remainder of the chapter, system outputs are explored and report complexity is considered. The components of an HRIS data base, including data elements, tables, and modules, are also examined. Finally the typical users alluded to in the John Donson case are discussed.

Before continuing, a few additional words regarding terminology should be said. Some common "systems" language is used, and these terms are defined in the glossary. However, some companies may use different terms. For instance, one company's *module* is another company's *application* and yet another's *subroutine*. Naturally, it is important to become familiar with the terminology used in your company.

## System Outputs

Without downplaying the importance of data acquisition and storage, it is the ability to manipulate, analyze, retrieve, and distribute HR information that makes the HRIS so important. The manipulation, analysis, retrieval and distribution activities provide the HRIS outputs.

Several types of outputs are available from an HRIS. These include data dumps or extracts and three levels of reports—standard/production, cataloged/library, and ad hoc. Each of these outputs is discussed below.

### Data Dumps or Extracts

In some cases all we want from the HRIS is raw data. The most common case is when an analysis will be performed on a microcomputer and the data reside on a mainframe, or when data reside in a microcomputer data base and the analysis is to be performed on another type of microcomputer software. In the John Donson case the HR research group wanted to validate the company's selection tests. To do so, data would be extracted from the mainframe, downloading test scores, EEO class, gender, and performance appraisal data into a file a microcomputer can use. This file can then be read into a statistical analysis package on the microcomputer (e.g., SPSS, SAS). In other cases data might be extracted in a format compatible with a spreadsheet (e.g., LOTUS 1-2-3) or micro data base (e.g., dBASE or R:Base for DOS) package for additional analyses.

### Production or Fixed Reports

A production or fixed report is run and distributed on a predetermined time schedule. The programming required to produce the report is done in advance and is not modified. Users are on a distribution list and receive the report on a regular basis (e.g., biweekly, quarterly, annually). In the John Donson case, the monthly report of positions requested and filled versus positions budgeted was a production report. Another example was the tickler

report reminding supervisors which of their employees were due for performance evaluations each month. Payroll system managers use many production reports because of the cyclic, financial control aspects of the payroll
function. Sample production reports they receive could include quarterly
tax reports, W-2s, and worker compensation reports. Some of the typical
HRIS reports are considered in Chapters 8 and 9.

Managers do not need to have any knowledge regarding the HRIS
to receive production reports; these are simply a product of the HRIS.
Unfortunately, some production reports are wasted because users receive
reports they do not need, are inundated with reports, or were never taught
how to interpret the reports.

Some large companies produce upwards of 1,000 production reports
per year. Often, the number of production reports grows over time. More
new reports are created than old reports discontinued. Fortunately, many
companies are recognizing the futility of overreporting. Chase Manhattan
recently reduced the number of production reports they use from 350 to
around 50. The trend is toward fewer production/fixed reports and more
library and ad hoc reports.

## Cataloged or Library Reports

A cataloged or library report does what the title implies—it resides in a
catalog or a library. The report is not distributed on a standard basis but
instead is available by request. These reports are typically written using an
HRIS report writer and are stored for repetitive use. Often these reports
may be modified by a trained user. To again use the John Donson scenario,
assume a historical comparison of the number of minority applicants exists
in the "library" of reports. The cataloged report was for an annual basis
(January 1 to December 31, year 1, versus January 1 to December 31, year
2). However, the EEO/AA manager, trained to use the HRIS report writer,
could retrieve the report and modify it to focus on the Domestic Division,
comparing May to September with October to February, to evaluate the
impact of a minority recruiting program that began October 1.

KeyCorp, a regional bank holding company, uses a centralized mainframe HRIS for most of its human resource information needs. Exhibit 2.2
is a description of a report that resides in KeyCorp's HRIS report library.
Descriptions such as this one are made available to potential users of the
system (e.g., managers). The report described in Exhibit 2.2 was developed
and used at a previous point in time and is now available, upon request,

**Exhibit 2.2** Sample Report Description from Catalog of Reports

```
                          KEY SERVICES CORPORATION-MAINE
                             PAYROLL SERVICES DEPARTMENT

                          I.E. REQUEST/DESCRIPTION SUMMARY


REPORT TITLE        : 401(k) Eligibility List

JOB REQUEST NAME    : MSAKEY16

REPORT SERIES NAME  : N/A

COMPANY(S)          : All KeyCorp Companies

DESCRIPTION         : Lists employee's name, employment code, date of hire,
                      year-to-date regular hours and overtime hours, year-to-date sick hour
                      and profit-sharing eligibility date.  Sorted by eligibility date.

FREQUENCY           : On Request

MASTERFILE/GEN      : KeyCorp Master File
```

```
PARAMS REQUIRED    :  RUN-TIME SELECT EMP-CONTROL-LEVELS-1-2-GROUP
                      RUN-TIME SELECT EMP-PROFIT-SHR-ELIGIBLE-DATE

EST RUN TIME       :

TAPE OUTPUT        :  N/A

NUMBER OF COPIES   :  1 Copy  Stock Paper

DISTRIBUTION       :  Satellite to KSC NY for further distribution

SPECIAL FORMS      :  N/A


            ORIGINAL PROD DATE    :  09/20/88

            ORIGINATED BY         :  Cindy Kilpatrick

            REPORT REVISION DATE  :

            REVISED BY            :
```

*Source:*  Courtesy of KeyCorp, Albany, New York.

from the library. If this were a production report, under "FREQUENCY" it would have noted when it is distributed (e.g., monthly, every payroll cycle, end of first quarter) and under "DISTRIBUTION" it would have noted who was to receive it. To receive the 401(k) eligibility report, the requester must provide certain information, including the employee profit share eligibility date of interest, so the HRIC can customize the report.

At a minimum, a user must be aware of what cataloged reports exist to be able to request a cataloged report. If these reports are available on-line (i.e., hands-on use of the computer to request current data), then a working knowledge of how to access the library and initiate a report is needed. Exhibit 2.3 shows a "menu" of reports from a microcomputer-based HRIS. This system was developed in R:Base for DOS, a programmable data base package, for use in KeyCorp's subsidiaries. A trained user can call up these menus on the screen and access any of the listed reports.

### Ad Hoc Reports

Ad hoc reports are developed to address a specific need for which a fixed or library report is unavailable. They usually address one-time needs. Ad hoc reports are developed using an HRIS report writer or query language and may provide "immediate" information to the requester. Although fixed and library reports usually result in a paper report, ad hoc queries may be provided via screen output and/or via paper report. When senior management wanted a list of all employees that had profit-loss experience, spoke Italian, and were willing to relocate, an ad hoc inquiry would have been used to generate that list. In some systems, if the user believes the ad hoc report will be used again, it can be added to the library. Ad hoc reporting allows quick access to information. Some reporting languages are easy to learn, but others are more akin to programming and may be quite difficult to master. However, easy-to-use report writers usually only allow users to develop simple reports.[1] Some software vendors provide an easy-to-use ad hoc reporter for simple queries and another more difficult reporter for more complex requests. Ad hoc reporting requires user training. This is particularly important on mainframe systems, where a poorly worded ad hoc inquiry may eat up valuable and expensive computer time and yield inappropriate results.

The HRIC at one large insurance firm recently reviewed the reports they generated during the year. They produced approximately 1,100 reports, of which 72 percent were production or library reports and the remaining were ad hoc requests. They also produced 130 regularly scheduled data extracts and 35 ad hoc data extracts. Requests came from users throughout the com-

**Exhibit 2.3**   Report Menus

```
━━━━━━━━━━━━━━━━━━━━KEY MAIN MENU━━━━━━━━━━━━━━━━━━━━
   (1)  Maintain Employee File
   (2)  Maintain Compensation File
   (3)  Maintain Education File
   (4)  Maintain Training File
   (5)  Maintain Termination File
   (6)  Access Reports Menu
   (7)  Perform Utilities Functions
   (8)  Exit to System to Quit or do Ad Hoc Reporting
```

```
━━━━━━━━━━━━━━━━━━━━REPORTS MENU━━━━━━━━━━━━━━━━━━━━
      (1)  Employee General Reports
      (2)  Compensation Reports
      (3)  Education Reports
      (4)  Training Reports
      (5)  Termination Reports
      (6)  Return to Main Menu
```

```
━━━━━━━━━━━━━━━━━━━━GENERAL REPORTS MENU━━━━━━━━━━━━━━━━━━━━
      (1)  Alpha List - Sorted by Name
      (2)  Employee List - Sorted by Level 4, Name
      (3)  Name & Address Report
      (4)  Mailing Labels - Sorted by Name
      (5)  Return to Reports Menu
```

```
━━━━━━━━━━━━━━━━━━━━COMPENSATION REPORTS MENU━━━━━━━━━━━━━━━━━━━━
      (1)  Salary Listing by Department
      (2)  Salary Performance Review
      (3)  Salary Listing by Employee Code
      (4)  Return to Reports Menu
```

```
━━━━━━━━━━━━━━━━━━━━EDUCATION REPORTS MENU━━━━━━━━━━━━━━━━━━━━
      (1)  Employee List of Completed Degrees and Schools
      (2)  Return to Reports Menu
```

```
━━━━━━━━━━━━━━━━━━━━TRAINING REPORTS MENU━━━━━━━━━━━━━━━━━━━━
      (1)  Report of Total Training Per Employee
      (2)  Internal Training Report in Total - Alpha List
      (3)  Internal Training Report by Course
      (4)  External Training Report in Total - Alpha List
      (5)  Seminar Report in Total - Alpha List
      (6)  Print a Transcript for a Particular Employee
      (7)  Return to Reports Menu
```

```
━━━━━━━━━━━━━━━━━━━━TERMINATION REPORTS MENU━━━━━━━━━━━━━━━━━━━━
      (1)  Report of Terminated Employees by Month
      (2)  Report of Terminated Employees by Employment Status
      (3)  Return to Reports Menu
```

pany, with the HR functional specialists the heaviest users. Within HR they found the EEO/recruiting and employee relations functions were their heaviest ad hoc users, followed by the benefits function and the administrative payroll group. The staff planning unit also made a significant number of ad hoc requests. These numbers are not included to suggest that this is the correct or incorrect mix of standard to ad hoc requests or an appropriate user breakdown. The ratios will vary from company to company. However, users should be surveyed regularly, and requests should be monitored to evaluate whether they are meeting user needs.

## Report Complexity

Reports vary in complexity. In particular, reports differ in the difficulty in retrieving relevant data, the degree of manipulation involved, the complexity of the analyses, and the customization of the report layout.

Data retrieval is a concern for some reports. A user may want to access data from different files within the data base. Depending on the structure of the data base and the software being used, this may require complex programming. For example, when HR and payroll data are kept in different files, a report requiring information from both files simultaneously may require an intensive programming effort. Good HRIS report-writing software can help bridge unrelated files, although it cannot bridge different data bases.

Assuming the data are accessible, several types of reports can be generated. Some questions can be answered with a report that requires minimal data manipulation, little or no analysis, and a simple report format. Other questions may call for more complex reports requiring tricky data manipulation, complex analyses, and detailed customized formats. A few types of reports of varying complexity are highlighted below.

### Simple Lists

Many reports are simple lists of information, with column formats specified for the user by the default option of the report-writing software. The user requests several types of information, such as name, number, and salary, and the report writer will space them according to a predetermined layout. In most cases, there is a limit to the number of columns that the user can request without customizing the format. However, a good report writer should allow customized layouts in terms of heading titles, spacing, dates, and page numbers.

Users may request lists that require some manipulation prior to printing the report. Many requests will require that data be sorted. For example, a user may want a list of all marketing employees sorted in order by division (alphabetical) and salary (descending) (see Exhibit 2.4). Sorting improves the readability of many reports. Ren Nardoni, a respected HRIS consultant, suggests that the sort sequence of a good HRIS report writer should be able to manipulate at least five data fields simultaneously and should operate on any type of field, whether character, data, or numeric.[2] Rarely will reports need to be based on every employee in the data base. In a large company, if each employee's record had to be reviewed to access data, production time would be enormous and users would have to sort through a lengthy report to find the information they needed. For this reason the user should be able to specify which employee groups are to be included in the report. For example, a user could select employees on the basis of their language skills, job experience, and willingness to relocate.

Users should be able to use Boolean logic to establish complex selection criteria. In Boolean logic, the use of the words *AND* and *OR* can link conditional requests together. For example, a selection criterion of

list EMPNAME if PLEXP GT "1 YR" *AND* ITALIAN EQ "ADVANCED" *AND* RELOC EQ "YES"

would list the names of employees who had greater than one year of profit-loss experience, spoke fluent Italian, and were willing to relocate. The list would contain John Donson.

A selection criterion of

list EMPNAME if (PLEXP GT "1 YR" OR LEVEL GT "MGR 2") *AND* ITALIAN EQ "ADVANCED *AND* RELOC EQ "YES"

would list all employees having profit-loss experience or at a managerial level greater than 2 as well as the necessary relocation and language factors. This group of employees would be larger than the first group because this selection statement allows managerial level to substitute for profit-loss experience and vice versa.

KeyCorp uses a data request form that allows managers to solicit information from the HRIC, specifying the groups of employees that should be

**Exhibit 2.4**   List Report: With Sorting

---

**RLB CORPORATION**
 **SALARY REPORT**                                     **DATE:** 01/09/90

**REQUESTED BY:** Payroll


**EAST COAST DIVISION**

| Cash, Brett    | $74,000 |
| Beard, Rebecca | $52,000 |
| Stone, Diana   | $44,330 |


**HOME OFFICE**

| Heine, Mitchell     | $123,000 |
| Tolpotch, Michelle  | $64,500  |
| Donson, John        | $32,400  |
| Andresse, Jim       | $21,200  |


**INTERNATIONAL DIVISION**

| Levato, John       | $73,250 |
| Messinger, Andrew  | $44,510 |
| Johnson, Hank      | $42,400 |
| Elmore, Rita       | $21,200 |


**WEST COAST DIVISION**

| Carl, John        | $68,985 |
| Heine, Steve      | $42,400 |
| Berman, Scott     | $41,225 |
| Hoham, Hal        | $32,200 |
| Truitt, Winifred  | $21,250 |

---

selected, the data elements that are needed, the type and order of sorts, and any calculations (see Exhibit 2.5). In addition, requesters are asked to draw what they want their report to look like. This helps ensure that the report meets user needs.

**Exhibit 2.5** Data Request Form

```
                        KEYCORP
                    HUMAN RESOURCES
                     DATA REQUEST

DATE REQUESTED: _____    PERSON MAKING REQUEST: _____

YOUR COMPANY NAME: _____    TARGET COMPLETION DATE: _____

REQUESTOR'S PHONE #: _____    REPORT NAME: _____
```

WHAT WILL THIS INFORMATION BE USED FOR?: _____

WHAT TYPE OF EMPLOYEES SHOULD BE INCLUDED ON THIS REPORT:
(You must select 1 item each from group A, B, and C)

A. Employment Code ?                 B. Employment Status?

___ ex - exempt                      ___ blank - active
___ ne - non exempt                  ___ t - terminated
___ pt - part time                   ___ tt - terminated/transferred
___ tp - temporary                   ___ n - not active
___ all employees                    ___ p - deceased
                                     ___ t1 - terminated / retired
C. What Subsidiary?

___ Specify Sub(s)                   D. Special

    _____                     _____

    ** - all Keycorp Subs               _____

                    WHAT FIELDS DO YOU NEED ?
Mark an (X) in the select column to choose elements to be printed on the
report.  See questions below on sorting and totaling.

SELECT      SORTED BY    TOTALED BY

_____     _____      _____     Employee name last name first
_____     _____      _____     Employee name first name first
_____     _____      _____     Address 1
_____     _____      _____     Address 2
_____     _____      _____     Address 3
_____     _____      _____     Employee number
_____     _____      _____     Social Security number
_____     _____      _____     Position number (code number)
_____     _____      _____     Level 3
_____     _____      _____     Level 4
_____     _____      _____     Level 5
_____     _____      _____     Sex
_____     _____      _____     Race
```

*continued*
```

**Exhibit 2.5** *continued*

```
                            KEYCORP
                        HUMAN RESOURCES
                         DATA REQUEST


    REPORT SKETCH
    _____

          Please draw a sample of what you want your report to look like.
    Place the data elements across the page as you would like them to appear
    on your report.  Remember to specify column headings if you prefer
    something specific for a result field or a D/OE field.
```

```
                            KEYCORP
                        HUMAN RESOURCES
                         DATA REQUEST

    SELECT      SORTED BY    TOTALED BY
    _____      _____    _____


    _____     _____     _____    date of birth
    _____     _____     _____    age
    _____     _____     _____    date of hire
    _____     _____     _____    length of service
    _____     _____     _____    job title
    _____     _____     _____    employment code
    _____     _____     _____    termination date
    _____     _____     _____    annual salary
    _____     _____     _____    hourly rate
    _____     _____     _____    minimum salary
    _____     _____     _____    midpoint salary
    _____     _____     _____    maximum salary
    _____     _____     _____    salary grade
    _____     _____     _____    salary review date
    _____     _____     _____    telephone number (home)
    _____     _____     _____    deduction/other earnings #_____
                                               ytd_____ qtd_____ mtd_____
    _____     _____     _____    deduction/other earnings #_____
                                               ytd_____ qtd_____ mtd_____
    _____     _____     _____    deduction/other earnings #_____
                                               ytd_____ qtd_____ mtd_____

    OTHER FIELDS NOT LISTED ABOVE, SPECIFY BELOW.

    _____

    _____


    SORTING
    _____

         Please specify the sort order of the report by placing a 1,2,3 on the
    line by the elements you want sorted.  One indicates first sort and 2
    would indicate a second sort within the first sort.  Place an (A) or
    (D) next to the column you wish to sort to indicate ascending or
    descending order of data.

    TOTALING
    _____

         Place either an (S) or (T) on the line by the element you wish to total
    or subtotal.

    CALCULATIONS
    _____

         Please specify any calculations below.  List the column headings if
    result fields are needed.  Calculations must be done on data elements
    that were selected above.

    _____

    _____
```

## Comparison Reports

These reports go beyond simple listing and provide a comparison of information. The comparison may be with (1) historical data (e.g., minority hiring this year versus last year), (2) a specified standard (e.g., actual minority hiring versus predetermined minority hiring goals), or (3) a company policy (e.g., comparing whether the number of hires exceeds the number of positions budgeted). These last two comparisons may be referred to as variance or exception reports because they are often used to identify variances or exceptions for management control and action.

## Computations

At the simplest level, computations involve column totaling or subtotaling. This type of request is so common that some report writers include totaling as part of the basic report-request capabilities. Addition, subtraction, division, multiplication, and exponentiation are all forms of computations. More complex computations involve the formation of a new piece of information (i.e., a new data element) based on one or more existing data elements. For instance, a *compa-ratio* is calculated by taking a person's annual salary and dividing it by the midpoint of that person's salary range. As someone's salary changes, or if the salary structure changes, their compa-ratio changes as well. The newly computed data element, employee compa-ratio, can then be used in a variety of reports.

## Statistical Analyses

Many statistical tools exist that can be applied to HR data. Most HRIS software packages have limited statistical capabilities. Special-purpose software packages (e.g., SPSS, SAS, BMDP) that are capable of performing statistical analyses are available. Simple statistics such as averages, ranges, and frequency distributions are often useful in reports. More complex analyses such as correlation, regression, time-series analysis, and a variety of complex modeling approaches can be used to analyze and interpret data and to provide decision support. These tend to be associated with a DSS or MIS perspective rather than an EDP perspective, as noted in Chapter 1.

### *Graphics*

Graphics tools provide the capability to graphically depict HR data and information. Most HRIS software packages have limited graphics capabilities. As with statistical analyses, special graphics packages are available (e.g., Harvard Graphics). Well-developed bar charts, pie charts, organizational charts, and XY, two-dimensional charts enable the reader to absorb information more easily or with greater impact.

## The Data Hierarchy and Related Terms

Prior to discussing the various modules of an HRIS (e.g., applicant tracking, benefits administration) a few terms associated with the data hierarchy need to be clarified. These terms will be used throughout the book.

The way an HRIS stores and processes information is by breaking that information down into a series of **bits**, or binary digits (i.e., 0's and 1's). These bits are strung together to form **bytes** (8 bits to a byte), and bytes are aggregated to form higher levels of information. All information systems are based on this data hierarchy. The data hierarchy of an HRIS is shown in Exhibit 2.6.[3]

## Modules

The underlying structure of an HRIS, including the relationships among tables, data elements, files, and interfaces, can be arranged in many ways. While the HRIS developers are aware of the underlying structure, it is transparent or unseen by most users. From the end user's perspective, most HRISs are organized by modules. Each module is designed to support a specific HR function.

A modular approach allows users to deal with the data of interest to their function without having to weed through every data element in the system. In addition, it is difficult (perhaps impossible) to implement a system that addresses all user functions right away. With a modular approach additional modules can be implemented as time and resources permit.

The John Donson case alluded to the idea of modules. A **module**, according to Walker,

**Exhibit 2.6** Data Hierarchy

| Definition | Term | Example |
|---|---|---|
| The system used to acquire, store, manipulate, analyze, retrieve, and distribute HR information. | HRIS | The computer, people, programs, and procedures that make up the system. |
| The data base contains interrelated information on employees, jobs, etc. and is composed of one or more files. | Data base | HR, Benefits, and Payroll files are interrelated to form data base. |
| A file contains information on a specific topic or group (e.g., employee benefits file). | File | Name — Health Coverage — Dental Coverage<br>John Donson  A  Y<br>Bill Jones  B  Y<br>Sue Brown  A  N |
| Some data bases use tables to store specific types of information (e.g., job table). | Table | Job Code — Job Title<br>3014  Marketing Rep II<br>3015  Product Mgr |
| A file or table is composed of many records that describe the people, jobs, etc. in the file. An employee's record within the benefits file contains information on the employee's name, coverage, marital status, number of dependents, etc. | Record | John Donson  A  Y  Married  2 |
| Each record is made up of many fields or data elements. First name, last name, coverage, etc. are data elements in the employee record. | Field or data element | Last-name field: Donson |
| Each data element is composed of a series of bytes. | Bytes | 1010100 (letter "j" in one form of computer code) |
| Each byte is composed of a string of bits | Bits | + or − (1 or 0) |

*Source:* With permission, adapted from K. C. Laudon and J. P. Laudon, *Management Information Systems: A Contemporary Perspective* (New York: Macmillan, 1988), 167.

1. is directed to one specific function of HR
2. has its own input forms or screens
3. uses some internal transformations to the data
4. has some reports or analyses that are particular to that user group or function
5. may have some data elements that are unique to that user or function.[4]

So within a module specific data elements, entry screens, tables, reports, analyses, models, and/or menus might be found. A module usually has some unique features but also shares data elements and tables with other modules.

Modules should reflect the way users use the system. They should be based on the HR department structure and should be consistent with the way activities are performed within the department. Are executive compensation activities performed as part of the compensation function or does a separate group of people deal with it? Does the company have flexible benefits? Is there a separate career planning/development function or is that strictly the responsibility of the manager? Since the modules should conform to the company, there is no "correct" set of modules for all companies. Exhibit 2.7 includes a list of many possible modules.

**Exhibit 2.7    HRIS Modules**

| | |
|---|---|
| Applicant tracking | Job evaluation |
| Basic employee information | Job descriptions/analysis |
| Benefits administration | Pension and retirement |
| COBRA compliance | Performance management |
| Health insurance | Training |
| Short- and long-term disability | Skills inventory |
| Employment history | Compensation |
| EEO/AA compliance | Payroll |
| Time and attendance | Bonus and incentive management |
| Position control | Succession planning |
| Labor relations planning | Job posting |
| Career development/planning | Health and safety |
| HR planning and forecasting | Turnover analysis |

Specific applications from the modules are examined in Chapters 8, 9, and 10. For now, brief descriptions of a few of the modules are included:

### Basic Personnel
### (Employee Information) Module

This module, not surprisingly, contains basic employee information [e.g., name, date of birth, Social Security number, address, supervisor, status (part time, full time, leave) marital situation, salary, job code, etc.] and is always one of the modules in an HRIS. It is the core of the system and is often the first module developed. Many of the data acquired for this module are used in other modules as well. These data are collected as part of the hiring process or during the first few days on the job and are updated throughout an employee's tenure. In some organizations, the entry screen for this module mirrors the paper form filled out during the hiring process. Sometimes the number of data elements collected from a new employee exceeds the space available in one screen. In these cases a series of screens are used to enter and edit basic employee information. In some systems, when the user completes data entry on one screen he or she is automatically moved to the next, related screen. This is referred to as **screen linking**. Different screen-linking patterns may be established for different users. Examples of two entry screens for a basic personnel module are shown in Exhibit 2.8.

To ensure that employees' personnel data have been entered correctly and are current, a **turnaround document** can be produced by the computer. These forms are sent to each employee and show their personnel information as currently kept in the system. Employees are asked to verify their data,

**Exhibit 2.8a**  Sample Data Entry Screens: Basic Employee Module (Personal Data)

```
┌──────────────────── Personal Data ────────────────────[F2]┐
│                                                            │
│   NAME  GONZALES,MARIA              SOC SEC NO  853-98-1714│
│                                                            │
│        STREET  7 Tammy Lane         HOME PHONE  203-752-8974│
│                Apt. 4               WORK PHONE  203-455-1022│
│          CITY  Darien               USER3                  │
│         STATE  CT        ZIP  06302 USER4                  │
│                                                            │
│  EMERG CONTACT  ROBERT GONZALES     EMERG HPHONE 203-752-8974│
│       RELATION  HUSBAND             EMERG WPHONE 212-410-4600│
│    MAIDEN NAME  SANTOS              MARRIAGE NAME          │
│                                                            │
│           SEX  F        MARITAL STAT  M      REF CODE  3010 │
│      ETHNICITY  4  HISPANIC  BIRTHDATE 10/15/61  SOURCE  WALK-IN│
│       HANDICAP  N              AGE  26    MIL STATUS       │
│                                                            │
├────────────────────────────────────────────────────────────┤
│  EMP NO  2          LAST UPDATED  02/02/90   UPDATED BY  HRISC│
└────────────────────────────────────────────────────────────┘
```

**Exhibit 2.8b**   Sample Data Entry Screens: Basic Employee Module
(Employment Data)

```
┌──────────────────── Employment Data ─────────────────────[F1]┐
│                                                                │
│  NAME  Gonzales,Maria              PREFIX  Mrs.    SUFFIX       │
│                                                                │
│    STATUS  A        HIRE DATE  05/01/85        REHIRE DATE     │
│  EMP TYPE  E      TIME WORKED  4 yrs 10 mos 14 days    USER1    │
│  REG/TEMP  R      % FULL TIME  100.0                   USER2    │
│                                                                │
│     LOA CODE  2                     TERM CODE                   │
│     LOA REAS  SURGERY               TERM REAS                   │
│     LOA DATE  09/30/87              TERM DATE                   │
│    RETURN DT  12/28/87                 REHIRE                   │
│                                                                │
│     DEPT NO  120002              SUPV EMP NO  1                 │
│   DEPT DATE  01/10/88              SUPV NAME  Barrington,Blake  │
│   DEPT NAME  ADMINISTRATION        SUPV DATE  05/01/85          │
│    MGR NAME  GONZALES,MARIA                                     │
│                                                                │
├────────────────────────────────────────────────────────────┤
│  EMP NO  2          LAST UPDATED  02/02/90   UPDATED BY  HRISC │
└────────────────────────────────────────────────────────────┘
```

*Source:*   This exhibit is an example from HR-1, a micro-based HR software package by Revelation Technologies, Inc., 2 Park Avenue, New York, NY 10016. Reproduced by permission.

adding missing information and correcting erroneous information, and to send the form back for revisions to their computer record. Other modules may also use turnaround documents.

Similarly, **status change documents** can be used to update employee records. These documents are used to notify the HRIS about changes in an employee's status (e.g., salary increase, new address). The difference between this and a turnaround document is that a status change form originates from a manager or an employee—not from the HRIS.

### Applicant-Tracking Module

Many companies are beginning to establish applicant-tracking modules. This module may be used to identify applicants who qualify for open jobs, to identify open jobs for which people can apply, and to provide support for EEO/AA compliance.

An applicant-tracking module is used to record applicant information prior to their becoming employees. In some cases the applicant-tracking module will feed the basic employee information module whenever an applicant becomes an employee. This is logical because the two modules share many data elements (e.g., name, address, phone number, date of birth, etc.). However, the basic employee information module must include data elements not collected until hiring (e.g., starting salary). In addition, the applicant-tracking module may contain data elements that will not be part of the employee's record. Some of the data elements specific to the applicant-tracking module include recruiting source (where the applicant learned about the job), status (e.g., passed interview), and reasons for rejection (e.g., unqualified).

The applicant-tracking module may share data elements with an EEO/AA module or a recruiting module. In fact, complex EEO/AA reporting needs require accurate, historical applicant information on those classes of individuals protected from unfair employment discrimination by law. Thus, race and gender of applicants would be shared with the EEO/AA module.

Remember, the establishment of modules should be consistent with the way the HR department performs the various functions. If recruiting and staffing are handled together there may be one applicant-tracking/recruiting module. If EEO/AA and applicant tracking are handled together there may be one EEO/AA applicant-tracking module.

### Recruiting Module

As mentioned above, the recruiting module may overlap the applicant-tracking module. The recruiting module uses data elements collected during the applicant-tracking process. However, the recruiting module might also track recruiting costs (e.g., advertisement costs), include an analysis of recruiting-source effectiveness, and generate reports of recruiting trends over time.

### Performance Management Module

The performance management module allows for the monitoring or tracking of employee performance and may facilitate the manager's job. Functional specialists from the HR department may also use the performance management module to evaluate the overall effectiveness of the performance appraisal system. Reports that show performance ratings by manager, job type, or department can identify trends. Are some departments too lenient? Are performance evaluation guidelines being followed? What is the relationship between pay increases, bonuses, and performance ratings? For the line manager, a performance management module could be used to generate lists of forthcoming performance reviews, to record key performance events, and to report previously agreed upon employee goals.

### Career Development/Skills Inventory Module

As with the performance management module, the career development module may be targeted to an HR subfunction and/or to line managers; it depends on the way the HR department operates. If there is a career development center and well-defined career tracks and job skill requirements exist, then this module may be used by the center to provide advice regarding career opportunities. Alternatively, career counseling duties may be performed by each manager. The manager might use work history information and job skill requirements as well as performance appraisal scores and career goals to suggest career development activities for employees.

This module may overlap the human resource planning or succession planning module discussed below. The identification of skills and career plans is critical for staff planning as well as individual career planning.

### Position Control Module

A position control module enables an organization to track positions for monitoring, budgeting, planning, and control. Typically, each position will be assigned a code, and position characteristics (e.g., title, salary, skill requirements, level, location, etc.) will be maintained. Position status can be monitored. Is a position vacant, filled, frozen, or planned? Position control reports may compare similar positions across departments, examine variances between authorized and actual staffing, and/or compare previous, current, and projected position budgets.

### Benefits Module

Changes in employee demographics and legislative changes are making the benefits arena one of the most critical and complex areas of HR. An effective benefits module helps ensure compliance with COBRA, ERISA, Section 89 of the Tax Reform Act of 1986, and other existing legislative requirements, as described in Chapter 3. The benefits module may also be used to administer programs (e.g., pension, 401(k), flex benefits) and traditional employee benefits (e.g., health insurance, life insurance, disability), to provide advice to employees about their benefit choices, and to produce an annual employee benefits statement. Benefit analyses can be used to monitor benefits programs and to help control the rising costs of benefits to the organization.

## Compensation Module

This module is used by the functional specialists in the compensation group. They use it to monitor compensation costs, policies, and programs and to support future compensation decisions. The compensation module can be used to help monitor the executive compensation, bonus, and profit-sharing plans and to ensure compliance with the Fair Labor Standards Act. In many systems, the compensation module is used to help develop salary structures.

Compensation analysts may correlate performance evaluations with pay increases and consider salary grade dispersion by department. Compensation models can be used to answer "what if " questions like, What if we give 3 percent bonuses? What if we switch to a pay for performance system? or, What savings are accrued if we close a plant? Comparisons of compensation across jobs and with other companies provide information useful for facilitating internal and external pay equity.

## Payroll Module

Sometimes considered part of the HRIS, payroll is treated as a module in some systems. When payroll is part of the HRIS, termed an *integrated* system, several tasks are facilitated. For example, to ensure compliance with the Equal Pay Act, payroll and EEO data must be compiled together. When this information is kept in separate systems a great deal of manual effort may be required to create the necessary reports. Still, payroll's relationship with HRIS varies across companies. For this reason, Chapter 10 is dedicated to addressing the unique considerations involved in payroll.

## EEO/AA Module

The Civil Rights Act of 1964, and in particular, Title VII of that act, prohibits employment discrimination on the basis of race, ethnicity, or national origin. A number of other laws, regulations, and executive orders, covered in Chapter 3, protect classes of people from unfair employment discrimination. Several government reports must be filed to ensure that companies have complied with legal requirements (e.g., EEO-1 report). In addition, an EEO/AA module can monitor hiring, promotion, and firing patterns to evaluate compliance with internal guidelines. Problem areas can be identified and remedial efforts can be targeted.

## Training Module

The training module typically includes information about the training experience of employees, which may also be included under the career development/skills inventory module, and about the training courses available to employees. In addition, training costs, enrollment figures, and training evaluation data may be maintained. A comprehensive training module would allow managers or employees to get information about course availability and appropriateness and would allow the training subfunction to evaluate and improve course offerings. Reports and analyses could identify the most cost-effective and popular courses and, based on course evaluations, could target those courses that need improvement. In addition, recent changes in tax law may require additional record keeping with regard to training. Some training courses may need to be considered as taxable income to the employee requiring a transfer of data from the training module to the payroll module.

## Human Resource Planning (HRP) Module

The HRP module may provide information to help estimate future labor supply and demand by analyzing current staffing levels and skill mixes, turnover, promotions, and other employee movements. In an elaborate HRP system, strategic plans are considered to forecast sales and production growth or decline and converted to project future labor needs. By comparing projected labor needs (demand) with current and projected staffing levels (supply), surpluses or deficits can be identified. This information can be used to develop HR programs to balance labor supply and demand. For example, heightened recruiting efforts could be used to increase labor supply.

Some HR planning modules are designed to facilitate succession planning, a key element of HR planning. Succession plans are used to monitor the readiness of current employees to fill positions of increased responsibility. On an individual level they are useful for targeting developmental plans to prepare employees for future responsibilities. On an organizational level, succession plans help identify critical positions for which there are no ready successors and can be used to identify patterns of weaknesses in terms of the overall skills and experience mix among current employees.

Succession planning data can be maintained and summarized on the HRIS, but these data are usually very sensitive, often secretive. Extreme care must be taken to ensure the privacy of the information.

## Which HR Functions and Tasks Are Computerized?

Researchers have recently begun surveying organizations to assess their HR computerization patterns.[5] An examination of these survey results reveals which HR functions are computerized and trends or changes in computerization.

Exhibit 2.9 lists the results of five surveys. It lists HR tasks/functions and then shows the percentage of survey respondents that have computerized each. Each survey used a slightly different breakdown of tasks/functions. For example, Lee's survey clusters all "Benefits" together, while the HRSP survey considers "Defined benefits," "Defined contributions," "Benefits statements," and "Flexible benefits" separately. This precludes direct comparisons across studies but still allows for an overall examination of computerization trends. Each survey was targeted to a different group of respondents. Differences in each researcher's sampling strategy are noted in Exhibit 2.10.

### Trends

The three most prevalently computerized HR functions are payroll, basic employee records, and EEO/AA. These basic HR functions tend to have strong administrative components, and many of the applications associated with these functions tend to be closer to the EDP end of the continuum than the DSS end.

Compensation and benefits are two other frequently computerized functions. Although most early HRISs were compensation or perhaps payroll-driven systems, more systems in which benefits applications are the most critical and highly emphasized are now starting to appear. With the exception of the New York State agencies, most companies are relying on their HRIS to support benefits functioning. The reason why the New York State agencies report less reliance on computers for payroll (64 percent versus 89 percent average for the three surveys that considered payroll) and benefits (27 percent versus 75 percent average for the others) is that New York State centralizes some of its payroll and benefits activities. Therefore, some agencies do not perform those activities, computerized or manually.

**Exhibit 2.9**    Survey Results: Computerization of HR Functions

| *Lee (1988)* | *HRSP (1987)* | *Thorp and Elliot (1984)* |
|---|---|---|
| Payroll (92%) | EEO records (91%) | Budget and acccounting (78%) |
| Employee ID (88%) | Basic personnel/ payroll (89%) | Position stats (75%) |
| Benefits (88%) | Merit increases (81%) | EEO/AA (74%) |
| Pension (86%) | Defined contri- butions (73%) | Benefits (70%) |
| Compensation administration (85%) | Defined benefits (73%) | Seniority/Staffing (51%) |
| ERISA (81%) | EEO analysis (72%) | Turnover (41%) |
| Employee history (81%) | Performance appraisals (66%) | Wage and salary (38%) |
| EEO (80%) | Benefits statements (65%) | Performance appraisals (36%) |
| Job ID (72%) | Position control (61%) | Absenteeism (30%) |
| Training and development (64%) | Salary forecast (60%) | Productivity (19%) |
| Succession planning (62%) | Executive compensation (56%) | Medical stats (17%) |
| Performance appraisals (62%) | Skills inventory (53%) | Manpower planning (15%) |
| Job evaluation (62%) | Training (52%) | Worker's Compensation (14%) |
| Position control (57%) | Applicant tracking (51%) | Accident/Injuries (12%) |
| Staffing search (57%) | Attendance (51%) | Work scheduling (12%) |
| Worker's compensation (54%) | Bonus incentives (49%) | Unemployment insurance (11%) |
| Labor planning (52%) | Planning (44%) | Employee surveys (11%) |
| Safety (49%) | Stock purchase (42%) | Collective bargaining (9%) |
| Attitude survey (34%) | Job analysis (39%) | Recruiting lists (7%) |
| Grievances (32%) | Flexible benefits (39%) | Job analysis (6%) |
| | Organizational charting (38%) | Test scoring (6%) |
| | Union increases (36%) | Application blanks (6%) |
| | Internal search (35%) | Skills inventory (5%) |
| | Succession planning (32%) | Computer assisted instruction (4%) |
| | Accidents (30%) | |
| | Claims (28%) | |

**Exhibit 2.9**  *continued*

| Kavanagh, Gueutal, and Tannenbaum (1988) | Magnus and Grossman (1985) |
|---|---|
| Basic employee information (91%) | Payroll (88%) |
| Employment status (82%) | Benefits (72%) |
| Location (68%) | Records and administration (69%) |
| Performance evaluations (68%) | Compensation (53%) |
| Salary (68%) | EEO/AA (52%) |
| Position control (64%) | Absenteeism (34%) |
| Payroll (64%) | Turnover (29%) |
| EEO/AA (55%) | HR planning (29%) |
| Job history (55%) | Employment/Recruitment (23%) |
| Salary history (55%) | Training and development (23%) |
| Attendance (45%) | OSHA (17%) |
| HR planning (36%) | Labor relations (12%) |
| Internal transfers (32%) | |
| Job evaluation (27%) | |
| Benefits administration (27%) | |
| Turnover analysis (23%) | |
| Medical insurance (18%) | |
| Compensation planning (18%) | |
| Training (18%) | |
| Pensions (14%) | |
| Applicant tracking (14%) | |
| Career planning (14%) | |
| Collective bargaining (9%) | |
| Safety/OSHA (0%) | |

While the primary use of HRISs remains administrative, the surveys reveal some strategic uses of HRISs as well. Lee reports that 62 percent of the companies use their HRIS for succession planning, 52 percent for labor planning, and 57 percent for staffing search. The HRSP survey shows that 60 percent use their system for salary forecasting, 56 percent for executive compensation, and 44 percent for planning. These two recent surveys of primarily private sector companies show the greatest use of strategic applications.

Based on the surveys and our experience, the following trends in HR computerization are apparent:

NB  JS

**Exhibit 2.10**   Survey Samples

*Lee (1988)*

> Sample: HR departments Fortune 500
> Number sent: 500
> Number returned: 150
> Percent using computers in HR: Approximately 100%

*HRSP (1987)*

> Sample: HRSP member companies
> Number sent: 900
> Number returned: 360
> Average company size: 13,800 employees
>                    12% < 1,000 employees
>                    35% 1–5,000 employees
> Percent using computers in HR: Approximately 100%

*Thorp and Elliot (1984)*

> Sample: American Hospital Association members
> Number sent: 300
> Number returned: 94
> Company size: 14% < 500 employees
>                    27% 500–1,000 employees
>                    22% 1,000–1,500 employees
> Percent using computers in HR: 86.2%

*Kavanagh, Gueutal, and Tannenbaum (1988)*

> Sample: New York State government agencies
> Number sent: 65
> Number returned: 43
> Percent with HRIS: 51% had HRIS
>                    21% planned to install during year

*Magnus and Grossman*

> Sample: *Personnel Journal* subscribers
> Number sent: 1,000
> Number returned: 434
> Average company size: 2,400 employees
>                    50% < 1,000 employees
> Percent using computers in HR: 99.7%

- Payroll, basic employee records, and EEO/AA are the most commonly used modules, followed closely by compensation and benefits.
- The benefits module will show the greatest growth in terms of complexity and importance in the next few years.
- The use of computers to support position control is increasing.
- There are more administrative applications than strategic applications but there is a slight trend toward the development of more strategic applications.
- There are still more EDP-type applications than MIS- or DSS-type applications, although more MIS-type applications and some DSS-type applications are being used. It is hoped that DSS-type applications will be used to a greater extent in the future.
- The use of computers in HR is increasing, and more functions are being computerized.
- Computers are used more in the HR function in the private sector than in the public sector, although the public sector uses the computer for many basic functions. Larger companies rely on computers more than smaller companies.
- The reported use of computers in labor negotiations and planning seems to have lagged considering the importance of the subfunction. However, the finding that 52 percent of the larger companies are now using their HRIS for labor planning is encouraging.[6]

## Users: A Diverse Group

As was illustrated in the John Donson case, a variety of people use the HRIS. Because user needs should drive the system, it is important to understand the distinction among user types. Users vary according to their computer sophistication, the level of aggregation they are interested in (the individual, the unit or division, the company, and/or the system itself ), the types of information they require, how frequently they use the system, and whether they are hands-on users of the system (as programmers, application developers, data retrievers, analysts) or simply receive reports. Some of the most common HRIS user groups are discussed below.

### HR Functional Specialists

Human resources professionals who are assigned to a specific HR subfunction (e.g., compensation) are referred to here as **HR functional specialists**.

A broad spectrum of technical sophistication exists among this group of users. Many functional specialists rely on the HRIS to perform their job and to provide services to other clients; some need hands-on skills, others simply request information from the HRIC or EDP/MIS group. Typically, these users only have access to the data regarding their function. As noted before, most HRISs have modules targeted to major subfunctions. Some functional specialists use the system by submitting requests for information to the HRIC. However, some sophisticated functional specialists are directly involved in information reporting, data administration (for the data elements in their module), development (typically in a microcomputer environment), and may even provide user support if line managers are using their applications.

## HR Executives

Human resource generalists with managerial responsibilities are also users of the HRIS. Typically, they have less technical sophistication than the users discussed previously. They look for HRIS efficiency to free their time from administrative activities so they can focus more on strategic pursuits.[7] In addition, HR executives may look for data from the HRIS to guide or justify strategic decisions.

The focus of the HR executive regarding the HRIS will vary according to his or her responsibilities and the size of the company. Higher-level HR executives, in larger companies, spend more time on strategic issues and probably have little involvement at the individual level (except regarding high-level transfers or succession planning). At lower levels, or in smaller companies, HR executives may be involved in counseling, grievances, and other individual-level issues and, thus, have more interest in individual-level HRIS data. Often, HR executives are hands-off users, requesting reports and analyses from the HRIC or EDP group. However, this is not always the case. At one large money center bank nine of the top fifteen HR executives have computers on their desks. (Although who knows to what extent they are used!)

## Line Managers

Line managers usually require little technical expertise regarding the HRIS. For the most part, they are concerned with individual-level data regarding their employees or summary-level data regarding head counts and labor expenses. They typically receive information from standard reports or by submitting requests for information to the HRIC. However, in some companies (for example, Federal Express) line managers are becoming hands-on users of the HRIS, retrieving information (e.g., developmental plans, performance appraisal information) on their terminals.[8] This is clearly not yet the norm. However, as retrieval tools become more user friendly and as more line managers have access to terminals, more hands-on use of HRIS by line managers is expected.

## Senior Management

Senior managers are rarely hands-on users of the HRIS. They receive information from standard reports or through specific requests to the HRIC. Their focus is at a high level of aggregation—mainly summary reports comparing divisions/functions or highlighting opportunities or problems. As with senior HR executives, the primary interest at the individual level is with key promotions or succession plans. They may be infrequent users of the system but their requests have high visibility and may impact critical decisions.

A trend toward **executive information systems (EISs)** or **executive support systems (ESSs)** in other functional areas is now starting. These systems are unique because they are targeted toward senior managers as users. They are designed to present data from several data bases in a manner that is usable and understandable to computer-naive executives. A recent survey by MIT's Center for Information Systems Research found over half of the Fortune 500 are developing EISs in one form or another, and a few (e.g., Sears and General Motors) have already developed an EIS.[9] It will be interesting to see the role of human resource information in the future development of EISs.

## Employees

Until recently employees were only users when they received turnaround documents (forms used to confirm or revise employee records), their pay checks, W-2s, and perhaps annual benefits statements. They were never hands-on users. But an era of greater employee involvement is beginning. Legal requirements (e.g., the Privacy Act of 1974) grant employees greater access to their personal data.[10] HRISs are starting to change accordingly. Some organizations have established information kiosks (similar to automatic teller machines) or dial-in (phone to computer linkup) services for employees to query the HRIS regarding their benefits, payroll, or other data.

## Human Resource Information Center

In some organizations there are one or more HR professionals whose primary responsibilities are to support and proliferate the HRIS. This group (or person) is referred to as the **Human Resource Information Center**.[11] Some companies may not use the abbreviation HRIC (and some employees may be surprised to find out they are the HRIC!), but HRIC is used in this book for communication purposes. This term refers to the function—not to any physical location like "the center."

Exhibit 2.11 lists some of the common activities or services provided by a "full-service" HRIC.[12] The activities noted in Exhibit 2.11 are not always performed by the HRIC. Some of these activities may be performed by the EDP/MIS group or by HR functional specialists (e.g., a compensation specialist may do her own report preparation) depending on the size, structure, and preference of the organization.

Lee's survey revealed that 74 percent of the HR departments at large (Fortune 500) organizations employ at least one computer professional in the HR department. Moreover, 43 percent of the respondents reported that

**Exhibit 2.11**    Human Resource Information Center Activities

Information Reporting
  Report preparation and distribution
  Research
  Report documentation

Data Administration
  Data preparation
  System maintenance
  Security

Development
  Enhancements/Modification
  System documentation
  Product development

User Support
  Training
  Marketing
  Answering questions
  Consulting

at least one of their HR employees had designed, operated, or maintained a mathematical computer model with HR applications. While smaller companies tend to have more HR generalists, and thus are less likely to employ HRIS specialists, there is an increase in the computer skills of HR professionals in smaller companies as well. In fact in a study of HR practices in hospitals, 85 percent of those hospitals with less than 1,000 employees reported using computer applications to support the HR function.[13]

HRIC members tend to have some technical sophistication. In companies where the HRIS is independent from the EDP/MIS staff, the HRIC staff must have somewhat greater sophistication; as keepers of the system their focus is similar to that of the EDP/MIS staff. This independence is not as rare as you might think. Thirty-two percent of the respondents in Lee's survey reported that the HR department, not the MIS department, controls daily access to their companies' mainframes and micros for HR purposes.

In contrast to the independent HRIC, in some companies the primary role of the HRIC is to act as a liaison between other users and the EDP/MIS department. In essence they act on behalf of other HR subfunctions and line managers in working with the EDP/MIS group. In these cases, the HRIC's focus will vary according to client and business needs.

Regardless of their focus, the HRIC staff must have HR expertise in addition to whatever technical expertise they possess.

## EDP/MIS

The EDP/MIS people are not users in the classic sense. However, they do use the system to develop applications or to generate reports for other users, and thus they rely on the system to be able to perform their jobs. They are concerned with the efficiency of the system's hardware and software.

They are technically sophisticated, hands-on users. Their focus is on the system: how the system is used; where the system must interface with other systems; what errors, warnings, and problems have arisen; what programs and applications must be developed and maintained; and who has access to the system.

Exhibit 2.12 plots the various user groups along two dimensions: computer sophistication and human resources sophistication. Naturally, most MIS/EDP types have high computer sophistication and low HR sophistication. Most HR functional specialists have low to moderate computer sophistication and fairly high HR sophistication. Typical line managers and senior managers are not well versed in the nuances of computer programming nor benefits administration—they rate low on both computer and HR sophistication. The different levels of expertise among users can create communication problems that lead to conflicts. MIS/EDP types don't understand HR concerns and HR types don't understand computing concerns. Fortunately, a few people with both HR and computer sophistication are starting to emerge. The ideal HRIC is placed in the high-high quadrant. Individuals with both skill sets can serve as liaison/communicators between the technical and nontechnical user groups.

**Exhibit 2.12**   Computer and HR Skills of Various User Groups

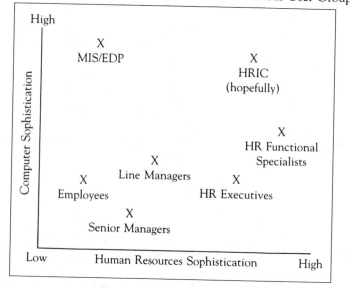

# User Group Implications

Each HRIS will serve one or more of the user groups noted above. The user mix and emphasis will vary from company to company, as will the location of the budget. It is important to recognize explicitly which user groups will be served. There are some critical implications for system effectiveness as a result of user characteristics.

Prior to purchasing, revising, or developing a system a needs analysis should be conducted (see Chapter 5 for details). As part of the needs analysis the issue of user-groups' needs must be addressed: Who will use the system and what are their specific needs? Many HR professionals are pushing the concept of strategic HR and advocate the use of the HRIS for strategic purposes.[14] If you want your system to drive or support strategic concerns the system must reach managers outside the HR function. Some of the users will be reached secondhand (via reports), but there is an increasing trend to direct system access. Expanding the hands-on user group has important implications for system design, selection, and user training.

For example, when users have little technical sophistication but are expected to have hands-on contact, the system must be extremely easy to use. In this situation a system must be designed or purchased that reduces the learning curve for the relatively naive user. Some systems are beginning to use **icons** (symbols, for example, a dollar sign to signify payroll) and other ease-of-use features to facilitate user understanding.

If users are to be reached strictly through standard reports and all hands-on work will be performed by more sophisticated users (i.e., the EDP/MIS group or the HRIC technical staff), then the system will require fewer ease-of-use features. Regardless, all users should receive some training regarding the HRIS. All users should at least have an overview of the system and understand how to request additional information. This could be included as a part of other management training or provided as written documentation, but *all* users should understand the system's capabilities. In this way they are less likely to request information the system cannot provide. In addition, uninformed users may fail to request useful information because they think the system cannot provide it, when in fact it can. This is supported by a recent survey that revealed that a major information system complaint among managers is that they are not aware of the information in the data base and how to access it.[15]

For some, training must go beyond the system overview. Some users will need to be trained in report generation and others on the actual operation of the system. In other words, training needs will differ for different user groups. At Exxon's Central Services user skills are evaluated as a way of determining training needs. They break down their users into various levels of sophistication, for example, novices, experts, and trailblazers. They use this schema to help target different types of training to specific jobs and individuals.

In general, more hands-on contact with the HRIS is occurring. As a result, HRISs need to be developed and acquired that are less intimidating for nonsophisticated users, and training must be targeted to different user group needs.

## Summary

This chapter explained what an HRIS is and how it is typically used. The focus was on the various types of outputs available from an HRIS and the modules that typically make up an HRIS. In addition, various users were examined, noting their needs and their computer and HR skill base. As mentioned at the start of the chapter, an HRIS interfaces with a variety of systems including the external environment. In Chapter 3 the changing human resource environment is examined more closely.

## Discussion Questions

1. What is an HRIS? Why should policies and procedures be considered part of the HRIS?
2. What types of output are available from an HRIS? What types of reports would a line manager find most valuable?
3. Which HR subfunctions are most likely to use computerized support tools? Which subfunctions do you think will increase their use in the future? Why?
4. Who are the users of an HRIS? How do their needs and skills differ? How can these differences affect the system?
5. With what systems does the HRIS interface?

## Notes

1. R. Nardoni, "Executive Summaries," *Computers in Personnel* (Summer 1987): 52–55.
2. Ibid.
3. Exhibit 2.6 is based, in part, on the data hierarchy found in K. C. Laudon and J. P. Laudon, *Management Information Systems: A Contemporary Perspective* (New York: Macmillan, 1988), 167.
4. A. Walker, *HRIS Development: A Project Team Guide to Building an Effective Personnel System* (New York: Van Nostrand Reinhold, 1982), 25.
5. Several surveys have been conducted evaluating computer use in HR. See, for example, M. J. Kavanagh, H. G. Gueutal, and S. I. Tannenbaum, "Government: Who Needs an HRIS?" *Computers in Personnel* (Fall 1987): 40–43; A. S. Lee, "Despite Microcomputer Proliferation, Mainframes are Still Preferred," *Computers in Personnel* (Winter 1988): 45–50; M. Magnus and M. Grossman, "Computers and the Personnel Department," *Personnel Journal* (April 1985): 42–48; Survey of Human Resource Systems (1987), The Associ-

ation of HRSP, P.O. Box 8040-8202, Walnut Creek, CA 94596; C. D. Thorp and L. B. Elliot, "EDP Applications for Personnel Activities by Hospitals: A Current Survey of Practices and Plans," *Personnel Administrator* (September 1984): 55–61.

6. Lee, "Despite Microcomputer Proliferation," 46.

7. B. Saari, "New and Emerging Boardroom Concerns and HRIS Implications," *HRSP Review* 4 (1988): 5–7.

8. R. J. Schmiedicke, "Keep it Simple," *Computers in Personnel* (Spring 1987): 45–47.

9. See "Executive Support Systems Put Corporate Data Base at Top Managers' Fingertips with Touch of a Button," *Computerworld* (March 25, 1985).

10. See J. Ledvinka, *Federal Regulation of Personnel and Human Resource Management* (Boston: PWS-KENT, 1982): 225–256.

11. J. Pasquelletto contributed greatly to the use and understanding of this term in the HRIS field. See "Creating an Effective HRIC: Beyond Data Management," *HRSP Review* (Spring 1987): 5–8, 28–30.

12. Pasquelletto, "Creating an Effective HRIC," 30.

13. Thorp and Elliot, "EDP Applications for Personnel Activities," 55.

14. See, for example, A. O. Manzini and J. D. Gridley, *Integrating Human Resources and Strategic Business Planning* (New York: AMACOM, 1986); H. G. Angle, C. C. Manz, and A. H. Van de Ven, "Integrating Human Resource Management and Corporate Strategy: A Review of the 3M Story," *Human Resource Management* (Spring 1985): 51–68; R. S. Schuler and S. E. Jackson, "Linking Competitive Strategies with Human Resource Management Practices," *Academy of Management Executive* 1 (1987): 207–219.

15. G. S. Howard and G. J. Weinroth, "Users' Complaints: Information System Problems from the User's Perspective," *Journal of Systems Management* (May 1987): 30–34.

# 3

# Why Do Organizations Need an HRIS: The External Environment of Human Resources Management

This chapter focuses on the dependence of the human resources function on the external environment of the organization. The history of the HR function in organizations is one of responding to the demands of the external environment, particularly in terms of compliance with various laws and regulations by both federal and state governments. However, when the major social legislation of the 1960s regarding employees' rights began, organizations with manual HR systems were in a panic trying to comply with the new laws and new reporting requirements. Computer technology, which had made only some minor inroads into the personnel function prior to this time, became an important part of the answer to the increased reporting requirements demanded by government agencies. As computer technology became more sophisticated and companies became more sensitive to the increasing significance of the external environment to the more effective functioning of HR, the demand for HRISs increased. This need for HR to become more sensitive to the external environment is the single most important reason for the rapid development of computer-based HR systems.

In this chapter, the critical interrelationship between the HR function and the external environment is first emphasized, and the factors of the environment external to the organization that specifically drive the need for an HRIS are then described. To understand the current situation, it will be necessary to refer to the evolution of the HR field contained in the historical description in Chapter 1. Of greater importance, the various aspects of the external environment contained in Exhibit 1.4 will be analyzed in terms of their impact on the development or acquisition of an HRIS. This chapter focuses on factors that impact primarily the development, implementation, and use of an HRIS, not the total HR function in the firm. This latter concern has been well covered in other texts and is not within the scope of this book.

# The External Environment
# Relevant for HR

The external environment of any organization contains an enormous amount of information relevant to its operation. Much of this information, such as prevailing financial interest rates, is only of interest to specific departments or functions within the organization. Like the other functions, HR has to attend only to portions or facets of the external environment. Because the HRIS is embedded within the HR department and, as discussed in Chapter 2, mirrors its internal structure, it is also directly affected by the external environment.

The history of the HR field, as covered in Chapter 1, really illustrates the interdependence between HR activities and the external environment. The employee abuses in the early part of this century that led to major labor legislation in the 1930s are an example of this interdependence. Social problems in this country in the 1950s and 1960s led to most of the social legislation of the 1960s and 1970s. In fact, as illustrated in Exhibit 1.4, the entire HR management system is impacted by its external environment. However, in this chapter, the focus is on the impact of these environmental factors on the development and use of the HRIS. A broader discussion of how the external environment impacts the total HR management system can be found in most HR textbooks.[1]

The facets of the environment primarily relevant to HR and HRISs are depicted in Exhibit 3.1. As each part of the external environment is discussed, the implications of these factors outside the organization for the design and use of the HRIS are covered. The major point of this section is that

**Exhibit 3.1**   Environmental Factors That Influence HRISs

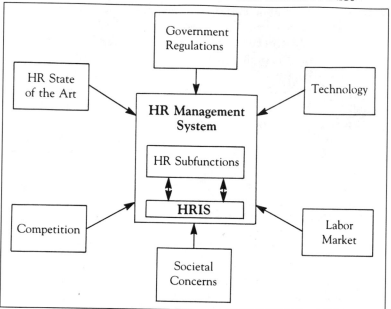

the information from the external environment relevant to the HR function is both complex and constantly changing, thus necessitating an HRIS.

## Government Regulations

As discussed in Chapter 1, government regulations, both federal and state, have had, and continue to have, a major impact on HR and the HRIS. Although other authors[2] cover the various government regulations in detail, the discussion here focuses on several examples of how government regulations impact the HRIS.

### Employment Discrimination

**Title VII of the Civil Rights Act of 1964,** as amended by the Equal Employment Opportunity Act of 1972, prohibits unfair discrimination based on race, color, national origin, religion, and gender in all employment practices. This includes initial hiring, termination, promotion, merit raises, and selection into training programs that are required for career advancement. This means that private employers with fifteen or more employees must maintain comprehensive records on all employees with regard to these employment decisions.

**EEO-1 Report**   One of the requirements is that all organizations covered by the law must submit an **EEO-1 report** annually. This report details the composition of the work force of the organization in terms of race, gender, and national origin. In addition to these categories, numerous other groups are protected by various laws.[3] These include people with physical or mental handicaps, disabled veterans and Vietnam veterans, and people over the age of 40. For the remainder of this book, these groups are referred to as **protected classes**.

Records must be kept not only on protected classes of individuals when they are employees of your organization but also on all job applicants for one year whether or not they are hired. In the case of initial hires, these records form the basis of statistical tests to determine if the employer has violated the law. Obviously, keeping these records on a computer and using statistical software to compute the tests for unfair discrimination is vastly superior to working with a manual, paperwork system. In fact, most major software packages have an applicant-tracking module that can perform these analyses for the EEO-1 report. Obviously, this is considerably easier than spending endless hours tallying protected classes of employees and applicants on yellow notepads.

One personnel director of a company of approximately 700 employees estimated that she spends approximately 25 days every January producing the required government reports with a manual system. Compare this with the capability of using one or two simple commands to a microcomputer software package to produce the same reports in one day!

**Employee Composition**   The other area where an HRIS is handy for EEO compliance is in determining the statistical distribution of a company's work force. The EEO laws require that companies have the same composition of their work force in terms of race, gender, and national origin that exists in the external labor market. Although the exact definition of the appropriate labor market is controversial and has often had to be decided in court, it is still clear that companies must match some labor market in terms of the composition of their work force of protected classes of individuals under the various government regulations. This determination of whether a company is in compliance is done by comparing the percentages of employees in protected classes against the composition of the appropriate labor market. Having an HRIS with access to statistical software makes this a relatively simple task.

In addition to this employee composition requirement, the company must be able to demonstrate that it has a fair, nondiscriminatory promotion policy. Using a computer analysis within an HRIS, **Markov procedures**, complex mathematical procedures that can be used to project historical employee patterns into the future, have been developed for this purpose.[4] Software that will do the statistical analyses examining the promotion rates of protected classes within a company is also available. These software packages are covered in more detail in Chapter 8. Similar analyses for both initial hire and promotion progression for all protected classes are necessary to demonstrate compliance with government regulations, thus increasing the need for the efficient analyses and report generation contained within an HRIS.

***Regulatory Model***    Exhibit 3.2 shows the regulatory model for EEO that affects the HR functions. Exhibit 3.3 humorously illustrates the alphabet soup of agencies and legislation that forms the regulatory environment for human resources. The most striking feature of both these exhibits is the complexity and confusion embedded in them. If you think it looks confusing, imagine how confusing and difficult it is for HR departments to handle. What all of this regulation means for companies is increased record keeping, increased analysis of employee data, and increased reporting responsibilities. Fortunately, these are the three things that HRISs do best. The increase in work that resulted from this regulation is one of the most pressing reasons HR departments have developed and implemented HRISs.

In the "Management Responses" column of Exhibit 3.2 a number of areas within the HR function that EEO information is required relative to various employment actions are indicated. These actions require accurate data collection, data analysis, standard reports, and ad hoc reports. The standard reports are those required by law. They serve to audit the firm's compliance with the EEO requirements detailed in Exhibit 3.2. The need for ad hoc reports is also seen in Exhibit 3.2, when management has to respond to specific situations in the area of training, communications, lawsuits, or grievances. The specific type of EEO information needed for these purposes changes depending on the situation. For example, a company may need EEO information contrasting females versus males in second-level management

**Exhibit 3.2** The Regulatory Model Applied to EEO

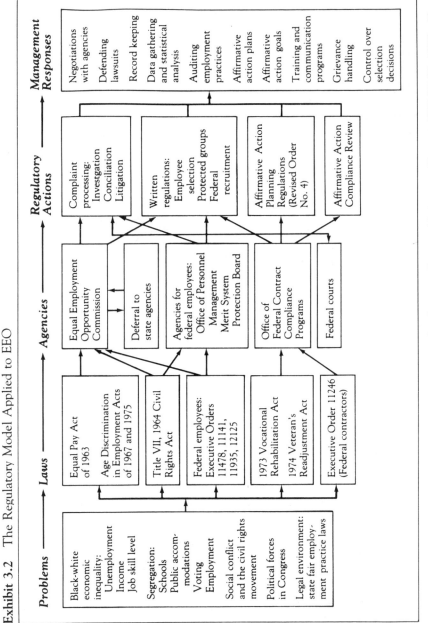

*Source:* J. Ledvinka, *Federal Regulation of Personnel and Human Resource Management* (Boston: PWS-KENT, 1982), 23. Reproduced by permission.

to provide a report in defense of a litigation, while in a grievance hearing, management may need the number of minorities versus nonminorities working as machinists in a plant in central Iowa. Although these varying needs for EEO information in different slices of the employee data base create major headaches for manual systems, most computer-based systems have this ad hoc inquiry capability. As part of the needs analysis for the HRIS, to be discussed in Chapter 4, these and other ad hoc inquiry capabilities must be specified.

**Exhibit 3.3**    Regulatory Environment: An Alphabet Soup of Agencies and Legislation

| |
|---|
| ADEA |
| HMO          OSHA |
| FLSA |
| Wage and hours |
| PBGC          IRS |
| Equal pay |
| ERISA          OFCCP |
| TEFRA |
| TSCA |
| EEOC |
| DRG |
| DOL |
| Privacy Act |
| SEC. 401(k) |
| COBRA |
|              REACT |
| DEFRA |
| SEC. 125 |
| SEC. 403(b) |

*Source:*    The Association of Human Resource Systems Professionals, HRSP 101 — Introduction to Human Resource Information Systems Seminar. Reproduced by permission.

**State Laws**    In addition to federal regulation, organizations must be sensitive to state laws that affect the HR function. Since these laws vary from state to state, specific laws are not covered in this book. However, the major area of regulation in terms of state laws is in unemployment and disability compensation. As with federal regulation, software packages are available to help the HR department meet state law requirements. Some of these are covered in Chapter 8, but for the HR practitioner, it is best to contact a software company. A listing of these companies and their software offerings was recently published.[5]

**Court Decisions**    The HR function and the HRIS are also affected by court decisions regarding the welfare of employees. For example, recent decisions have defined the liability of companies for employees exposed to asbestos on the job. This means that the HR department, within the requirements of OSHA, must now determine which of their employees were, or are now, exposed to asbestos. Because precise records must be kept, a new requirement is added to the OSHA module within the HRIS. Under OSHA requirements, records must be kept on all employees exposed to any toxic material at the workplace. As the personnel director of a large chemical company related, the list of toxic materials is in the thousands for his company; and he could not handle the OSHA requirements without his HRIS.

Likewise, any new court decision modifying or clarifying any state or federal regulation relevant to the HR function invariably means some changes to the HRIS. This means a need to accommodate change, particularly in the HRIS modules concerned with government regulations. This must be kept in mind during the needs analysis, which is discussed in Chapter 4.

**New Laws**    Both the HR function and the HRIS are impacted quite seriously by new laws or changes to existing ones. The **Tax Reform Act of 1986** has had serious implications for benefits in terms of pension plans and defining various benefits as taxable. The **Age Discrimination in Employment Act (ADEA)**, of 1967 amended in 1986, prohibits employers from discriminating on the basis of age against people over 40 and eliminates mandatory retirement for most employees. The **Omnibus Budget Reconciliation Act (OBRA)** of 1986 affected pension accruals and participation beyond a pension plan's normal retirement age of 65.[6] At a time when the management of benefits and compensation is one of the most important programs for cost containment within the HR department, these new laws can mean increased costs in record maintenance and reporting requirements. Finally, changes to existing regulations can cause major revisions to record-keeping requirements. For example, in January 1989 the Labor Department announced widespread changes in workplace-exposure limits for 376 toxic chemicals.[7] For organizations without an HRIS, this presents a nightmare in changed record keeping and reporting. The presence of an HRIS that allows flexible modification of its software to integrate these changes into the benefits and compensation modules can greatly reduce the costs of complying with new laws and responding to changes in existing ones.

## Technology

In terms of impact on the HR function and HRIS design, the technology facet in Exhibit 3.1 ranks second to the influence of government regulations. As noted in Chapter 1, very few organizations in the 1950s and 1960s were using computer technology in HR because of the expense of the rigid, stand-alone computer systems and programs being developed at the time. The introduction of the IBM/360 and similar mainframe computers in the 1960s made computing capability more accessible and affordable to HR departments. However, in the late 1970s and early 1980s, the major software packages for human resources were applicable only to mainframe environments. Because these were quite expensive, particularly when the cost of the mainframe hardware was included, they were adopted only by large companies. When this state of affairs is contrasted with the power of microcomputers and minicomputers today at more affordable costs, one begins to understand the tremendous influence of technological advances on the design, development, and implementation of HRISs within HR departments.

There seems to be no end to new developments in technology for the HR function. With each advance in processing speed or storage capacity, new software for HR appears on the market. A word of caution is appropriate at this point. Technological advances and the purchase of an HR hardware-software configuration alone will not solve all the problems of the HR department. As discussed in Chapters 5 and 6, a careful needs analysis, including a cost-benefit analysis, must be done before purchasing new technology.

## Labor Market

The next important factor in the external environment is the labor market. Because the labor market is where organizations obtain new employees, its importance to the HR function is obvious. However, its influence on the HRIS may not be so apparent. Several ways in which the labor market influences various programs within the HR department and, thus, the HRIS modules associated with those programs, are discussed below.

## Human Resource Planning

The HR program in which the labor market is most important is **human resource planning (HRP)**. HRP estimates future demand for and supply of employees; it then develops plans for reconciling any demand-supply imbalance.[8] HRP would obviously relate to the HR planning and forecasting module; in terms of obtaining new employees from the external labor market, both the applicant-tracking and succession planning modules would be useful.

## External Environment Scanning

To analyze the labor market, organizations use some form of external environmental scanning (EES). EES involves monitoring relevant events in the external environment, analyzing them for significance, and injecting the relevant information into the HRP process.[9] Exhibit 3.4 illustrates how an HRIS can be used in this EES process for storing, analyzing, and transmitting labor market information to the relevant modules. This exhibit depicts an ideal example of how this EES could operate using the HRIS within the planning process. Although this type of operation may not yet be implemented, it provides a guide for future development. In terms of the labor market, this would mean monitoring information on employment trends, such as shortages of people to fill certain jobs. The next step would be to enter these labor market data into a data base for storage within the HRIS.

The analysis of these data would be guided by queries relevant to the HR system modules listed in Exhibit 3.4. For example, the people involved

**Exhibit 3.4**   Labor Market EES with an HRIS

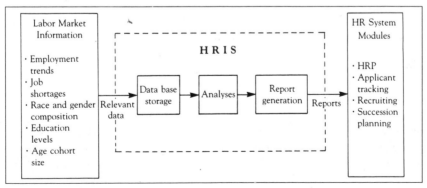

with HRP may estimate a need for fifty new computer programmers in the next year. The analysis part of the HRIS would analyze the labor market data base and produce a report on whether this number will be available in the external labor market. In a similar manner, the people involved in recruiting may need to know the number of people in protected classes that will be available in the labor market for the next year. The HRIS should be designed to answer this question and provide a report to the relevant group in the HR department. Thus, the labor market drives the design of the HRIS and should not be ignored in the needs analysis. Because of its storage, analysis, and reporting capacities, an HRIS is superior to a manual system for monitoring the labor market.

## Societal Concerns

The societal concerns factor involves the many and diverse issues that are raised concerning the firm's image as a good citizen and a good neighbor. Although it is impossible to anticipate all the questions that are referred to the HR department by outside groups, several general types of questions can be expected. The important point of this discussion is to illustrate that an HR department receives diverse and complex inquiries from outside groups and that it must respond rapidly to them. This ability to respond rapidly using the ad hoc inquiry capability of the computer-based system is one of the real advantages of an HRIS.

### Employee Information Requests

One of the most common inquiries to the HR department involves the gender and racial composition of the company's work force. With an HRIS in place this information should be readily available, since, as discussed earlier in this chapter, it is needed for the EEO-1 report. Another common request is for the number of employees who are working in hazardous conditions. Again, because of OSHA requirements, this information should be available on the HRIS. Another common inquiry is about any environmental pollutants the firm may be dumping into the local environment. Although controlling pollution is not usually a responsibility of the HR department, the HR department sometimes reports this information to the public and thus must monitor it. A final inquiry that is frequently directed to the HR department is the possibility of layoffs or new hires. With an HRIS involved in the HRP function, this information should be readily available.

To fully understand the advantage of having an HRIS, just imagine how long it would take to respond to the queries in the previous paragraph with a manual system. Often, the length of time it takes to respond to queries is related to the public's perception of the firm as a good neighbor or citizen. A lengthy response time may adversely affect the firm's operation in the community. This is particularly true for firms in the service economy, such as supermarkets.

## Privacy Issues

Another societal concern, from both outside and inside the firm, is the issue of privacy of employee information. The federal **Privacy Act** of 1974 specifies limits and controls for federal agencies regarding the access and use of personal information. This act does not currently apply to private industry, but it may signal the direction for future legislation.[10] Most firms are very sensitive about maintaining the privacy of personal information about their employees. In fact, revealing confidential information concerning employees has been the source of numerous law suits. Further, most firms recognize that employee morale can be seriously damaged if employees feel that personal information about them is not being kept confidential.

An HRIS is typically superior to a manual system in maintaining the privacy of employee records. In a manual system, employee files are frequently maintained in file cabinets, which can be inadvertently left unlocked. Also, in our experience with a variety of firms, few maintain a "sign-out" security system on employee files. Employee files can be left on desks while the HR specialist is at lunch, on a break, and so on. Although having an HRIS can solve some of these problems, security is obviously still an issue. However, by using a multiple-level password system, access to employee files, or at least parts of them, can be controlled. For example, although HR specialists in the compensation area do not typically need access to medical records of employees, those in benefits need this access for health insurance purposes. The multiple-level password system in an HRIS can establish this differential control. Most important, a password system can exclude unauthorized users completely. Finally, changing passwords on a regular basis, for example, monthly or quarterly, is a further advantage of the security characteristics of an HRIS.

## Note of Caution

These various societal concerns firms must respond to provide one more reason for adopting an HRIS. As noted before, these societal concerns also provide guidelines for the needs analysis and subsequent design of the HRIS. If these concerns are issues for the firm, they must be included in the needs analysis since they will have a major impact on the design and acquisition of the hardware-software configuration that will comprise the HRIS.

Finally, a note of caution. The societal concerns raised in this section are very real and are becoming more important as our society becomes more sensitive to ethical issues in the workplace. However, adopting an HRIS is not the complete solution to these issues. The HRIS is simply another tool for management to use. The HRIS is a very efficient tool and is considerably better than a manual HR system in responding to these societal concerns. However, it is still management's responsibility to address and resolve these issues.

# Competition

This factor, which drives a need for and affects the design features of an HRIS, refers to the multiple competitors for new employees in the external environment. The major focus of this competition for new employees is in the wage and benefits areas, jointly referred to as the compensation area of the HR function. Thus, this aspect of the external environment is most relevant for the benefits and compensation modules of the HRIS discussed in Chapter 2. Although other factors, such as geographic location and quality of life, affect the decision to accept a job, clearly the compensation package of the company is one of the major determinants.

## Compensation Management

In the past decade it has become clear that the effective management of compensation is central to the profitability of the firm.[11] There are several reasons for this. It has been estimated that payroll costs in the manufacturing sector can be as high as 40 percent of the firm's operating costs; in the service sector payroll can be nearly 70 percent.[12] In addition, benefits add about one-third to total compensation costs.[13] What this means is that compensation is a major cost factor that needs close and continual attention if the firm is to remain profitable.

## Labor Market Surveys

In order to be effective, information from wage and benefits surveys must be based on the relevant labor markets for the employees of the firm. Thus, for entry-level through most white- and blue-collar jobs, wage and benefits information on the local labor market within a defined geographic area is critical. More skilled employees like computer analysts, accountants, and HR specialists would likely be hired from a regional labor market, whereas scientists, higher-level executives, and highly skilled technical employees may be hired from a national market. This means the firm must have information on what its competitors are offering in their compensation packages in all these labor markets.

The wage and benefits surveys relevant to each labor market create large data bases that need to be analyzed to determine how they will influence the compensation strategy and practices of the firm. Without a computer and statistical software, these analyses are almost impossible. Given the tremendous need for companies to compete for skilled employees while controlling compensation costs, any medium-sized or larger firm without access to computer analyses of appropriate compensation packages based on labor market surveys will have considerable difficulty attracting and retaining good employees. Further, most firms want to keep their compensation strategy and planning confidential, particularly from their competitors. This is another strong argument for acquiring and implementing an HRIS.

## Compensation Planning

The area of compensation planning is where a computer-based human resources system may be the most useful to a firm. Whether it is a compensation module of a comprehensive HRIS or a stand-alone software application in compensation planning, the ability to examine "what if" alternatives in compensation planning is critical to a cost-effective plan. With compensation software it is a relatively simple matter to examine the varying costs of alternative compensation plans that are combinations of wage and benefits packages. With the powerful spreadsheet software built into these compensation computer packages, the implication in terms of overall changes in costs, even minor changes, to either wage or benefits packages can be quickly assessed. As a tool for decision makers, this ease of considering the impact of alternative compensation packages is invaluable. A firm without this capability in an environment where competitors have the capability through an HRIS is at a serious disadvantage. More information on the HRIS as an aid to decision makers in compensation as well as in other areas of human resources is contained in Chapters 8 and 9.

## HR State-of-the-Art Information

The final factor in the external environment that drives the need for an HRIS is the current state-of-the-art information in the field of human resources. Every new textbook published in the field refers to computer-based HR systems, and it is rare to find any issue of the professional journals in the HR field without an article on HRISs. National societies for professionals interested in computers in the HR field have been formed, and new journals have been started. Professional seminars in HRISs have begun to appear in the past five years, and educational curricula in human resources have been modified to reflect this changing emphasis in the HR field. All of these changes in the professional field, along with the other factors in the external environment, have produced tremendous pressure on firms to computerize their HR function. The remainder of this section is devoted to documenting these significant and recent changes in the HR field to provide a better understanding of the widespread nature of this shift to HRIS in the HR field.

### *Initial Book and Professional Organizations*

Although earlier articles in the professional HR literature on HRISs were published, the major publication that heralded the beginning of the serious attention to computer-based HR systems was Alfred Walker's *HRIS Development: A Project Team Guide to Building an Effective Personnel Information System* in 1982.[14] Two years earlier, in 1980, the **Human Resource Systems Professionals (HRSP, Inc.)** was formally incorporated as a national organization. This was the first professional HR organization devoted primarily to computer-based HR systems, and it remains the dominant professional organization in this field today.[15] In addition to its quarterly publication, which covers new developments in the field of HRIS, HRSP sponsors an annual conference and professional seminars on the use of computers in the HR field. Attending the annual conference or one of the professional seminars is an excellent way to acquire information about computer-based HR systems.

In addition to HRSP, the other professional human resources organization that has covered the use of computers in HR is the **Human Resources Planning Society (HRPS)**.[16] Although this organization is focused primarily on strategic human resource management, is has encouraged work on the use of computers in the human resource planning process. However, it is not focused primarily on HRISs, as is HRSP.

The final professional organization that also covers developments in HRISs is the **American Society for Personnel Administration (ASPA)**.[17] This is the oldest and largest professional HR organization, and it serves the HR professional in all aspects of the HR function in organizations.

### *Professional Publications*

ASPA publishes the *Personnel Administrator* journal, which usually contains at least one article on HRISs in each issue. The HRPS publishes the *Human Resources Planning* journal, which carries a mix of articles on human resources planning and the application of computers to the planning process. HRSP, in addition to their chapter newsletters and the *HRSP Review*, published a bibliography of professional references in the HRIS field in 1987,[18] which was updated in 1989. Further, the New York chapter, the Human Resource Information Management Society, published a systems survey in 1986.[19] Finally, a new professional journal, *Computers in Personnel*, that focuses exclusively on the HRIS field was begun in 1987.[20]

As evidenced by these numerous and recent developments, the state of knowledge in human resources has shifted to the development of professional skills in HRISs. These developments in the HR profession have also begun to appear in higher education in terms of curricula designed specifically for learning the knowledge and skills in the field of HRISs.[21] These developments have significantly altered the field of HR permanently and provide yet another reason for developing an HRIS within the firm.

## Summary

In this chapter, the factors in the external environment that are significantly changing the HR profession toward computer-based HR systems were examined. It has become obvious that firms without an HRIS capability are lagging behind. This situation could seriously impact the ability of these firms to manage their human resources in a cost-effective fashion in the future. A careful consideration of the factors in the external environment is critical in the needs analysis and design of a new or renovated HRIS. There are several professional organizations and publications where the HR professional can obtain more information on HRISs.

## Discussion Questions

1. Describe how the external environment has led to a greater need for HRISs.
2. What are three ways HR and HRISs must react to the environment factor in government relations? Give several examples of how the HRIS can help comply with changes in government regulations.
3. How will new technology affect the HR function in the future? What are some cost areas that should be affected?
4. How can an HRIS assist with external environmental scanning? Could this be used for factors in the environment other than the labor market?
5. How would an HRIS assist in maintaining the privacy of employee records?
6. Why is a knowledge of competition important for the HR management system? How would an HRIS be useful in interfacing with this environmental factor?

## Notes

1. For example, see W. F. Cascio, *Managing Human Resources: Productivity, Quality of Work Life, Profits* (New York: McGraw-Hill, 1986); G. T. Milkovich and J. W. Boudreau, *Personnel/Human Resource Management: A Diagnostic Approach*, 5th ed. (Plano, Texas: Business Publications, Inc., 1988); V. G. Scarpello and J. Ledvinka, *Personnel/Human Resource Management: Environment and Functions* (Boston: PWS-KENT, 1988).
2. J. Ledvinka, *Federal Regulation of Personnel and Human Resource Management* (Boston: PWS-KENT, 1982); D. P. Twomey, *A Concise Guide to Employment Law EEO & OSHA*, 2nd ed. (Cincinnati: South-Western, 1990).
3. J. Ledvinka, *Federal Regulation*, 24–26, contains an exhibit that details the various laws, protected classes, and employers affected by government regulations.
4. J. Ledvinka and R. L. LaForge, "A Staffing Model for Affirmative Action Planning," *Human Resource Planning* 1 (1978): 135–150; G. Milkovich and F. Krzystofiak, "Simulation and Affirmative Action Planning," *Human Resource Planning* 2 (1979): 71–80.

5. R. Frantzreb, *The Personnel Software Census* (Roseville, CA: Advanced Personnel Systems, 1988).

6. For further information on the impact of these laws on compensation and benefits, see R. M. McCaffery, *Employee Benefit Programs: A Total Compensation Perspective* (Boston: PWS-KENT, 1988); M. J. Wallace, Jr. and C. H. Fay, *Compensation Theory and Practice* (Boston: PWS-KENT, 1988).

7. "OSHA Sets or Toughens Exposure Limits on 376 Toxic Chemicals in Workplace," *The Wall Street Journal*, 16 January 1989.

8. L. D. Dyer, "Human Resource Planning," in K. M. Rowland and G. R. Ferris, eds., *Personnel Management* (Boston: Allyn and Bacon, 1982), 52–77.

9. G. Milkovich, L. D. Dyer, and T. Mahoney, "HRM Planning," in S. J. Carroll and R. S. Schuler, eds., *Human Resources Management in the 1980s* (Washington, DC: The Bureau of National Affairs, 1983), 2-1–2-29.

10. W. F. Cascio, *Managing Human Resources: Productivity, Quality of Work Life, Profits,* 2nd ed. (New York: McGraw-Hill, 1988), 163.

11. Ibid., 382–385.

12. K. M. Bartol, "Making Compensation Pay," *Computers in Personnel* (Winter 1987): 35–40.

13. McCaffery, *Employee Benefit Programs,* 1.

14. A. J. Walker, *HRIS Development: A Project Team Guide to Building an Effective Personnel Information System* (New York: Van Nostrand, 1982).

15. For information on HRSP, contact HRSP, Inc., P.O. Box 801646, Dallas, TX 75380-1646, (214) 661-3727.

16. For information on HRPS, contact Human Resources Planning Society, 228 East 45th Street, New York, NY 10017, (212) 490-6387.

17. For information on ASPA, contact American Society for Personnel Administration, 606 North Washington Street, Alexandria, VA 22314, (703) 548-3440.

18. L. M. Plantamura, *Human Resources Information Systems Bibliography* (Dallas, TX: HRSP, 1987).

19. D. W. Muehring, *HRIMS Member Systems Survey* (New York: HRIMS, 1986).

20. For information, contact Andrew Rosenbloom, *Computers in Personnel,* Auerbach Publishers, One Penn Plaza, New York, NY 10119, (212) 971-5000.

21. For information on these educational programs, see H. G. Gueutal, S. I. Tannenbaum, and M. J. Kavanagh, "Where to Go for an HRIS Education," *Computers in Personnel* 3 (1988): 22–26; C. H. Fay, "Educating Old and New HR Managers," *Computers in Personnel* 4 (1988): 20–26.

# II

## Systems and Management Skills for HRISs

# 4

# The Systems Development Process

This chapter presents an overview of the systems development process. First, the more common barriers to success are explored. By understanding the problems that have blocked previous projects, future systems development projects can be better planned. Next, the systems development process is defined, and a special type of systems development process—reautomation—is discussed. Finally, the activities and phases associated with an HRIS development project—from inception to implementation and continued system maintenance—are examined.

This chapter also provides an overall context for the next three chapters. In Chapters 5, 6, and 7 the focus is on some of the most important issues associated with the systems development process. Additional details on each of the three major phases of systems development—needs analysis, design and development, and implementation and maintenance—are provided.

## Barriers to Success

Before addressing the activities and phases involved in the successful and implementation of an HRIS, it will be useful to look at some of the reasons HRISs do not succeed. Why do some HRISs fail? Sid Simon and Alfred Walker, two of the leading HRIS experts, have reflected on the most common reasons for HRIS failures. Being aware of the potential for the kinds of problems Simon and Walker describe is the first step in avoiding them.

Building on Simon, the most common problems include

Lack of management commitment leading to inadequate resources and personnel. This can be a serious concern if a protracted development process is anticipated.

Failure to assign a project team for the duration of the project. It is important that the core project team members stay with the project from inception to implementation.

Political intrigue, conflict, and hidden agendas set up the project for failure. Power struggles can lead to dysfunctional behavior by all involved.

Poorly written, incomplete needs analysis reports lead to incorrect decisions and a costly system that does not fit the needs of the organization.

Failure to include key personnel on the project team. This can exacerbate political problems and reduce "perceived ownership" to a small group.

Failure to survey/interview key groups in the organization. For example, overlooking the accounting/payroll group in the needs analysis could lead to a system incompatible with the general ledger system of the organization.[1]

Walker has put together a widely cited list of ten mistakes commonly made when developing an HRIS. This list is presented in Exhibit 4.1.

Simon and Walker point out many common mistakes made in developing a system. In fact, 94 percent of those involved in the system development process said they would do it differently if they were to do it again.[2] So just what is involved in developing a successful HRIS?

## What Is the System Development Process?

The HRIS development process refers to the steps taken from the time a company considers computerizing its human resources functions through

**Exhibit 4.1**   Ten Common Mistakes in Developing an HRIS

1. Being all things to all people—all at once.
2. Having no personnel experience on the project team.
3. Separate systems are vulnerable to errors. (Tie new system to payroll to avoid errors.)
4. Avoid superfluous complexity: Resist demand for reports.
5. Insufficient or waning management support.
6. Desing by committee. (Keep the group small.)
7. Technical marvels fail if not user oriented.
8. Loose project control.
9. Promising force reductions: Savings that do not occur.
10. Building when you can buy.

*Source:*   A. J. Walker, *HRIS Development: A Project Team Guide to Building an Effective Personnel System* (New York: Van Nostrand Reinhold, 1982), 8–15.

the analysis, design, development, implementation, maintenance, evaluation, and improvement of the system. In the past, most HRIS development projects were attempts to automate manual functions within the HR
department. A company could automate by developing its own computer
programs or by purchasing a vendor-developed package. Today, in addition
to these two approaches, many HRIS development projects are **reautomation** projects. For example, Metropolitan Life is working on an ambitious
"Personnel System Re-engineering Project" to improve their existing HRIS.
Pfizer is developing a new system with a relational data base, integrated per-
sonnel-payroll, and fewer subsystems. In general, many companies with at
least some computerized HR capabilities are expanding, revising, or revamping their HRISs.

## Why Reautomate the Current System?

In Chapter 3 the reasons for computerizing the HR function were discussed.
But why do companies that are already computerized expand, revise, or
revamp their systems? Because an HRIS, like any system, has a life cycle.

   The life cycle of an HRIS is similar to that of any system in that all
systems, whether biological, mechanical, or organizational, eventually must

die. The generic system life cycle is shown in Exhibit 4.2. The four stages are development, growth, maturity, and decay.

The process of designing and implementing an HRIS corresponds to the development stage in the generic system life cycle. The growth stage includes distribution, adjustments, and enhancements—the period during which new users and functions are added to the system. The maturity stage in an HRIS occurs when the system is operational and is being maintained, more or less in its current form. At some point, however, the HRIS will enter the decay stage, which is when the system begins to become obsolete. A system can become technologically obsolete, procedurally obsolete (no longer meets users' needs), or obsolete in some other form.[3] The average life span of a computer system, postdevelopment, is four to seven years, although some last ten years or more.[4]

There are several recurring reasons why some companies are reautomating their HRISs. Because of these reasons, described below, the companies felt that their systems had entered the decay stage, which caused them to go back to the development stage.

***Technology Changes.*** As noted in Chapter 1, computer technology is in a period of rapid technological advancement. The increased availability and capabilities of microcomputers and minicomputers and the advancements in mainframe operating systems (e.g., relational data base management systems) have encouraged many companies to change their computer hardware. This change may make the "old" HRIS obsolete and precipitate a change to a new HRIS.

The software that is available to support HRISs is also rapidly improving. When better alternatives were not available, companies were willing to

**EXHIBIT 4.2**    Generic Systems Life Cycle

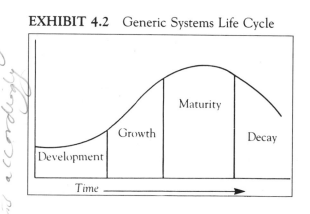

accept limitations in their systems (e.g., inability to reflect retroactive organizational changes, inability to report on historical information, capability for record-level security instead of field-level security, necessity to dual enter common payroll and personnel data elements, etc.). As more attractive alternatives become available in the marketplace, organizations are stimulated to improve their existing HRISs.

**Changes in the Environment**   These changes were detailed in Chapter 3. Changes in legislation and increasing health costs have forced organizations toward more *systems intensive* benefit alternatives. Some of the older HRISs cannot handle changes, such as COBRA or Section 89 compliance, or flexible benefit programs.

**Business Changes**   Organizational growth through mergers, acquisitions, or business expansion may render a previously useful HRIS obsolete. Major changes in the size and scope of the business can create new human resources information needs.

**HRIS Strategy Changes**   HRIS strategies may be linked to business changes, but not always. Some organizations are changing their HRIS strategy to decentralize HRIS activities and to distribute processing throughout the organization. Some have decided that payroll belongs in Human Resources, not in Accounting. Other companies are going in exactly the opposite direction. Regardless, changes in HRIS strategy may necessitate changing to a new system to accommodate those changes.

**Old Age**   Systems become more expensive to maintain as they get older. Modifications accumulate as does the documentation necessary to support the system. As new needs arise some systems are "patched" to address the needs. These patchwork systems, while creative solutions at the time, may become inefficient, requiring dual entry, and so on.[5] Over time the system can begin to experience performance decrements. At some point, a cost/benefit analysis would suggest that a new system be developed.

**Poorly Designed System**   Sometimes systems meet a premature demise because of mistakes made during the development of the system. If user needs were not clearly identified, the system would have been poorly designed or the wrong system would have been purchased. These systems quickly become obsolete. At that point convincing management to "try it again" is not much fun.

***Combinations***    Most typically, the reason for reautomation is a combination of the reasons just mentioned. As is reiterated later, HRISs must be monitored to identify problems and improve the system or decide if a change of systems is called for.

Whether going from a manual system to a computerized system or reautomating a current system, you will be taking on a significant task. In the rest of the chapter the activities, phases, and milestones that occur during the systems development process are examined.

## Categories of Activities

The activities that should occur during the course of a systems development project can be divided into four major categories: (1) analysis, (2) tactical, (3) automation, and (4) distribution.

### Analysis

Analytic activities involve collecting and reviewing data to improve decision making. These activities help define and focus the project. Analytic activities help identify user needs and establish the appropriate system specifications. These activities serve as the basis for the tactical, automation, and distribution activities discussed below.

### Tactical

*Non-computerization* activities, designed to support the system, are tactical activities. Many of the problems noted by Simon and Walker are a result of inadequate or incorrect tactical activities. Tactical activities help sell the system, garner the necessary user and management support, improve daily operations during the development process, and facilitate implementation.

The conversion and implementation process for a vendor-developed, mainframe-based HRIS can take nine to eighteen months. Home-grown systems can take even longer. During this time several tactical activities should be performed, including the implementation of interim solutions (e.g., procedural revisions) to existing problems and events to facilitate the success of the computerization effort (e.g., training).

## Automation

Automation activities are what are typically thought of as systems development. Activities related to the actual computerization, such as writing code, system testing, preparing detailed system specifications, and constructing applications, fall into this category. Usually the MIS or EDP department is heavily involved in these activities.

## Distribution

As the system becomes operational it is delivered to various users. Distribution activities involve putting the system into the hands of the different users and getting them to use it. Distribution activities include pilot testing, delivering the system to HR users, and distributing the system to additional locations in the organization.

# Project Phases

In general, the system development process consists of three phases: (1) needs analysis, (2) design and development (sometimes considered as two separate phases), and (3) implementation and maintenance. Chapters 5, 6, and 7 correspond to these phases. Exhibit 4.3 illustrates these phases and shows how the system development process is best thought of as circular, for reasons addressed later in the chapter.

The phases are sequential, but the types of activities discussed in the preceding section are not limited to any one phase. Although each phase is typified by a dominant activity, analysis and tactical activities should take place throughout the project and automation and distribution activities will start and stop with the addition of new modules and new user groups (see Exhibit 4.4).

For a specific project it may be best to think about project phases as determined by key milestones. For example, (1) the development of a project proposal, (2) the selection of a vendor (if a purchase is to be made), (3) the completion of core development and the initial implementation, and

**EXHIBIT 4.3** Project Phases

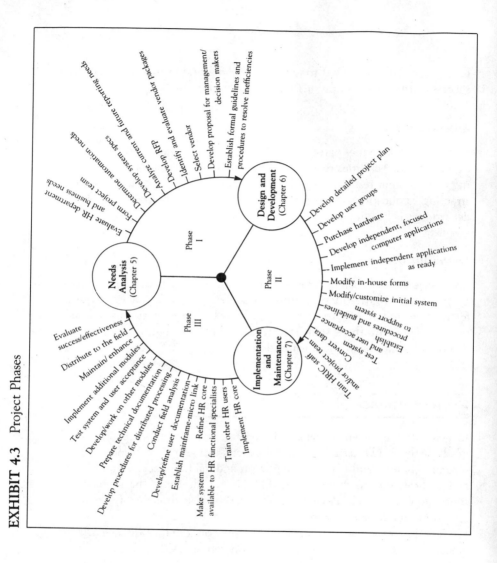

**Exhibit 4.4**    Phases and Dominant Activities

| Phase | Dominant Activity |
|---|---|
| Needs analysis | Analysis |
| Design and development | Automation |
| Implementation and maintenance | Distribution |

(4) the beginning of distributed processing could all be milestones that signify the end of one phase and the beginning of the next. Often these will correspond to the phases noted above. Regardless, the four types of activities will occur at various points in the project cycle, and project milestones should vary based on the type of project, the steps being followed, and the company culture.

## HRIS Project Plan

Exhibit 4.5 shows an HRIS development project plan. It is based in part on an HRIS development project underway at Swiss Bank Corporation. Swiss Bank has computerized some HR functions but is working to implement a new, fully integrated, state-of-the-art HRIS. After some analysis, they decided to go with a vendor-developed mainframe product and to set up a microcomputer network that is tied into the mainframe system.

This project plan can be broken down into three phases, triggered by key milestones. Receiving management approval ends Phase I and triggers the beginning of Phase II. Implementation of the HR core (the basic employee module) ends Phase II and initiates Phase III. These three phases correspond to the phases described above: needs analysis, design and development, and implementation and maintenance. However, as noted above, several types of activities occur simultaneously during a given phase.

Exhibit 4.5 shows the major activities to be performed during the project. Each activity is labeled according to its category (e.g., AN = analytical) and its order. These labels are used throughout the chapter to refer to Exhibit 4.5.

Certain activities have been added and deleted to make the project plan more generic. However, some features of this scenario still differ from

**Exhibit 4.5**   Sample HRIS Project Plan

## PHASE I

*Types of Activities*

**Analysis**

| Evaluate HR department and business needs (AN-1) | Determine automation needs (AN-2) | Develop system specs (AN-3) | Analyze current and future reporting needs (AN-4) | Develop RFP (AN-5) | Identify and evaluate vendor packages (AN-6) | Select vendor (AN-7) |
|---|---|---|---|---|---|---|

**Tactical**

| Form project team (TA-1) | | | | | | Develop proposal for management/decision makers (TA-2) | Establish formal guidelines and procedures to resolve inefficiencies (TA-3) |
|---|---|---|---|---|---|---|---|

**Automation**

**Distribution**

those in other organizations and projects. Remember, this project is based on a vendor-developed, mainframe system with in-house customization. A microcomputer system project would include many of the same activities, but some activities would be emphasized more or less and many would take less time. An HRIS developed completely in-house would introduce still other activities.

**Exhibit 4.5**   *continued*

| | |
|---|---|
| Management Approval → Phase II Begins | **PHASE II**<br><br>*Types of Activities*<br><br>**Analysis** |

**Tactical**

| Develop detailed project plan (TA-4) | Develop user groups (TA-5) | | | Modify in-house forms (TA-6) | | Establish procedures and guide-lines to support system (TA-7) | | Train HRIC staff and/or project team (TA-8) |
|---|---|---|---|---|---|---|---|---|

**Automation**

| | | Purchase hardware (AU-1) | Develop indepen-dent focused computer applica-tions (AU-2) | | Modify/customize initial system (AU-3) | | Test system and user accep-tance (AU-4) | Convert data (AU-5) |
|---|---|---|---|---|---|---|---|---|

**Distribution**

| | | | | Implement independent applications as ready (DI-1) | | | | |
|---|---|---|---|---|---|---|---|---|

In reality there is no universal project plan. Nonetheless, by examining the activities performed during this project, you should get a feeling for what can transpire during the system development process. Remember, however, that your project plan will differ from this one.

While the Swiss Bank example highlights activities associated with system purchase and refinement, certain activities specific to in-house system development are also addressed. These are noted separately.

**Exhibit 4.5**  *continued*

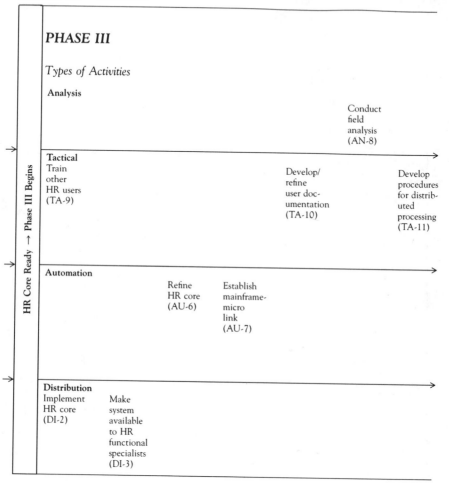

| | | | | |
|---|---|---|---|---|
| **PHASE III** | | | | |
| *Types of Activities* | | | | |
| **Analysis** | | | | Conduct field analysis (AN-8) |
| **Tactical** Train other HR users (TA-9) | | | Develop/ refine user doc- umentation (TA-10) | Develop procedures for distrib- uted processing (TA-11) |
| **Automation** | Refine HR core (AU-6) | Establish mainframe- micro link (AU-7) | | |
| **Distribution** Implement HR core (DI-2) | Make system available to HR functional specialists (DI-3) | | | |

*HR Core Ready → Phase III Begins*

In the following section the HRIS development plan is examined in more detail. Some of the specific activities that may take place during an HRIS development project are described, and critical decisions and milestones are identified.

**Exhibit 4.5** *continued*

**Analysis**

Evaluate
success/
effective-
ness
(AN-9)

→

**Tactical**

→

**Automation**

| Prepare technical documentation (AU-8) | Develop/ work on other modules (AU-9) | Test system and user acceptance (AU-10) | Maintain/ enhance (AU-11) |
|---|---|---|---|

→

**Distribution**

Implement additional modules (DI-4)          Distribute to the field (DI-5)

## Specific Activities

### Major Milestone: Company Considers Developing an HRIS —Phase I Begins

### *Evaluate HR Department and Business Needs (AN-1)*

Every systems development project should be driven by the needs of the business. Therefore, a key analytic activity is to study how the human resources function operates, including examining the department's mission and its position within the overall business operation. Where does/can the HR function support the business direction? How well are HR operations being performed? What is currently automated? Do similar HR computer applications exist elsewhere in the company?

It is also critical to consider the objectives of the business. The human resources department and its HR systems should support business objectives. "We are not in the human resources business or the systems business," says Mike Method, an HRIS specialist with Ford Motor Company. "We are simply in the business."[6] If your company is planning rapid growth, your HRIS should be able to support that growth. You must know and understand your business—being technically knowledgeable is not enough.

Most companies require a cost justification before allocating the resources necessary to develop an HRIS. A proposal that is founded in the needs of the business will have a better chance of being funded than one that simply focuses on technical requirements. This is also one of the first places to begin garnering critical management support. Demonstrating an understanding of business needs and how the HR function fits into the larger picture of the organization will help gain support and, most important, will lead to a system that provides maximum payoffs to the company.

Based on the analysis of the HR function, it may be necessary to "refine" the HR group prior to embarking on the HRIS development project. HRIS development can be a major undertaking. If the HR group is not in good shape you may encounter difficulties during the project. Before taking on the HRIS project the right people should be in place and operating effectively. The HRIS project cannot cure all that ails the department. However, a good HR group can use a new or improved HRIS to better support the company and provide services to its clients.

## *Form Project Team (TA-1)*

One of the first steps is to form a **project team**. The project team will guide the project throughout its life cycle. Some team members should be involved for the entire project — including system maintenance. The HR department should control the project, and some HR functional specialists should be on the team. It is also important that the team include systems professionals (technical experts) from the EDP department and/or the HR department. Some project team members may form the core of the HRIC as the system becomes operational.

For those mainframe-based systems that are developed in-house, there may be a project management team similar to the team described above and a second project development group that would include systems analysts and programmers. Regardless of its makeup, the project team will meet on a regular basis. Some organizations like to use a diary and circulate minutes from each meeting to keep the project on track.

The project manager is a key member of the team and must understand the business and HR functioning and have adequate technical competence. He or she must also have good people and political skills, strong stamina, and a sense of humor.[7] Obviously, this person is a key to the project's success. The project team is discussed in more detail in Chapter 6.

## *Determine Automation Needs (AN-2)*

Through a process of interviews, surveys, and document reviews the project team examines the company's HR automation needs. The key here is to identify and prioritize needs. This helps ensure that the system does what you need it to do and helps avoid the tendency to computerize everything. As part of this process the project team should examine the current configuration and potential alternatives and consider the feasibility of developing a new system. If a new system is not possible, it is important to recognize this as soon as possible.

## *Develop System Specs (AN-3)*

System specifications specify the desired outputs, inputs, and processing requirements of the system. They also must consider potential errors and identify procedures to locate or prevent them.[8] Although some of the system specifications should be identified up front, some of the detailed system specification work does not occur until the design and development phase of the project.

One tool frequently used to support these activities is the **data flow diagram**, an example of which is included in the Appendix. The data flow diagram is a graphic representation of how data flow to, from, and within a system as well as of the processes that transform the data and the places where the data are stored. Data flow diagrams can be used to depict manual or computerized systems and can be used to develop a logical flow for the new system.

As part of these activities the project team should be sure to consider the HRIS's linkages with other systems and software, as noted in Chapter 2. This can be a major problem with any computer system if not considered carefully as part of the system specifications.

## *Analyze Current and Future Reporting Needs (AN-4)*

What reports are currently used? What are needed? What are the legal requirements? How will these be changing? The needs analysis should answer these and other related questions. In addition, this analysis should consider the system audit reports that will be needed to monitor the system.

## CRITICAL DECISIONS

At this point in the system development process some critical decisions need to be made:

1. *System configuration.* A critical question that must be answered is, How will the system be configured? Will the system be a microcomputer system? Single user or networked? Mainframe based? Mainframe and microcomputer combined? There are pros and cons for each configuration as well as organizational parameters that will influence the decision. These are addressed in Chapter 6.

2. *Build or buy?* While Swiss Bank decided to purchase a vendor-developed system and to supplement it with customization and other solutions, other companies, such as McGraw-Hill, Metropolitan Life, and Pfizer, have decided to develop their systems in-house. McGraw-Hill's system, called CHRIS (for Comprehensive Human Resource Information System), was developed internally and inter-

faces with their payroll system. Although the system development process for CHRIS was quite time consuming, the result is a fully customized system that McGraw-Hill finds quite effective. It is not intrinsically right or wrong either to build or to buy a system. It is a question of fit, including considerations of resources and time frames. This is a critical decision point in any project.

## Develop Request for Proposal (RFP) (AN-5)

Steps 2 and 3 (AN-2 and AN-3) will often culminate in the development of a **request for proposal (RFP)**. This document tells vendors what your company needs and asks them to submit proposals regarding how they can meet those needs and at what cost. A complete discussion of RFP's may be found in Chapter 6.

## Identify and Evaluate Vendor Packages (AN-6)

If outside vendors are a viable alternative, potential vendor packages must be examined. This is not an insignificant task. There are 300 to 400 software packages designed to operate on microcomputers[9] and many others for minis and mainframes. Significant effort must go into identifying what each package has to offer. The vendor evaluation process should involve a review of each system's documentation, vendor visits, and demonstrations of the system at other companies.

AN-1 through AN-6 and TA-1 are major activities within the needs analysis. The needs analysis is one of the most critical aspects of the system development process. Companies occasionally neglect or shortchange the needs analysis and almost invariably suffer the consequences later. Chapter 5 is dedicated to explicating the needs analysis phase. The DECIDE model is presented there as a useful means of conducting a needs analysis.

## Select Vendor (AN-7)

Based on the evaluation of the proposals submitted, vendor visits and demonstrations, a vendor is selected. Vendor selection is a bit like marriage. As Vince Ceriello, an experienced HRIS consultant, says, "Once you are well into system development, changing vendors is usually just about as simple as changing utility companies."[10]

## Develop Proposal for Management/Decision Makers (TA-2)

Some organizations will require a proposal prior to the start of the needs analysis. However, before the needs analysis it may be impossible to determine whether the system should be built or bought and how it should be configured. It will also be difficult to estimate costs. Regardless of timing, most companies will require some form of proposal prior to releasing funds and resources for system development.

Typically, the proposal will include an indication of costs and other necessary resources in comparison to potential benefits from the system. Each company has different unwritten rules regarding proposal development, and it is our experience that in any organization there are a few key people who understand these rules. These people are valuable resources and should be consulted during the proposal-generation process.

Although the proposal helps sell the system, you must be careful about making promises you cannot keep; for example, reductions in head count rarely occur as a result of a computerized HRIS. In addition, do not underestimate the costs—you may end up with a partially developed system or without a job.

## Establish Formal Guidelines and Procedures to Resolve Inefficiencies (TA-3)

A significant amount of time will transpire before the system is implemented. During this time some of the inefficiencies identified during the needs analysis can and should be removed through tactical activities. For example, improved information flow may reduce data redundancy. The payoff from this will be immediate and will also facilitate the subsequent implementation of the system.

## Major Milestone: Management Approval—Phase II Begins

## Develop Detailed Project Plan (TA-4)

Although the proposal usually contains a tentative project plan, now that the vendor has been selected and more information is available a more detailed plan can be developed. This should include *realistic* timetables. Most project plans underestimate time requirements by failing to consider unforeseen but inevitable delays, personnel turnover, and resource competition from other projects. The use of project planning tools (e.g., Gantt or PERT charts) may be useful here.

The plan should also address marketing considerations—specifically, how will the system be marketed to the various user groups?

### Develop User Groups (TA-5)

Typically a user group is made up of representatives from a variety of business units throughout the organization. These groups provide input throughout the project. They help keep user needs in the forefront and ease implementation when system distribution occurs. Chase Manhattan used user groups effectively in the development and implementation of their large, companywide HRIS. User groups can be developed at several points throughout the project; when they should be formed depends on what you want them to accomplish.

### Purchase Hardware (AU-1)

Few, if any, companies decide to purchase a mainframe computer solely to install an HRIS. However, companies may undergo system upgrades or may need to purchase additional terminals or microcomputers as part of the HRIS development project. Hardware purchases can occur at several points during the project and may be influenced by system expansion (new modules) or wider distribution (new users). A major user complaint is a shortage of microcomputers and terminals, and hardware needs must be considered as part of the planning process.[11]

### Develop Independent, Focused, Computer Applications (AU-2)

In purchasing a system it will soon become apparent that despite the continued improvements in vendor packages no "comprehensive" HRIS can meet all needs. In addition, some systems will offer desired functions, but users cannot wait for their implementation two years hence. Finally, some information is best kept in a noncentralized location.

To address these needs some companies develop independent computer applications. Many of these applications are built using software packages (e.g., LOTUS 1-2-3, R:Base for DOS, dBASE) on a microcomputer. Others are designed on minicomputers or on a mainframe. A variety of stand-alone, application-specific products developed by vendors are also available.

Many companies have some independent applications in addition to their primary system. For example, American Express developed an applicant-tracking system and ultimately plans to integrate it into their main system. Pfizer has stand-alone applications to assess cost per hire, to support their tuition reimbursement program, and to monitor and service their employee fitness center. The Depository Trust Company does their merit budgeting and management incentives on separate microcomputer applications (enhancing security) as well as part-time and temporary-personnel tracking. Leonard Memorial Hospital uses an independent, microcomputer application to deal with COBRA compliance. PepsiCo is developing a system to track and monitor their consultants.

When developing independent, stand-alone applications a few points must be considered. On the positive side, they can provide early, visible successes during the longer system development process. They are particularly useful for retaining and processing data elements you may not want to keep on the centralized system (e.g., executive compensation information or health-related information). They can provide capabilities that may not be available on the primary system. However, as with the HRIS, these systems require well-developed rules and procedures. In addition, you must be careful about the proliferation of these systems without considering integration and data consistency. Some companies have found that developing multiple stand-alone systems and linking them "as needed" yields a chaotic array of information.

Some companies purchase and develop specific applications to meet information system needs throughout the life of the project. However, be careful to consider user needs, integration, and consistency if you plan to use independent applications.

## Implement Independent Applications as Ready (DI-1)

As just noted, these applications may be developed throughout the life of the system and will be implemented accordingly.

## Modify In-House Forms (TA-6)

Do not simply model your system after your existing information forms. The systems development process is a prime opportunity for evaluating and modifying the forms used in your company.

## IN-HOUSE DEVELOPMENT

If the system is being developed in-house there are some activities that will need to be performed that may be unnecessary or less time-consuming for vendor-purchased systems (e.g., programming).

For a vendor-purchased system, identifying the system specifications (system specs) helps the company decide which vendor system best fits their needs and specifically identifies where customization is called for. For an in-house system, the development of system specifications and the system design process are even more critical. The development team must design input screens, menus, the underlying data structure, validation and relational edits, and so on, essentially providing a map for system development.

Programmers will take the system specifications and translate them into program code. Some companies employ system analysts/programmers to do this, while others prefer using separate analysts and programmers. For vendor-purchased systems some programming may still be needed if customization is desirable. Depending on the system purchased and the type of customization desired, changes may require programmers or may be handled by technically oriented HR people. If a vendor-developed system is extensively customized through programmatic changes, the vendor may no longer support the system.

During the development process some programmers like to use **prototyping** to facilitate progress. Prototypes are samples or shell versions of a system's screens, reports, and so on. They are developed quickly and submitted for user approval and sign-off prior to detailed programming. Although these are typically developed on the computer, the use of paper prototypes, that is, hand-drawn representations of screens or reports, is also advocated. Paper prototypes do not determine programming feasibility but they can help ensure that programmers and users are in agreement. Florida Power & Light Company uses a fill-in-the-blank survey they developed that helps users lay out screens and reports and facilitates system design.[12] KeyCorp uses similar prototypes.

One concern about prototyping should be mentioned. Users often do not understand the delay involved in going from a prototype to a functioning system. A significant amount of time must be spent in data base building, testing, and so on to advance to an operational system. If prototyping is going to be used, be sure to create realistic user expectations.[13]

When programming is "complete," installation begins. In systems parlance, installation refers to testing and data conversion. Approximately 60 percent of the bugs in a system are caught during system design; 35 to 40 percent are caught during installation.[14] This suggests that careful testing is critical to system success. Testing is designed to answer the question, Does the system produce the results it should under specified conditions? There are three types of testing:

1. *Unit testing* refers to the testing of each program in the system. For example, Does the EEO compliance program produce results consistent with predetermined data?

2. *System testing* focuses on the system as a whole. Do the modules function together as they should? If the system specs say that the payroll module should update the basic employee module, does it?

3. *Acceptance testing* is the final certification prior to data conversion and says the system has passed testing.[15]

**Data conversion** is the process of changing from the old system to the new one—even if the old system was a manual one. It addresses the question, Will the new system run under real conditions? There are four common strategies for conversion:

1. *Parallel.* Both the old and the new system run together until you are convinced that the new system is working properly. This is the safest method because the old system serves as a fall-back, but it is also the most costly.

2. *Direct cutover.* When the new system passes the testing stage, the old system is discarded and the new system becomes the operational system. This is less costly but very risky. There is no fall-back if problems occur.

3. *Pilot study.* The new system is installed in a limited area in the company (i.e., one location). When debugging is complete and the new system is "working," then the new system is installed throughout the company.

4. *Phased installation.* The new system is used throughout the company, but only part of the work force is on the system or only part of the functions are operational. For example, the new system may be used for nonexempt employees first. After this group is being served smoothly, the system becomes available, in phases, to serve other functions, units, and so on.

## Modify/Customize Initial System (AU-3)

Almost *all* purchased systems require modifications. Be wary of the phrase "full turn-key" system. This phrase implies that the system is ready to use without company modification. The level of technical sophistication required to modify the system will vary by product and may call for HR, EDP, and/or vendor involvement.

## Establish Procedures and Guidelines to Support System (TA-7)

This is one of the most critical steps in the process. It takes considerable thought and time to develop proper procedures and guidelines to support the system. Procedures and guidelines must be resolved prior to implementation. They should answer questions such as, Who has access to which data elements? Who can change data elements? When are payroll data due? and many others. To support their system, McGraw-Hill set up an "office of primary responsibility (OPR)" for each data element. A functional specialist (e.g., the Affirmative Action officer) or a line manager is responsible for the integrity and accuracy of each element and has the final word on changes and edits. This is a procedural rule designed to facilitate their system's effectiveness.

It is not the technology that makes a system effective, although better technology improves your chances. It is the way the system is managed that determines whether it will work. Some "archaic" systems work acceptably because clear and effective procedures support them. And some "state-of-the-art" systems fail because they are not managed effectively. The rules and procedures that support the system must reflect organizational realities and system limitations and must be clear and enforceable. This activity should not be a last minute add-on relegated to a low-level employee but must be viewed as a critical part of the system development process.

## Test System and User Acceptance (AU-4)

These activities were discussed in the in-house development section. They are also necessary for vendor-developed systems. At this point, testing should be conducted for the initial module(s).

## Convert Data (AU-5)

As with testing, this activity was discussed in the in-house development section but is necessary for vendor-developed systems as well. One of the tasks that must be accomplished here is the population of tables. That is, the tables in the system (e.g., the job table) must have the necessary data entered into them. For example, if a company has job codes, each job and its respective code would be entered into the job table.

Since all systems are based on the GIGO principle (garbage in–garbage out) it is critical that data conversion be performed correctly. This means making sure the data that should be passed to the new system are passed correctly. This is also a prime time for checking old data and eliminating errors. It makes no sense to convert incorrect or outdated data to the new system.

## Train HRIC Staff and/or Project Team (TA-8)

The initial training is usually provided by the vendor. Often this training is designed to "train the trainer," that is, to allow those that are trained to train others in turn.

---

Major Milestone: HR Core (Basic Employee Module) Ready
—Phase III Begins

---

## Implement HR Core (DI-2)

Make the HR core available to the HRIC.

## Train Other HR Users (TA-9)

If possible this training should be conducted by in-house staff. Ideally, the people who will answer phone calls regarding the system should also conduct the training.

## Make System Available to HR Functional Specialists (DI-3)

After receiving training, HR functional specialists who were not on the project team will have the system made available to them. The order in which the system is distributed varies by company, but obviously each user group must receive training prior to being put on the system.

## Refine HR Core (AU-6)

After using the HR core module the initial users will have some suggestions for improving the system. The HR core should be refined based on their suggestions prior to distributing the system to field sites.

## Establish Mainframe-Micro Link (AU-7)

This is not applicable to all projects, but having a mainframe-micro link is a fairly common configuration. If the system is configured to use both mainframes and microcomputers, several procedural issues must be resolved, including which data elements can be uploaded (from micro to mainframe), which can be downloaded (from mainframe to micro), and which will reside only on the mainframe or the microcomputer. In addition, a number of technical issues must be resolved, such as identifying the appropriate communication medium and determining compatibility across systems.

A mainframe-micro link can be established in several ways:

1. *Terminal emulation.* The microcomputer accesses the mainframe by acting like ("emulating") a "dumb" terminal. This does not involve true downloading and does not take advantage of the processing capabilities of the microcomputer.

2. *Selective data extracts.* Selected data elements are downloaded from the mainframe onto diskettes for analysis on the microcomputer.

3. *Communication links (integrated software).* Several methods exist for having the mainframe talk to the microcomputer, allowing data to be uploaded (from microcomputer to mainframe) and downloaded (from mainframe to microcomputer). This is a technical area that is rapidly changing. Improvements in the communication between mainframes and microcomputers should continue.

In general, uploading and downloading data are usually much more difficult than they sound. Some of the limitations are technical and others are procedural. Regardless, the advantages of linking mainframes and micros encourages many organizations to address the problems and overcome the difficulties.

For example, Shearson Lehman Hutton, with approximately 40,000 employees worldwide, feeds data from their mainframe to microcomputers at locations throughout the organization. They download data via communication links and, for a few divisions, with selective data extracts. In this way, divisions throughout the company are able to access and analyze data relevant to their division without continually accessing the mainframe. As with most systems, their linkages were not easy to establish and are not trouble-free. However, they find the advantages of distributed data processing to be worth the trouble.

## Develop/Refine User Documentation (TA-10)

User documentation can make a system easy to use or a nightmare. User documentation should include easy-to-read and understandable instructions, including an introduction to the system, sample screens, sample menus, data elements, and reports.[16] More and more systems are using on-line documentation to help users. That is, users can access the documentation at the terminal to answer questions they may have. This does not replace hard-copy documentation but supplements it. Vendors typically provide documentation, but many companies choose to customize the documentation to meet their needs. In Chapter 7 documentation is addressed again.

## Conduct Field Analysis (AN-8)

This should be an ongoing activity. Prior to distribution to a new group, and periodically thereafter, users' interests and needs should be assessed. You should not simply wait for user requests but should proactively attempt to identify them. Ask users what they need or present them with sample reports or potential new applications and access their reactions. Treat the users as customers and perform the equivalent of market research. As Randy Velez, McGraw-Hill's Director of HRIS and a well-respected HR systems expert, notes, "You can't wait around like the Maytag repairman. You need to deal with your users proactively."

The information gathered during field analysis serves several purposes. By identifying how users work, field analysis can help establish procedures for managing a distributed system. In addition, field analysis will help sell the system and allow you to customize the system to fit user interests.

## Develop Procedures for Distributed Processing (TA-11)

As was done for the centralized processes described above (TA-7), guidelines must be established prior to decentralizing parts of the system. This is important because field reps who are not part of the HRIC or EDP group may not be as interested in the system, and discipline problems may result if procedures are not clear. Revise as necessary.

## Prepare Technical Documentation (AU-8)

Technical documentation serves a similar role as user documentation except it is targeted to a technical audience. Technical documentation provides information on what data are in the system, where they are located, what attributes they have, and the relationships data elements have with each other. Clear, concise technical documentation is essential for subsequent system maintenance and improvement.

## Develop/Work on Other Modules (AU-9)

In Chapter 2 the concept of modules was discussed. As emphasized there, it is best not to try to develop/implement a system all at once. Typically, the basic employee information, or core module, is implemented first, and that is the case in this project. After the core is working, each additional module should be developed according to plan.

## Test System and User Acceptance (AU-10)

Do this for each module as ready.

## Implement Additional Modules (DI-4)

Do this for each module as ready.

## Maintain/Enhance (AU-11)

Some estimate the average life span of an information system to be four to seven years. During this time the system must be maintained. In many companies, over half the data processing department's staff is involved in maintenance/enhancements.

*Maintenance* is often used as an umbrella term to refer to both system maintenance activities and system enhancements. Enhancements include making the system faster, adding new features or interfaces, or incorporating other optional components. Maintenance activities include modifying to correct bugs, to deal with emergencies, to deal with new regulations, or for other reasons. Studies of the data processing maintenance function reveal that 20 percent of maintenance time is spent on debugging and emergencies; 20 percent on changes in data, files, reports, and hardware; and 60 percent on user enhancements and improved documentation.[17]

Although maintenance is not glamorous, it is absolutely necessary and must be included in the budget. Maintenance can be a potential problem with HRISs that are fully independent of the EDP function. In these cases, the HR department must have sufficient expertise within the department or have a sufficient budget to purchase support from the vendor.

Maintenance on a mainframe HRIS can occupy two or three people. It is not unheard of to have ten to fifteen people involved. At one West Coast bank more than fifty people are involved in HRIS maintenance and enhancements![18] Naturally, the effort necessary to maintain a system is contingent on the size of system and its complexity. But even a small system requires maintenance.

## Distribute to the Field (DI-5)

Again, this is contingent on the distribution strategy. In this project, the system will be distributed to field sites throughout the company. To prepare for distribution, pilot testing and training should be conducted.

## Evaluate Success/Effectiveness (AN-9)

It is critical to evaluate the system's effectiveness. Is it working? How can you tell? Is it becoming obsolete, entering the early stages of decay? What can be done to improve the system?

Several techniques can be used to evaluate system effectiveness. Analyses of reporting trends, audit reports, user surveys, error (or accuracy) analyses, and response time checks all reveal something about system effectiveness. In general you need to assess if the system is being used and if it is providing accurate information to the users.

Some experts suggest performing a *postimplementation audit* after installation is complete.[19] We agree. In addition, evaluation should be an ongoing activity.

Recall that in Exhibit 4.3 the system development process was depicted as a circle. While a specific project may appear linear, over a period of time the process becomes cyclical. At first, a company may evaluate its needs and decide its manual system is no longer acceptable. A computerized HRIS is developed and implemented. The system is maintained for a number of years and, after evaluating its performance over time, the company may decide it is time to reautomate. At this point the cycle begins again.

## Summary

In this chapter the systems development process was explored. Four major categories of activities (analysis, tactical, automation, and distribution) occur throughout the major phases of the process. Each of the activities occurs during the (1) needs analysis phase; (2) the design and development phase; and (3) the implementation and maintenance phase. This chapter is an overview. Chapters 5, 6, and 7 focus on the key issues and details associated with each of the three major phases of the systems development process.

## Discussion Questions

1. What are the most common problems that arise during HRIS development?
2. Parallel the systems life cycle with that of living systems (e.g., humans). How are they similar? How are they different?
3. What do you think is the most important phase in the systems development process? Why?
4. Why is the systems development process best thought of as a cycle?
5. How would the project plan for a system to be developed in-house differ from that for a vendor-developed system? How would the plan for a reautomation project differ from that for a manual to computer project?

## Notes

1. S. Simon, "Steps to Success for Your HRIS," *Personnel* vol. 62 (November 1985): 16–20.
2. M. Zippo, "HR Data: Out of the Filing Cabinet, into the Computer," *Personnel* 58 (November/December 1981): 51–53.
3. See M. P. Martin, "The Human Connection in System Design: Designing Systems for Change," *Journal of Systems Management* (July 1987): 14–18.
4. K. C. Laudon and J. P. Laudon, *Management Information Systems: A Contemporary Perspective* (New York: Macmillan, 1988); V. Ceriello, "Computerizing the Personnel Department: Make or Buy?" *Personnel Journal* (September 1984): 48.
5. D. Leote addresses this concern in "Piecemeal Planning Hinders HRIS Performance," *Personnel Journal* (March 1988): 65–69.
6. M. J. Method, "Changing HRIS Responsibilities: Start with the Rule of One," *HRSP Review* 3(3) (Fall 1987) 11–13.
7. N. Bloom, "Selecting and Supervising an HRMS Project Manager," *HRSP Review* vol. 4(2) (Spring 1988): 9–12.
8. H. C. Lucas addresses some of these issues in *The Analysis, Design, and Implementation of Information Systems* (New York: McGraw-Hill, 1985):269–289.
9. D. Leote, "Piecemeal Planning," 67.
10. V. Ceriello, "Computerizing the Personnel Department: How Do You Choose a Vendor?" *Personnel Journal* (December 1984): 33–38.
11. G. S. Howard and G. J. Weinroth, "Users' Complaints: Information System Problems from the User's Perspective," *Journal of Systems Management* (May 1988): 30–34.
12. E. Witkin, "System Design: Tell Me What You Want," *Computers in Personnel* (Summer 1987): 19–24.
13. J. M. Carey and R. McLeod, "Use of System Development Methodology and Tools," *Journal of Systems Management* (March 1988): 30–35.
14. V. Ceriello, "Computerizing the Personnel Department: Make or Buy?" *Personnel Journal* vol. 63 (1984): 47–48.
15. The information in this section and additional information on testing and conversion strategy can be found in K. C. Laudon and J. P. Laudon, *Management Information Systems: A Contemporary Perspective* (New York: Macmillan, 1988), 398–400; for a detailed description of a data conversion effort at the Potomac Electric Power Company, see C. L. Donnel and S. V. Snyder, "Before the Deluge of Data Conversion," *Computers in Personnel* (Fall 1987): 21–24.
16. See M. MacAdam, "HRIS Training: Keep Documentation on Track," *Personnel Journal* vol. 61 (November 1987): 45–51; D. Horsfeld, "Before the First Data is Keyed," *Computers in Personnel* (Winter 1988): 51–54.

17. See B. P. Lientz and E. B. Swanson, *Software Maintenance Management* (Reading, MA: Addison-Wesley, 1980).

18. V. Ceriello, "Computerizing the Personnel Department: Make or Buy?" 47.

19. L. G. Need, "The Importance of Being Audited," *Computers in Personnel* (Spring 1988): 60–62; N. J. Mathys and H. LeVan, "Responsibility, Technology, Visibility," *Computers in Personnel* (Spring 1987): 56–58.

# 5

# Needs Analysis

One of the most difficult problems faced by organizations deciding to automate or update their human resource systems is deciding where to start. One of the worst mistakes a company can make is to go blindly into the world of computers and software vendors and purchase a system. Almost certainly, the resulting system will not fit the needs of the organization. After all, it is hard to know what to buy when you are not sure what you want the system to do. So where do you start? The best approach is to begin with a needs analysis.

This chapter focuses on the needs analysis phase of developing or purchasing an HRIS. It describes the basic tools and techniques required to successfully complete the needs analysis. At several points additional readings are suggested for those wishing more information on specific topics. By using the approach outlined in this chapter, a successful needs analysis can be completed.

The chapter is divided into two major sections. The first section defines the needs analysis and discusses the rationale for conducting one. The second section presents the DECIDE approach to needs analysis, a step-by-step evaluation method. This sets the stage for Chapter 6, systems design.

## What Is a Needs Analysis?

A **needs analysis** is an in-depth study of the information collection, processing, storage, and reporting demands of an organizational unit. The needs analysis provides a definition of what the new system should do and has four major objectives.

First, it allows the HR manager and project team to evaluate critically the information processing needs of the department and provides the necessary background data to justify funding the HRIS.

Second, it provides a clear set of specifications to guide the project manager in designing or purchasing a system. As mentioned earlier, it is difficult to choose the best product when you are not really sure what you want the system to accomplish.

Third, the needs analysis can also assist the HR group on a strategic level. That is, through the needs analysis process HR professionals can establish a strategic information plan for the HR function. Often, the day-to-day demands of managing the HR group allow managers little time for strategic planning. The needs analysis process will require that top HR management make a number of decisions that will have long-term impacts on the HR function. For example, the needs analysis should lead to a decision about whether personnel data will be kept and maintained by the HR group or by the MIS/DP group. If the decision is to have the HR group "own" the system, there may be some fundamental changes in the strategic position of the HR function in the organization. HR staff will also need to be "systems" people, knowledgeable about the technology, software, and procedures needed to maintain a sophisticated information system. Job descriptions and responsibilities may be changed as well as "the way we do things around here." New staff may need to have computer expertise as well as traditional personnel training.[1]

Finally, the needs analysis provides the opportunity to develop an information policy. An information policy is a long-term plan for managing data and information resources. Such a policy includes a mission statement for the HRIS function; a current assessment of information storage, use, and technology; and a general plan for information management during the next three to five years. This plan should be consistent with any corporate information policies that have been set up. In retrospect, it is somewhat surprising that HR groups did not formulate information policies long ago. After all, there is probably no functional management area that is more information-intensive than human resources. As regulation increases and the work force matures, it is likely that the information intensity of the HR function will continue to grow.

Needs analysis is the critical first step in developing or purchasing an HRIS. Shortchanging the needs analysis will almost certainly lead to the selection or development of a system that no one is happy with and that does not accomplish the goals set forth by the organization. The needs analysis is also critical because of several other reasons. First, systems are expensive, with software costs ranging from several thousand to several hundred thousand dollars. Thus, the HRIS may well be a major capital expenditure for the organization. If a good decision is not made the first time, there may well not be a second opportunity. Second, the organization and, in particular, the HR department are going to have to live with the system for a substantial period of time. The system is going to impact the HR department's ability to meet the demands of the organization and comply with regulatory requirements. Living with a bad system may be worse than having no system at all. Third, a poorly conducted needs analysis may lead to unrealistic expectations of what the system will do. When the system is then installed and does not meet those expectations, careers, the clout of the HR department, and organizational effectiveness may be diminished.

Now that the needs analysis has been defined and its importance emphasized, the next step is to consider the critical questions the needs analysis should answer.

# What Questions
# Does a Needs Analysis Answer?

The typical questions answered by a needs analysis include the following:

Which HR functions (e.g., applicant tracking, EEO/AA reporting, training history, payroll) should be automated?

Which functions are most critical? Which are the highest priority for enhancing the performance of the HR function or improving compliance with state and federal laws?

How will this system impact and be impacted by other systems in the organization?

What data should be kept? Are both current and historical information needed (e.g., payroll history)?

How will the information be entered into the new system? Who will be responsible for system control? data entry? accuracy? edits? updates?

What kinds of reports does HR now generate? Are they necessary to the effective operation of the HR function?

What kinds of reports should the system generate? Fixed? Ad hoc?

What is the projected cost of the system? Is it cost-effective? How can the system contribute to the "bottom line"?

How will the system impact staffing? Will more or fewer employees be needed?

How will new or proposed legislation be accommodated by the new system?

How will the system interface with other information systems and applications in the organization (e.g., payroll, general ledger, electronic mail)?

What are the technical requirements of the system? How much storage is needed? What type of hardware is to be used?

What are the security requirements for personnel data to be stored in the system?

The answers to these and other questions included in the needs analysis will help steer the project and ensure that the system developed or purchased fits the needs of the organization.

The next section describes an approach to answering these questions and successfully completing the needs analysis phase of automating the HR function.

## Needs Analysis: Step by Step

Needs analysis is a general procedure that leads to a better understanding of the information requirements of the organization. There are several ways to conduct such a study. Authors such as Walker,[2] Simon,[3] and Lederer[4] have suggested approaches ranging from a general three-step procedure to highly specific, detailed methods encompassing more than fifteen steps. In this book, a six-step process, termed the **DECIDE** method, is used to describe the needs analysis process. This approach synthesizes previously suggested methods and incorporates several new techniques. It moves from a view of what organizations typically do in terms of needs analysis to what they should do.

## The DECIDE Approach

The DECIDE process is a synthesis of past approaches. It divides the needs analysis project into manageable chunks. There are six steps in DECIDE:

Develop a needs analysis plan

Early information inventory

Comprehensive information inventory

Information evaluation

Develop the HRIS strategy

Evaluate the development effort

Exhibit 5.1 summarizes the DECIDE procedure.

### Develop a Needs Analysis Plan

Arguably, the most critical step in developing an HRIS is a well-thought-out needs analysis. All too often in the rush to get a system "up and running" the needs analysis gets shortchanged or abbreviated. The result is a system that does not meet the needs of the organization. For example, one firm rushed to purchase a state-of-the-art vendor-developed system. It was only after $175,000 and six months of installation that it became clear the system could not accommodate new information and reporting requirements mandated by new tax legislation. No one had thought to discuss a human resources computer system with the controller and auditors of the firm. A more careful needs analysis might have determined that a change in tax regulations was anticipated and that any new system must plan for this. Obviously, mistakes like this are not career enhancing.

The needs analysis plan serves several objectives. First, it sets forth the purposes of the study and defines the products that will result. Second, it details the schedule of activities to be undertaken. Third, it specifies the costs associated with the needs analysis effort. Finally, it provides the background and support required to sell the needs analysis effort to management.

The needs analysis plan typically has several sections. The first is a *statement of objectives*. This section provides the justification for the study.

**Exhibit 5.1** The DECIDE Procedure

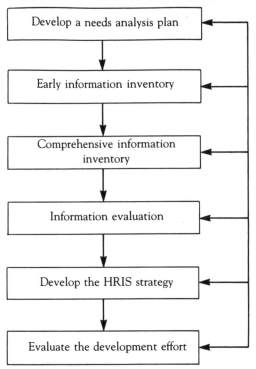

Samples of potential justifications and objectives are provided in Exhibit 5.2. Second, the plan contains a section on the *personnel and resource requirements* necessary to conduct the needs analysis. This section should indicate the amount of time required and by whom, and any additional funds or expenses that are anticipated. If consultants are to be part of the needs analysis, this should be indicated here. Third, the preliminary *information collection strategies* are described. That is, are interviews planned? A paper-and-pencil survey? Also included here is a summary of the groups to be interviewed, their number and department. For example, who among top management is to be included? MIS/DP? Payroll? Line management? Vendors of HR services? This summary will assist in completing the next section in the needs analysis plan, the *schedule of activities*. This section lays out the time line and key steps in the needs analysis.

**Exhibit 5.2**    Justifications and Objectives for the Needs Analysis

---

Determine the information requirements of the HR function.

Determine the adequacy of existing information/data for complying with current and proposed regulations.

Determine the most efficient procedures to facilitate information flow in HR tasks. Identify redundancies/inefficiencies in information handling.

Determine the priorities for automating the HR function.

Provide the basis for making system design/purchase decisions.

Provide a long-term information plan for the HR function and determine how the HR information plan fits with the corporate information plan.

---

Typically, the schedule is presented in the form of a **Gantt chart** or a **PERT (Program Evaluation and Review Technique) chart**. Exhibit 5.3 presents a typical Gantt chart for a needs analysis based on the DECIDE model.

Taken together, these components provide the plan for a systematic needs analysis and can help sell top management on the merits of investing in the process.

**Exhibit 5.3**    Gantt Chart for the DECIDE Needs Analysis Process

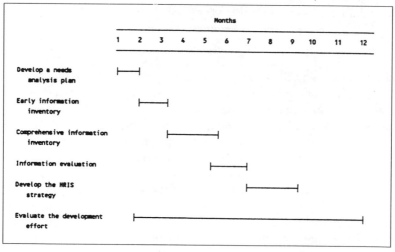

### Early Information Inventory

The early information inventory (EII) stage is designed to collect the information required to orient the initial project team members and facilitate planning the more intensive comprehensive information inventory stage. It is at this time that the initial project team is established. The members chosen will form the core of the final project team and should include the team leader, who will champion the system, HR staff members, and in many cases representatives of the MIS/DP department. At this point the criteria for inclusion in the team are enthusiasm for and interest in the new system. Later, additional team members will be added based on the need for specific technical skills or special knowledge. Until the EII stage is completed, however, the skills needed or training required for the final project team may not be evident.

The EII stage allows the key project team members to get a feel for the amount and types of data the HR subfunctions deal with. Many times individual HR professionals are assigned to a functional area within HR, such as EEO reporting, recruiting, compensation, and so on, and consequently may not be aware of the broad range of information utilized. Even within an HR functional area, information requirements may not be widely known. For example, a staff member in benefits who deals with the pension and 401(k) plan may have little understanding of the information required to determine eligibility for health care coverage under COBRA. The EII step often provides the first opportunity for individual team members to understand the range of data used by the HR function.

The key objective of the EII stage is to obtain a sample of the general categories of data inputs and outputs impacting the HR group. This may be done in a number of ways. In smaller organizations, much of the data may be readily available in the HR office. For example, the HR office would be able to provide input sources such as application blanks, benefits elections forms, performance appraisal forms, employee profile documents, and so on. Likewise, a variety of outputs, such as state and federal reports, internal studies, regular (weekly, monthly, quarterly) reports, payroll summaries, benefit listings, and so forth, can also be collected. Be sure to evaluate each item of information to determine if it is the product of other information (e.g., seniority status might be the product of tenure with the firm and hours worked this month). An inventory of the information on the forms and reports provides a fairly good picture of the information base of the HR group.

Preliminary discussions can be started with readily accessible staff. A word of caution: Do not wear out your welcome with staff members. In the next phase, detailed surveys or interviews will be conducted, and participation by key staff will be especially critical at that point. Hopefully, the project team members (since they are likely to be key users) will be able to obtain much of the information for the EII stage in the course of their regular job duties.

Three major tasks remain in the EII stage. First, the material collected should be shared among project team members and reviewed. This will allow the team members to become familiar with the information and provide informed input for the next two tasks. Second, the project team must be finalized. The initial team was probably composed of the HR staff most closely associated with the project. At this point, however, it may be necessary to expand the team to include other members of the organization who provide or use HR information. For example, the initial inventory may make clear the critical role of an outside vendor of payroll services in the information flow of the HR department. Consequently, a member of that organization's staff should be added to the team. If an HRIS/payroll system is planned, it may be necessary to include personnel from the controller function of the organization. The final project team should include representatives of all parties with an interest in the system. Keep in mind that the project team leader will need to have sufficient political clout in the organization to resolve the problems that are bound to arise.

The final project team will vary in size from five to twelve members, depending on the size of the organization and the complexity of the anticipated HRIS. Try to select members who are supportive of the system and who you anticipate are likely to stay with the organization for a significant period of time. Ideally, the team members should work on the new system from the needs analysis stage through system implementation. Where possible, a mix of tenure with the organization is also desirable. That is, try for a team composed of recent hires as well as "old-timers." This will provide a good mix of fresh ideas with a leavening of organizational history and experience.

The third major task of the EII stage is to finalize the data collection strategy and develop the instruments to be used. Interviews are probably the most common data-collection method. Indeed, it is difficult to conceive of conducting a needs analysis without including personal interviews. Much has been written about how to conduct interviews, and it would be valuable to review some of the literature on interviewing before developing your instruments. Good sources include Sudman and Bradburn,[5] Walker,[6] and Warwick and Lininger.[7] There is no generic interview form that works for all organizations. Rather, each needs analysis is unique and the project team will need to develop an instrument that targets the issues relevant to the specific organization. A few tips for designing interview instruments and conducting interviews follow:

Develop an interview form for the team members to use. This form should be broken down into major topics, contain key questions as well as follow-up probes, and provide space for the interviewer to record comments and answers. Developing a form will help standardize the collection process and ensure that critical topics/questions are not omitted. A common form also facilitates subsequent analysis.

Use a mix of open- and closed-ended questions. Open-ended questions have no set answer, allowing the interviewee to choose how to respond. For example, open-ended questions might include, What type of information that you use in your job is the most difficult to obtain? If you had a computer terminal on your desk, what aspect of your job would you like it to assist you with? What do you see as the biggest obstacle to automating your job? Closed-ended questions might include, Which of the following types of computer equipment have you had experience with? (list follows), Which of the following items of employee information do you commonly deal with? (list follows). Open-ended questions allow you to obtain information when the answers cannot be foreseen or when you do not wish to force interviewees into fixed responses. Closed-ended questions work well when you wish to cover a lot of information or when you wish to poll interviewees on items with fixed and definable responses.

When possible use two interviewers. This will allow one interviewer to concentrate on taking notes while the other conducts the interview. Two interviewers also help by allowing unclear responses to be clarified through discussions when post-interview notes are written. Where geographic dispersion makes personal interviews impossible, it may be useful to record phone interviews for later analysis. (Be sure the interviewee is aware of the recording.)

Schedule interviews so that the interviewer(s) have time to record their notes immediately following the interview. Do not rely on the memory of the interviewer. Anyone who has conducted a day of interviews can appreciate how quickly details tend to blur together.

Be aware that developing a new system means changes in work and jobs. Such changes may be threatening to various groups of users, and this may impact their degree of candor. Interviewers will need to be sensitive to this and try to set interviewees at ease. This does not mean misleading staff members by telling them that the new system will cause no changes. Rather, interviewers should try to enlist staff members' assistance and support and build their perceived ownership of the system. Interviewer training should definitely include techniques for conducting sensitive interviews.

Paper-and-pencil surveys can also be used. They are most appropriate when you wish to contact more employees than is feasible through interviews. Like interviews, a mix of questions is appropriate. It is critically important here to make sure questions are clearly worded and unambiguous since there will be no interviewer present to clarify items. For tips on drafting surveys and their analysis, see Fiedler,[8] Sonquist and Dunkelberg,[9] or Warwick and Lininger.[10]

The last task of EII is to identify the groups and individuals to be included in the interviews/surveys. Probably the best way to approach this is by breaking the potential respondents into three groups based on their relationship to HR information—those who generate the data (e.g., line supervisors), those who process the data (e.g., MIS/DP, HR personnel), and those who consume the output of the system (e.g., those receiving reports). The processing staff will probably constitute the largest single group. In identifying the interviewees, be sure to include those whose eventual support for the system will be critical. Individuals included in the development are likely to feel more positive about the system. Use the interviews to sell the system and build a support base.

Now that the initial project team is familiar with the information needs of the HR department, the participants identified, the instruments prepared, and the full project team finalized, the major information collection phase begins.

## Comprehensive Information Inventory

This phase is targeted at collecting a large body of information upon which the final report will be based and the system designed. This is the most time-intensive part of the needs analysis. Several classes of information should be examined: information inputs, data handling and HR processes, outputs, and design issues.

Each of these classes of information should be discussed in the interview/survey. Key questions to be answered include the following:

*Inputs.* Where do you get the information you need to do your job? From what sources? Where do they get this information? Are there any problems typically encountered with this information (e.g., inaccuracy, lateness, incompleteness)?

*Processes.* What happens to the information once it is received? How is it recorded and checked? Is the information transformed to create other information (e.g., are hours worked converted to qualified years for pension vesting)? How important is the information? How difficult is the processing? Would automating it be feasible? That is, can the current technology support the task? Can it be done more cost effectively through automation than is possible manually? Why or why not?

*Output.* What happens to the data after they are processed? Do they become part of any reports? Are they passed along to other groups? Who? How critical are these reports? Are there problems concerning these reports? Do you have any suggestions for simplifying the reports? Are there any other reports that would be valuable?

*Other issues.* What obstacles do you see in implementing an HRIS for the group? Are there any groups or individuals who you feel are not likely to support the new system? Why? If you were designing the system, what features would you like to see incorporated? What are the first HR tasks that you would like to see automated? Are there any tasks that should *not* be automated?

One of the chief benefits of this stage of the needs analysis is that it gets the HR staff thinking about information and the relationship of their job to others, both in and out of the HR group. Employees also begin thinking about better ways of acquiring, processing, and reporting the key raw material of HR — information.

Operationally, it is important to monitor the process and make sure that it proceeds on schedule. Interviews must be scheduled and materials will need to be duplicated. A number of interviews are bound to be delayed or canceled and must be rescheduled. Completed interview notes and surveys need to be collected and summarized. Consequently, it is a good idea to have an administrative assistant assigned at least part-time to the project.

The project manager will need to deal with major issues and the possibly ruffled feathers of some interviewees. It is also quite likely that the project manager will need to conduct some of the interviews, especially those with higher-level management.

The product of this phase is a large quantity of information, opinions, reports, and materials. Based on this, the new system will take shape. The next step is to analyze and process this material.

## Information Evaluation

The information evaluation phase can be intimidating. Even a team working in a small organization will generate a substantial body of data, reports, procedures, and comments through the comprehensive information inventory stage. The task becomes more manageable if broken down into smaller chunks. Below is a suggested approach to organizing and analyzing the data.

**Step 1**    List the major information-handling tasks of the department. These include such activities as generating reports, collecting information, manipulating data, responding to requests, and so on. For example, tasks might include processing new-hire benefits elections, generating staffing lists by department, and maintaining COBRA status records.

**Step 2**    Group tasks that go together into functions. For example, all tasks relating to benefits or performance evaluation might be grouped together.

**Step 3**    Rate each task in terms of its importance to the HR function and the level of effort required to automate the task. This may be done with a simple rating form that allows the evaluator to judge each task on a five-point scale ranging from "not at all important" to "critically important." Likewise, level of effort can be rated on a similar five-point scale ranging from "low effort, required few resources and work-hours" to "high effort, substantial resources and work-hours required." These ratings should be done by more than one project team member. A good practice is to have team members complete the ratings independently and then meet to compare ratings and reach a consensus. Prior to rating the tasks, the group members should meet and discuss the rating system and determine examples of tasks at various points on the rating scale. This will enhance the reliability of the subsequent ratings. Exhibit 5.4 presents sample rating scales.

**Exhibit 5.4** Sample Importance and Level-of-Effort Scales

*Key Question: How important is this task to the efficient and successful operation of the HR group?*

| 1 | 2 | 3 | 4 | 5 |
|---|---|---|---|---|
| Not at all important | Somewhat important | Moderately important | Very important | Critically important |

*Key Question: What level of effort (resources and work-hours) would be required to automate this task?*

| 1 | 2 | 3 | 4 | 5 |
|---|---|---|---|---|
| Low effort, few resources and work-hours | Moderately low | Average effort, moderate resources and work-hours | Moderately high | High effort, substantial resources and work-hours |

***Step 4***   Prioritize the tasks based on the ratings in Step 3. This may be done in several ways. A common approach is to rank the tasks first in terms of the importance ratings and second in terms of their level of effort. In this way resources may be targeted to those modules that are most important and for which sufficient resources exist to successfully complete the module design and implementation. Another approach is to multiply the ratings (importance × effort) in order to get an overall priority score for the task.

***Step 5***   Develop a task-by-information matrix. This is a simple way of determining the extent to which specific bits of information are used by several functions. An example is provided in Exhibit 5.5. For each task identified in Step 1, the specific items of information required to do that task are identified. These items of information are added to the table as shown in Exhibit 5.5, along with the name of the task. Information items already entered in the table are not entered again. As this process continues, a matrix is built that graphically shows the information use, by task, of the HR group. This matrix can then be used to determine which functions can be served by a common core of data. This process results in initial identification of the modules that can be included in the HRIS.

**Exhibit 5.5**   Needs Analysis Evaluation—Task-by-Information Matrix

| | HR Tasks | | | | | | |
|---|---|---|---|---|---|---|---|
| Information Item | *EEO and AA* | *Core Module* | *Performance Evaluation* | *COBRA* | | | |
| Last name | | X | X | X | | | |
| Social Security number | | X | X | X | | | |
| Job code | X | X | X | | | | |
| Age | X | X | | X | | | |
| Race | X | X | | | | | |

*Step 6*   Once the tasks to be automated have been identified, a preliminary data dictionary can be developed. This dictionary contains information on each of the data elements identified in the information matrix. The data dictionary contains a description of each data element as well as a variety of critical information about the acquisition, maintenance, and use of the data. This information will be critical for the design phase and subsequent incorporation in the system. Exhibit 5.6 presents a data dictionary recording form completed for the data element "current salary."

*Step 7*   At this point, the project team should begin to take a systems view of the tasks identified. Inefficiencies and redundancies that were revealed in the interviews can now be addressed. A useful technique for describing

**Exhibit 5.6**   Sample Data Dictionary Recording Form

```
Variable Name: CURSAL

Description of Variable: CURRENT ANNUAL BASE SALARY

Aliases: SALARY, GROSS PAY

Data Type: NUMERIC

Format: CURRENCY

Allowable Values: $0.00 TO $500,000.00

Located in Table: COMP1

Element Owner: PAYROLL DEPARTMENT

Frequency of Update: ANNUAL
```

Note: The exact information kept will vary from organization to organization. The information above is the basic details that should be included in all data dictionaries. Some information shown above, for example "Located in Table:" would be completed during the design phase, because it refers to the location of the data element in the data base design. After the system has been developed, information such as a listing of the reports the data element is used in may also be included in the dictionary. Maintaining the data dictionary becomes part of the ongoing management of the system.

the information flow and clarifying how data are transformed in the HR function is data flow diagraming. This technique graphically shows the input, throughput, and output of information. Carefully constructed data flow diagrams can lead directly to clarifying and possibly streamlining the HR function. For a discussion of data flow diagram methods, see the Appendix and Davis,[11] DeMarco,[12] or Yourdon.[13]

***Step 8*** At this point, it is likely that conflicting information concerning data acquisition, use, and storage will surface. Also, expect some information to be missing, necessitating follow-up interviews. Further, expect to spend an amount of time equal to 25 percent of the data collection time in clarifying information. For example, two interviewees may give conflicting answers regarding the use of a specific bit of information. It may be necessary to verify how an item of information is changed, or not changed, as it progresses through the system.

***Step 9*** Based on the priorities, preliminary design work can begin on selected modules. In order to prepare the final report for management, the modules to be implemented must be identified, described, and justified. This requires a cost-benefit analysis for each module. Cost-benefit analysis involves calculating the benefits associated with the implementation of the module and demonstrating that the cost of design and implementation are justified by the savings. When a complete system is being designed/developed, the cost/benefit of the entire system must be considered. One technique for doing this is to evaluate each module and combine the information to obtain estimates for the entire system. For example, in Exhibit 5.7 an applicant-tracking module is justified on both cost and effectiveness grounds. Cost savings suggest the module would "pay for itself" in 2.6 years. In addition, a number of other benefits would accrue to the organization. A similar approach could be used with the remaining modules in the proposed system. A full discussion of cost/benefit techniques is beyond the scope of this book. Good sources for information on cost-benefit methods include Cascio,[14] Fitzenz,[15] and Spencer.[16]

The summary for each module should be as concise as possible but contain at least the following information:

Title of the module.

Short description of the HR function to be automated.

**Exhibit 5.7**    Sample Module Specification

---

**Title:** Applicant tracking

**Description of function:** This module automates the
record keeping associated with the hiring process.
Both EEO and recruiting functions will be
supported. Specifically, the module tracks the
status of applicants as they proceed through the
hiring proces and helps ensure that timely
information is given to both applicants and line
management.

**Reports and output:** Recruiting status report, weekly
report of applicants to be contacted for interviews,
follow-up and no-interest letters, yield ratios by
source, EEO status letters, applicant summaries
broken down by race, gender, veterans' status,
handicapped status, output to EEO/AA modules, ad
hoc reports as required (e.g., applicants by
recruiting source).

**Development cost:** $7,500 to add and customize this
module for the HRIS. This includes customization
of the software, data collection and loading, and
personnel training.

**Cost savings/benefits:** $2,860/year. Reduction in
clerical time of 5 hours/week in preparing reports
is anticipated [5 hrs/wk × ($8.50/hr + $2.50
benefits/hr) × 52 weeks]. Enhanced timeliness
of recruiting reports will allow better targeting
of recruiting dollars, facilitate legal compliance
(potentially avoiding/reducing fines), and improve
recruiting success through better service to
recruiters and applicants.

---

Description of the output or products of the module (e.g., EEO reports,
monthly attendance summaries).

Description of the development costs for the module.

Description of the cost saving to be realized through the module and
the amortization period to recoup the cost. Also include any other
intangible benefits that the module affords.

Exhibit 5.7 shows a sample module description.

The information evaluation phase will take between four and eight weeks for a medium-size organization. It provides the critical review necessary to prepare the final report for management. This stage is important in that the recommendations in the final report are based on this analysis and will guide the development of the system.

## *Develop the HRIS Strategy*

The next step in the needs analysis process is to develop the HRIS strategy and final reports. Typically, two reports detail not only the proposed HRIS but also the strategic information plan of the HR group. The first report is a formal and lengthy version. This report is the operational document to guide system development. The second report is the executive summary. This document, limited to no more than five pages, focuses on the strategic issues and provides key points for decision makers without burdening them with extensive detail.

The formal report will be a fairly extensive document comprised of several sections:

Summary of the overall project, including a statement of the need for the HRIS system.

Description of the study process used to arrive at the priorities and suggested configuration.

List of specific user needs and problems.

Technical requirements—types of software or hardware the system must be compatible with, interfaces with other systems in the organization (e.g., payroll, general ledger), number of terminals to be supported, communications requirements, and so on.

HRIS strategy and proposal

HRIS strategy/system mission statement

Priorities and justification

Modules to be included (from previous step)

Suggested configurations

Advantages of approach/configuration

Drawbacks, limitations, constraints

Cost estimates and justification for proposed approach and any alternative configurations.

Legal issues that the proposed system could impact (e.g., privacy, Section 89 regulations).

Organizational issues that may impact system success (e.g., necessity for ongoing MIS/DP support).

List of team members and contribution.

Closing pitch for the system.[17]

The final report also provides the basic material for a presentation to top management. Both the presentation and the report are *sales* opportunities. It is a chance to persuade top management that the HR group is technologically sophisticated and can achieve productivity gains. Strategically, to start with choose modules that are relatively low risk (in terms of the chance of a complete failure) and that will be visible to management. Thus you can show a timely return on the investment in the system. This success can then be used to confirm the correctness of the decision to proceed and justify developing additional modules.

As you determine which and how many modules to tackle, remember the KISS principle—Keep It Simple Stupid. It is better to target one or two modules and have them be completed on schedule and on budget than attempt a complicated system with all the "bells and whistles." Attempting too much is probably the most common mistake system developers make.

### Evaluate the Needs Analysis Effort

The final phase of the needs analysis is the evaluation of the needs analysis effort. The objective here is to review the process just completed and determine what went well and what caused problems. Because maintaining a system is an ongoing process, needs analysis is an ongoing process. In most cases, a small number of modules will be designed and implemented to get the system going. As the HR group gains experience with the system, additional modules will be added or existing ones enhanced. Each time a module is designed, an abbreviated needs analysis will be conducted.

This phase provides feedback for the entire needs analysis process and as such is really an ongoing activity throughout the effort. Make some notes about what you would do differently next time. For example, How well did the interviews or surveys work? Were there questions that you did not think of initially and that required you to contact an interviewee for a second time? Did anyone suggest a change in procedures that could not be implemented now but that might be a good idea later?

Document the process you used. Make sure you archive the interview forms, lists of those interviewed, summaries of the data, and copies of the final reports. This will serve to give the department an "institutional memory," assist future project team members, and justify your decision. Although the evaluation phase is presented as the last step in the DECIDE process, it really occurs throughout the needs analysis. After each phase of the DECIDE process, make notes for the project evaluation. This will enhance the quality of the evaluation effort.

In sum, the DECIDE process for needs analysis provides a step-by-step approach to completing the first phase of system design. As noted earlier, it is one of several approaches and should be modified as required to fit the needs of each organization.

## Summary

This chapter has focused on the first step in establishing an HRIS—the needs analysis. The reasons for conducting a needs analysis as well as the questions the needs analysis answers were discussed. The DECIDE process laid out a step-by-step system for completing this first step.

Needs analysis is not a single process that must be conducted in "one right way." Each organization is unique, as is each needs analysis effort. The objective of this chapter is to familiarize you with the process and give you a framework to use in designing your own needs analysis.

Keep the barriers and mistakes noted in Chapter 4 in mind as you proceed through the needs analysis. The process is a bit like walking through a minefield—if you watch your step you'll get through; if you don't, your colleagues may be talking about you in the past tense!

## Discussion Questions

1. What tips would you give an HR manager developing an interview for a needs analysis?
2. Which HRIS modules are likely to be the most difficult to automate? Which are the easiest?

3. Why spend the time and effort on conducting a needs analysis? What will you gain by this effort?
4. What types of information would you expect to collect during the early information inventory stage?
5. What are the key components of the final needs analysis report?
6. What are the steps in the DECIDE model? Give a one-sentence summary of each.
7. How would you justify automating the HR function of a company that currently uses a manual system?

# Notes

1. For suggestions on the education and training of HR professionals and staff, see H. G. Gueutal, S. I. Tannenbaum, and M. J. Kavanagh, "Where to Go for an HRIS Education," *Computers in Personnel* (Spring 1988): 22–25.
2. A. J. Walker, *HRIS Development: A Project Team Guide to Building an Effective Personnel Information System* (New York: Van Nostrand Reinhold, 1982), 243.
3. S. H. Simon, "Steps to Success for Your HRIS," *Personnel* (November 1985): 16–20.
4. A. L. Lederer, "Information Technology: 1. Planning and Developing a Human Resources Information System," *Personnel* (May/June 1984): 14–27.
5. S. Sudman and N. M. Bradburn, *Asking Questions: A Practical Guide to Questionnaire Design* (San Francisco: Jossey-Bass, 1983), 397.
6. Walker, *HRIS Development*, 243.
7. D. P. Warwick and C. A. Lininger, *The Sample Survey: Theory and Practice* (New York: McGraw-Hill, 1975), 344.
8. J. Fiedler, *Field Research: A Manual for Logistics and Management of Scientific Studies in Natural Settings* (San Francisco: Jossey-Bass, 1978), 188.
9. J. A. Sonquist and W. C. Dunkelberg, *Survey and Opinion Research: Procedures for Processing* (Englewood Cliffs, NJ: Prentice-Hall, 1977), 503.
10. Warwick and Lininger, *The Sample Survey*, 344.
11. W. S. Davis, *Systems Analysis and Design: A Structured Approach* (Reading, MA: Addison-Wesley, 1983), 415.
12. T. DeMarco, *Structured Analysis and Systems Specification* (Englewood Cliffs, NJ: Prentice-Hall, 1979), 352.
13. E. Yourdon, *Modern Structured Analysis* (Englewood Cliffs, NJ: Prentice-Hall, 1989), 672.
14. W. F. Cascio, *Costing Human Resources: The Financial Impact of Behavior on Organizations*, 2nd ed. (Boston: PWS-KENT, 1987), 274.
15. J. Fitz-enz, *How to Measure Human Resources Management* (New York: McGraw-Hill, 1984), 237.

16. L. M. Spencer, Jr., *Calculating Human Resource Costs and Benefits* (New York: John Wiley & Sons, 1986), 361; see also J. Manry, "The Big Sell," *Computers in Personnel* (Winter 1988): 14–17; and J. Frazee and J. Harrington-Kuller, "Money Matters: Selling HRIS to Management," *Personnel Journal* (August 1987): 98–107.

17. Adapted from Walker, *HRIS Development*, 243.

# 6

# System Design/Acquisition

The next step in establishing the HRIS is designing and/or acquiring the system. This stage of the development process results in the delivery of a system that is then implemented. Many decisions must be made at this time, including, Should the company develop a system internally or purchase an existing vendor-developed system? Possibly some combination of the two? What type of hardware will be used? Will the system interface with other information systems (e.g., general ledger)? How will data security be assured? Each of these decisions will directly impact the configuration, implementation, and eventual success of the system.

This chapter addresses the critical issues in the design/acquisition process. The chapter is divided into four major sections. The first section covers many of the critical issues that must be resolved early in the design/acquisition process. The second section explores the issues involved in selecting the appropriate computer hardware. The third section discusses the request for proposals, a critical document that is used to screen potential vendors of the HRIS. The final section covers a variety of technical issues that arise during the design/acquisition process.

## Key Decisions

As the design/acquisition process begins, the project team will be faced with a number of key decisions that will have long-term effects on the system. Although the focus here is on two of the most important decisions, it will become apparent that each decision involves other key considerations. The first decision deals with the purchase/development option selected. The second pertains to the type of technology configuration to choose. The initial focus is on issues relating primarily to software rather than hardware. This is because finding software that will fit the needs of the organization is typically much more difficult than finding hardware to run the software. In addition, software is becoming increasingly compatible with a variety of hardware systems. In the future, software portability across systems is likely to increase, which will make hardware compatibility less of an issue.

### *Buy a New System or Update an Existing System?*

The first decision is whether to purchase/develop a new system or to upgrade an existing system to serve the needs of the human resources group. Existing systems may include the payroll system, internally developed HRIS applications, preexisting HRIS packages, and systems that seem to have grown over time to become HRISs. Among these, the most likely choice for adapting an existing system is to upgrade the payroll package. If the payroll system is an up-to-date package from a major vendor, it is likely that an HRIS upgrade is available as an enhancement. Organizations choosing this alternative point out that a great deal of the data are already in the payroll system and that a combined HRIS/payroll system will be more cost-effective. Although this is a viable option, it is likely that the resulting system will not be as flexible as one designed from the onset to be an HRIS based on a comprehensive needs analysis as described in Chapter 5.[1]

Adapting a home-grown system is another choice. For example, a staff member in HR may have developed computer tools (e.g., a data base system for generating EEO/AA reports) that could be expanded to an HRIS. In most cases, however, the amount of rewriting and changing required to convert these systems into a full-blown HRIS does not make this option feasible. After all, the reason the needs analysis was done in the first place was that the existing systems were not providing the amount or type of support required. If you are going to design/develop your own system, you are almost always better off starting with a clean slate. This way you begin with up-to-date software rather than build on a base that is already several years old.

### Design a New System or Buy an Existing One?

Assuming that updating is not an option, the project team must decide how the new system is to be acquired. That is, should the group develop/write its own software or purchase a package developed by a vendor? Actually there are four options:

1. Develop a new system from scratch internally.
2. Adapt a system used by another group or similar organization
3. Use an external service.
4. Buy a vendor system and modify it, or purchase a vendor system and use it as is.

The pros and cons of these four approaches are examined below, with special attention given to evaluating vendors and vendor-developed systems.

**Option 1: Develop a System Internally**   Developing your own system has traditionally been an option only for the largest, most technically sophisticated users. A 1984 survey of Fortune 500 companies showed that 46 percent had developed their own systems.[2] Technical sophistication was required because large systems were primarily mainframe based and used arcane, difficult-to-use languages. The designers needed to be programmers with formal computer science or MIS education. In most HR departments, such skills do not exist. Consequently, the internal design effort was typically left to the MIS/DP group—with HR as an onlooker.

Fortunately, advances in software technology have made it possible for nonprogrammers to develop highly sophisticated software applications. This is especially true when a microcomputer system is anticipated. Data base products like R:Base for DOS,[3] Revelation,[4] and others have built-in development tools that allow users to create custom systems. For example, several packages have **application generators** that lead the user through a series of questions concerning what the system should do and then proceed to write the software code to make it happen. Although system development is certainly more complicated than simply answering questions, it is not beyond the skills of a motivated HR professional.

A chief advantage of an internally developed system is that the HR department ends up with an extensive and detailed knowledge of the system. In designing the software, the group will acquire a great deal of experience in system design and development. This experience will be invaluable, because modifications and enhancements are invariably added to the system. Internal development led by the HR staff can help make the function information independent. The function is self-reliant in terms of the information processing needs of the HR group.

Developing a new system within the HR department is most feasible when a microcomputer system is being designed. If a mainframe system is chosen, it will probably be necessary to include MIS/DP staff on the project team. However, the HR staff should learn as much about the development as possible to avoid continuing an information-dependent relationship.

Although there are compelling reasons to develop a system internally, there are also serious drawbacks. Internally developed systems are not less costly than vendor-developed ones. Indeed, Corson estimates that building your own system can cost 400 percent more and take 33 percent longer to complete than a vendor-developed system.[5] Clearly, these estimates depend on the number of modules attempted and the way the system is costed. For example, if labor is not included in the development costs (as it should be), the system can appear quite inexpensive. However, when labor is included, the real cost of the system becomes much higher. Other potential problems in internally developed systems include difficulty in predicting development times and costs, unforeseen bugs and glitches in the system, lack of professionally developed documentation and training manuals, lower overall sophistication in the software, and lack of "expert" support when something goes wrong. However, when expertise is available and total customization is required, an internally developed system can result in a superior fit with the needs of the organization.

**Option 2: Adapt a System from Another Group**    Adapting a system from another group in the organization is an option for units of large organizations. This is especially true in organizations that have decentralized HR functions. In some cases another unit may have purchased or developed a system that can also be used by your group.

There are a number of advantages to this option:

*Reduced cost.* This is especially true if no new licenses or software purchases are required.

*Fit with group needs.* The system is likely to be highly modified for your organization and should contain data elements and terms familiar to the HR department.

*Support.* The other group may be able to help you through the start-up period and provide assistance thereafter.

*Economies of scale.* Future modules could be developed or purchased with other units on a shared-cost basis.

*Standardization.* Widespread use of a common system can lead to easier communication and consolidation of data across units.

*Low risk.* You know the system works in your organization; you also know what does not work.

The disadvantages of adopting a system from another group include the following:

*Documentation.* Internally developed systems may not be well documented.

*Mysterious designs.* Systems that have evolved over time are often an indecipherable mix of patches, add-ons, and fixes. The outcome is a system that no one really understands or can maintain. Be careful not to adopt a "black-box" system that cannot be maintained or upgraded.

*Ownership.* The ownership of the system may not be clear. For example, if the original system was vendor supplied but has since been highly modified, whose system is it? Is the vendor still in business? Will royalties have to be paid? Will the vendor be able to support your system?

*Local practices.* Differences in practices or business type can make cross-organizational transfers of software tricky.

Option 2 is not available to most organizations. However, for those that have the opportunity to share software, it can be the most cost-effective approach.

**Option 3: Use an External Service** External HRIS services have historically been a rather small part of the total HRIS market. An external service maintains the hardware and software for the HRIS. The user typically has only terminals and/or output devices (e.g., printers) at the work site. The user is basically purchasing computer time and HRIS services from a vendor without the expense of actually owning the system.

External services are typically marketed by payroll service firms. These firms have traditionally handled the information processing for the payroll of the organization. This includes computing pay and deductions, keeping payroll records, complying with state and federal compensation laws, and issuing paychecks. In recent years, these organizations have begun to expand their services to include benefits management as well as HRIS functions.

On the plus side, such services can achieve economies of scale by serving multiple users. They can be cost-effective. Since they already maintain a substantial amount of employee data for payroll purposes, the cost of adding additional data fields to manage HRIS tasks is relatively low. Start-up is also fairly quick since much of the data are already on hand and the HR staff may already be familiar with the operating software. In addition, a unified payroll/HRIS keeps all the data in one system, facilitating data consistency and integrity while avoiding redundancy between the HRIS and payroll systems.

On the negative side, payroll/HRIS services do not use state-of-the-art HRISs. The original software they use was designed to process payroll information efficiently. These systems are typically batch oriented and quite efficient at cyclical tasks in which large numbers of transactions are required. HRISs, on the other hand, deal mostly with ad hoc inquiries on a frequent but irregular basis, nonrepetitive reports, and, increasingly, modeling. Payroll-oriented systems are not typically user friendly in terms of writing reports, generating form letters, and performing what-if analyses. They were not designed to be used by nonprogrammers in an interactive environment. Operating costs can also be difficult to control as users "run up the bill" working on reports and studies. Payroll-service-based systems also may be difficult, expensive, or impossible to modify to fit the specifications of the needs analysis. As with some vendor systems, you must conform your operating procedures to be consistent with the software. Also, the service may not support the modules you need.

If you do decide to go with a payroll/HRIS, be sure to check on customizability and upgrades. What will the service do if you request a module (e.g., applicant tracking) they do not currently have? Will you pay the cost of development? Will they? How quickly can they respond to such requests? Are your data available in a format compatible with in-house systems? Are any of the foregoing conditions specified in the contract?

Payroll-service-based HRISs are a definite option for organizations currently using a payroll service. There are good arguments for tying the HRIS and payroll system together. Just be sure that the advantages of such services justify the limitations and trade-offs.

*Option 4: Purchase a Vendor-Developed System*   An option for virtually every organization is to purchase a system from a vendor. These systems range from large, mainframe-based packages costing more than $1 million to microcomputer-based systems costing a few thousand dollars. All told there are more than 300 systems currently on the market. Indeed, the most difficult choice facing the user is determining which of the many systems is best.

Several surveys of HRISs are published regularly. Sources of these surveys include *Personnel Journal,*[6] the *Human Resource Systems Professionals* newsletter and survey, computer magazines, and reviews in *Computers in Personnel.*[7] Other good sources of information about vendor systems may be found in various HR systems-oriented journals such as *HR/PC: Personal Computing for Human Resource Professionals*[8] and at local and national meetings of Human Resource Systems Professionals (HRSP).[9] The HRSP meetings are useful in that they often include vendor fairs where HRIS sellers display and demonstrate their products. The 1984 survey of Fortune 500 companies reported that 54 percent had purchased vendor-developed systems.[10] However, many of these organizations made major modifications to their new systems.

Two major evaluations must be done if you select a vendor-supplied product. The first concerns the product. Will it do what you require? The second is the vendor. Will the vendor be able to provide the amount and type of support you require? Each of these issues is examined below.

### Evaluating the Product

Three key questions must be answered in evaluating any vendor product. First, does the product purport to do the tasks that the needs analysis has determined are required? For example, does it have a position control module that can track temporary job openings? Second, will the product *really* perform the tasks? That is, can the system handle the job in a way that is consistent with your policies and procedures? The third question deals with technology issues. Will the software run on your system? Can it be networked? Is the hardware compatible with company standards? Does the software require specialized hardware?

Answering the first question involves screening. Some method must be used to sort through the many systems on the market. This can be done in several ways, including contacting vendors, reviewing publications, attending seminars, meeting with HR system users, and distributing a request for proposals (RFP). Most companies will use some combination of approaches but should arrive at an RFP during this process. The RFP tells vendors what you expect the system to do. RFPs are more completely described later in the chapter.

Answering the second question requires critical evaluation skills. Will the software actually perform as advertised? Will it accomplish the tasks in the way you want it to? The best way to answer these questions is to spend as much time as possible with the candidate systems. Clearly you do not have the luxury (or drudgery) of spending a lot of time with numerous systems. Consequently, it will be necessary to eliminate as many systems as possible. This may be done in several ways. First, a well-developed RFP will weed out many potential systems. Second, discussions with current users of the remaining systems can help eliminate the boasts from the reality. Do not underestimate the value of discussions with current users. They are probably the best source of evaluation information. Third, product reviews can be helpful in clarifying actual performance.

Once the list is narrowed down to a handful of systems, the hands-on portion of the evaluation begins. Vendors should be required to demonstrate their systems on-site if possible. The presentation will be designed to show off the best features of the system. For example, the demonstration system will often contain a relatively small data base with few records and little historical data. This allows the system to run very quickly. Likewise, expect to see some very impressive reports from the system. Undoubtedly, the vendor will explain how easily the reports are generated. Your job is to look past the presentation to the system's usefulness for your application. Go back to your needs analysis for guidance. Find out information such as

> How many employee records are in the system as it is demonstrated to you as a potential buyer? How does this number compare to the number of employees you plan to include in the system?

> Are the employees represented in all tables? That is, is information about employees contained in all the tables designed into the system?

If some tables are "empty," the system may appear to perform better than it would with full data.

How much historical information is kept in the demonstration system?

How well does the system respond to ad hoc inquiries? To test this, generate some ad hoc inquiries—the more complex the better.

Can the system generate reports like the ones currently used? If so, ask the representative to generate such a report.

Does the system assist the user in developing reports/forms?

How can the system be customized? Can this be done by users? How easy is it to do customization?

Many additional questions can be asked. The key point is to probe for the weaknesses in the system. Do not accept the sales representative's assurances that the system can do all the tasks you need it to do. Try some ad hoc inquiries, design a report, draw a form. If it seems difficult at first, it will probably be difficult later. Be sure to schedule sufficient time to work with the system personally. There is no substitute for hands-on experience with the product. It is often advisable to devise a standard set of reports, ad hoc inquiries, forms, and so on for comparison across systems.

During this evaluation stage it is important to involve as many project team members as possible. The quality of the decision reached will depend largely on the amount of experience team members have with various systems. The more systems you evaluate, the better you will get at focusing on critical system performance factors and the less likely you are to be surprised later.

Answering the third question, which deals with technical issues, is fairly straightforward. Does the system meet the technical requirements of the needs analysis? Typical questions include the following:

Does the system use the type and/or brand of hardware specified in the needs analysis? Is the system mainframe oriented? Written for one brand of mainframe?

What amount of storage does the system require? How is this storage backed up?

What computer language is the software written in? Is this compatible with languages supported by the organization?

Can the system be interfaced with other systems in the organization? Payroll? General ledger? If so, how?

Is the system designed to be used in a network? If so, is the number of workstations supported by the network and software sufficient?

Can the software be modified for specific applications of the user? If so, must this be done by the vendor or can it be done by the user? How much will this cost?

What type of documentation is provided with the system? Several types will be required, including user training manuals (written at a low level for computer novices), general information and syntax manuals (for reference by experienced users as they work with forms, inquiries, and reports), and technical manuals (written for programmers). Can extra copies be obtained? At what cost?

What provisions does the system have for uploading or downloading data? Does the system provide any tools to assist users in this process?

Answering these technical questions will help ensure that the system meets the general technical requirements for the HRIS. Additional technical issues are addressed in the RFP. Specific, detailed technical issues should be covered in discussions with the vendors of systems that are finalists in the selection process. At this point it is advisable to involve representatives from other departments (MIS/DP/Payroll) if the new system is to interface with other systems.

After carefully examining the software, it is time to evaluate the vendor.

### Evaluating the Vendor

Equally as important as the quality of the software is the quality of the vendor. Buying an HRIS package will almost certainly entail a long-term relationship with the vendor. The eventual success of the system will depend partly on the amount and quality of support available from the vendor.

Ask the following questions in evaluating potential vendors:

How long have they been in business?

Is there any evidence of the financial stability of the firm?

How can they convince you they will be in business in five years?

In what ways are clients supported by the vendor? Do they provide a designated account representative? What are the qualifications of these representatives? Is support available by phone? During what hours?

How often does the company update the software? Are these updates included free of charge for a period of time?

How long has the product been on the market? How many revisions has it gone through since its introduction?

Can the vendor provide the names of companies and contact people for you to call about satisfaction/performance of their products?

What type of training support is provided with the package? Are introductory as well as advanced courses available? Can training be done at your site or must it be done at the vendor's location? Are new training courses being developed to keep up with changes in software and HR practices? Are the trainers qualified to educate users?

What is the vendor's commitment to research and product development? How can their answer be substantiated?

Critically evaluate the answers you are given. It is better to learn of vendor weaknesses early on, before they become apparent during installation or utilization. The vendor is going to be a partner in your system; be sure it is the type of organization you wish to go into partnership with.

Purchasing a system from a vendor is a viable option for most organizations. On the plus side, vendor-supplied systems are generally well developed and benefit from the input of a variety of users. Often user groups composed of the purchasers of a specific system can be of assistance to recent adopters. Vendor systems also provide support for the user. This support can be invaluable for HR departments new to HRISs and that consequently do not have in-house technical experts. Likewise, system maintenance and enhancements are handled by the vendor. This does not mean the HR group will have little or no system work to do; rather, they will be involved as content-matter experts rather than applications programmers. Since the package is basically complete, the user can move quickly to data loading and training. Implementation is often facilitated by the vendor's experience. Many vendors also provide well-developed training materials and programs for staff members.

Vendor systems rarely fail completely—you *will* get a system that can do significant HRIS work. If time is a critical issue and the desired HRIS is complex, a vendor system is probably the best option. But purchasing a vendor system also has disadvantages. You are locked into a long-term relationship with a single vendor and may have little control over increases in maintenance fees and costs. Indeed, you will probably not own the software; rather, you will license it for a period of time. When the license expires you must either pay the new fees demanded or start over with a new system and a new company. Many systems also require that your HR procedures are changed to accommodate the system. Another disadvantage of vendor systems is that since they were developed externally, you may not be able to modify them easily and do not really know how they are structured internally. The extent to which these are major disadvantages for your department will depend largely on your relationship with the vendor and your view of the vendor's reputation.

The "make or buy" decision is probably the single most important choice you will make in putting together the HRIS. As you have seen, there are several options, each with advantages and disadvantages. Exhibit 6.1 summarizes the options and rates them on a number of dimensions. Other decisions involve the type of hardware to be used. This question is addressed in the next section.

**Exhibit 6.1**   Comparison of System Options and Attributes

| | *Options* | | | |
|---|---|---|---|---|
| **System Attribute** | *1* | *2* | *3* | *4* |
| Ease of development | L | M | H | H |
| Data security | L–M | L–H | H | M–H |
| Backup ease | M | M | H | H |
| Cost of development/acquisition | H | L | L | M |
| Operating cost | L | L–H | M–H | M |
| Initial data acquisition cost | H | M | L–M | L–H |
| Chance of complete failure | M | L | L | L |
| Ease of modification | H | L–H | L | M–H |
| User friendliness | M–H | L–H | L–M | M–H |
| Implementation time | H | L | L | M |
| Quality of documentation | L–M | L–H | L–M | M–H |
| Amount of user training required | M | L–M | L | M–H |
| Cost of updates | L–H | L–H | L | L–M |

*Options:*   1—Develop a system internally.    *Ratings:*   L—Low
            2—Adapt a system from another group.              M—Medium
            3—Use an external service.                        H—High
            4—Purchase a vendor-developed system.

# Choosing Computer Hardware

In the "good old days" only one type of system could handle the volume of HR records—the mainframe. Because the DP or MIS department cared for and fed the mainframe, they also became responsible for HR computing. Only mainframes could process the information fast enough and store enough of it to be useful in HRIS applications. Indeed, one of the first jobs given to mainframe computers was an HR job—payroll processing.

Today, however, many more computing options are available. The advent of microcomputers has changed the rules in data processing. Today's desktop microcomputer has several times the power and storage of a mainframe of a decade ago.

Minicomputers, virtually unknown in the 1960s and 1970s, have even more power and can support sophisticated computer networks. Consequently, the options for hardware for the HRIS have broadened considerably.

A complete discussion of the technical merits of each type of hardware is beyond the scope of this chapter. However, some of the advantages and disadvantages of microcomputer, minicomputer, and mainframe systems will be briefly examined from an HR user's point of view.

## *Microcomputers*

Microcomputers are rapidly changing the nature of HRISs. They have captured approximately 40 percent of the HRIS market. Increases in processing speed, storage, and network technology have made such systems an option for all but the largest users. Especially when payroll is not a part of the HRIS, microcomputer systems have significant advantages.

The advantages of microcomputer-based systems include the following:

Overall, the software costs less.

System ownership is generally within the HR department.

System users are likely to be less intimidated by a microcomputer system.

Users are likely to use the microcomputer for other tasks (e.g., word processing, telecommunications), thereby increasing the cost-effectiveness of the hardware purchase.

Daily use of the microcomputers will enhance the HR staff's sophistication with a developing technology.

Most recent college graduates will be microcomputer literate.

Security can be controlled since the location of the system, the data base, and the system's operation are controlled by the HR department.

Because the system is operated by HR staff, ad hoc inquiries and specialized reports are often more easily obtained. External groups are not needed to process special requests.

A great deal of software exists for modeling and decision support system (DSS) development (e.g., Lotus 1-2-3[11]). Much of this software is designed for use by nonprogrammers. Ease of modeling and DSS development are two of the chief advantages of microcomputer-based systems.

Software and applications packages designed for microcomputer use tend to be more user friendly and easier for nonprogrammers to work with.

Microcomputers also have several disadvantages:

Internal technical support for the system may not exist.

Backup of data is sometimes not done on a regular basis, which can result in a serious information loss.

Documentation may be inadequate, especially when the system is developed internally.

Maintaining equipment and software is the responsibility of HR personnel, who may not be familiar with this task.

Microcomputers may not be able to handle extremely large number-crunching tasks. However, this disadvantage will become less of an issue as technology advances.

Access speed (the amount of time it takes to retrieve a given item of data) may be slow when a large number of employee records are involved (e.g., > 2000). Over time, this is likely to be less of a concern as microcomputer processing power increases and disk access times decrease.

Data security can be a problem if multiple users have access to the data base. Microcomputer installations typically do not have sophisticated data security systems in place.

If a network is not used, the system will be available only to a single user. Where multiple freestanding systems are used, data inconsistency, errors, and redundancy are serious problems.

Interfacing with other systems, communicating, uploading, or down-loading are invariably more difficult than anticipated. The mainframe guardians may be reluctant to allow you to upload or download infor-mation from your system to theirs.

## *Minicomputers*

Minicomputer-based systems represent the smallest segment of the HRIS market (13 percent). These systems are most often used where multiple workstations are desired and a microcomputer-based network is not feasible. Minicomputers can typically serve a number of workstations and are quite similar to networks in many ways. The minicomputer provides the processing power and storage for the system. A good way to view a minicomputer system is as a small time-sharing installation.

Using a minicomputer HRIS has several advantages:

Centralized data storage facilitates security and data management.

Multiple workstations allow several users to access/edit/manipulate data simultaneously.

Because the system is typically managed by the user department, system ownership is clearer than in mainframe installations.

Processing power and storage are greater than in microcomputer systems.

Overall costs are lower compared to mainframe systems.

The disadvantages include the following:

A smaller selection of HRIS software is available than for microcom-puter or mainframe systems.

System management is more complicated than with microcomputers and may require assistance from other groups.

The investment in hardware may be larger. Also, the relative distinction between mini and micro systems is becoming blurred. A potential problem is that micros will overtake minis and that the software designed for a minicomputer system will not be transportable to a microcomputer environment.

As with microcomputers, interfacing the minicomputer system with other in-house systems, including the mainframe, may be difficult.

## Mainframe Computers

Mainframe computers continue to account for the largest segment of the HRIS market (47 percent), although they are losing market share to microcomputer and minicomputer systems. Mainframes are known for their processing power, storage, and difficulty of use. For large organizations requiring centralization of information, they are the only choice.

Mainframe computers have the following advantages:

The hardware is usually purchased and maintained with someone else's budget.

Mainframes have greater processing speed and storage capabilities than other types of computers.

Data backup and physical security are typically handled by the DP department.

Interfacing with other software is facilitated since everything is on the same system. This is marketed by mainframe HRIS vendors as "borderless processing."

Mainframes can support many terminals, allowing multiple users. However, speed is not always faster than other types of systems if the mainframe is overloaded.

Mainframe systems are often more feasible where payroll/HRIS are combined.

Technical support for applications can be provided by experts in programming and system design.

Telecommunication with remote sites can be handled more easily with a mainframe system. This can be critical if data consolidation from a variety of remote sites is an important function of the system.

Applications software is often upwardly compatible with new mainframes as long as the mainframe vendor is not changed.

Among the disadvantages are the following:

System ownership is often unclear. Control of the data may be in the hands of others.

The HR department must depend on others for support and software assistance. It may be difficult for HR to respond quickly to requests for reports.

Depending on the system, down-time (when the system is unavailable because of a hardware or operating system reason not related to the HRIS) can be a problem.

Developing decision support systems and modeling may be difficult on the mainframe, because these systems often do not have user friendly modeling languages for nonprogrammers to use.

Where the department is charged for computer time, costs can be difficult to control.

Selecting the type of hardware cannot be separated from selecting software and the results of the needs analysis. In many cases the information policy of the organization may dictate the hardware used. Likewise, the size of the organization, whether very large or quite small, may rule out a particular type of hardware. Although some software is transportable between types of computer systems, most is not.

The following section discusses the development and use of requests for proposals in generating a group of systems to choose among.

## Requests for Proposals: The RFP

The request for proposals is a document that tells potential vendors what you expect in an HRIS. This is a critical document for any user choosing an external service or purchasing a vendor-developed system. The RFP should flow directly from the needs analysis and is composed of several sections. Each of the major sections is shown in Exhibit 6.2 and described below. The information in this section is adapted from Plantamura.[12]

### Introduction

This section provides an overview of the RFP, listing such information as:

The contact person, title, and address.

The date by which proposals must be received.

Company background, size, business, number and distribution of employees, and general organization of the firm and human resources group.

General technical information on the type of information systems currently in use that may impact the proposed HRIS.

**Exhibit 6.2**    Major Sections of the Request for Proposals

- Introduction
- Functional requirements
- Technical criteria
- Vendor information
- Cost information
- Support and training
- Warranty and contract

*Source:*    Adapted from L.M. Plantamura, "Choosing an HRIS Vendor," *Personnel Administrator* (November 1985): 18–22.

A statement requiring nondisclosure of company information and a dis-claimer regarding release of the company from scheduled commit-ment dates. It should also specifically allow the company to disqualify any vendor without cause and make clear that any costs incurred in preparing or presenting their proposal are the sole responsibility of the vendor.

Indicate the general evaluation process as well as your expectations for the proposal and any presentation the vendor is to make.

## Functional Requirements

This section describes the tasks the HRIS is to accomplish. It is important to include as much detail here as possible and to be clear in the use of terms. This will allow the vendors to better assess whether their systems will be competitive. The needs analysis will provide major input for this section. Specific information to incorporate here includes:

The modules targeted for initial implementation as well as those planned for later.

The critical tasks each module is to accomplish and how that accom-plishment is to be assessed.

The type of on-line capabilities the system should have. For example, must a specific query language be used?  Does the system need to provide an applications generator? What type of editing and security capabilities does the system need? Does the software need to run on a network? Interface with other systems? Does it need data output in a specific form?

Is a specific type of system required? For example, if your intention is to purchase a networked system running an application built on a commercially available microcomputer data base product (e.g., R:Base for DOS), indicate this here.

## Technical Criteria

The technical criteria section provides detailed specifications relating to hardware and software. This section is most critical for users purchasing systems to work with existing networks or mainframe equipment. If a mainframe system is anticipated, this section will probably require input from the MIS/DP department.

Topics addressed in this section include:

Technical specifications relative to the requirements of the system. This may include the language and operating system the HRIS must use, the storage capabilities available, the telecommunications system, and so on.

Technical aspects of security systems that must be in place. Security provisions required in the HRIS should also be noted.

Any special requirements for installation.

Technical requirements for interfacing with other systems or packages (e.g., general ledger).

## Vendor Information

The vendor information section lays out the questions that you have about the vendor. This section requires the vendor to qualify as a bidding organization. It should include the vendor-evaluation questions found earlier in this chapter.

## Cost Information

This section asks the vendor to specify, up front, the fee structure for the software and the terms under which it is available. Key questions include

Is the software sold or licensed?

What is the term of the license?

How are updates provided? Are any updates provided free of charge for a period of time?

What are the fees for support and maintenance?

Are multiple installations/copies permitted? Under what conditions?

Is installation included? What if problems occur?

How are future price increases controlled? What is the history of price increases over the last several years?

How much training is included in the contract price? How much does additional training cost?

How are customization services costed? On average, how much does customization add to the purchase price?

## Support and Training

This section asks the vendor to specify the amount and type of support provided for the new system. It should ask that the amount and type of support and training be included in the contract. Continued and additional training should also be described. This discussion should include specifics about the site of training and the provision of training materials and equipment. The vendor should also be asked if any user groups are in operation and for contact people in these groups.

## Warranty and Contract

Finally, the RFP should request a sample copy of the system warranty and standard contract. Demand a comprehensive system warranty and insist that the warranty be a contractual obligation. View the warranty and sample contract provided by the vendor as a starting point for negotiation. Remember, these documents were written for the vendor's benefit. Have your legal department go over the contract.

The next section focuses on several of the technical issues that should be considered in designing/purchasing a system.

# Technical Issues

## Data Base Management Systems

Virtually all HRIS implementations rely on a data base management system (DBMS). The DBMS is usually thought of as the software package that underlies the HRIS. The DBMS allows users to access the data base, build applications, and generally manage the data. For example, in a microcomputer environment, a project team might choose R:Base for DOS or dBASE IV for the DBMS package and use a programming language within the DBMS to create the HRIS. The choice of DBMS is quite important, as the power and ease of use of the DBMS will directly impact the success of the HRIS. The project team should devote significant time and energy to selecting the DBMS, expecially if the decision is to build the system in-house or customize a vendor-developed system. DBMSs are often reviewed and compared in computer publications. Such reviews are a good place to start in deciding on a DBMS.

DBMS products rely on a data base model or method of structuring the information. **Relational data bases** are most commonly used in HRIS applications. In a relational system, information is kept in various tables and is linked across tables by a common data element or relational factor. This structure allows for minimal redundancy in data storage. As an example, contrast a system that uses a **flat file** structure with one that is relational. Flat file systems maintain all information about an employee in one large table. Think about a line of information that extends almost forever. Personal data, benefits elections, work history data, compensation information, skills and education summaries, and so on are all kept on one line in the data base. Such a system accesses information extremely slowly since each inquiry requires that all the information in the system be read to complete the request. Further, the structure leads to a great deal of information redundancy. For example, each employee has work location information associated with his or her record. This would include information such as work phone, work address, fax number, and so forth. If fifteen employees all worked in the same office, this information would be repeated fifteen times in the system, thus increasing storage requirements.

On the other hand, relational data bases deal with many of these problems. For example, personal information (name, address, Social Security number, race, gender, etc.) might be kept in one table, benefits data in another, and work history in a third. When the user requests information on, say, gender and race, only the personal information table is accessed. Less information is sorted and response time is much quicker than in a flat file system. Data redundancy is also reduced. Each table is linked to other tables by a common element. For example, the table containing personal information might be linked to a work location table by a *location code* found in both tables. The personnel information table has only the location code and personnel information and the work location table has location codes and information about work sites (address, fax number, number of employees at site, etc.). Thus, redundant site information does not have to be kept with each employee record, but for any employee the system could print out the employee's name, gender, and work address. The system would take name and gender from the personal information table and, using the location code, link to his or her work location table to get the work address. Exhibit 6.3 compares flat file and relational data bases. In general, relational systems are more efficient and likely to underlie the HRIS. For more information on data base types and design issues, see Laudon and Laudon[13] or Cardenas.[14]

DBMSs vary on a number of criteria. Many of these have already been discussed in the context of evaluating vendor products. Many others are included in the product reviews previously noted. However, based on our experience, some of the most important questions to answer about DBMS packages include the following:

*Programming language.* How easy is the programming language to use? Can a nonprogrammer become proficient in the language? Can changes to the system be made by the personnel who will be working with and maintaining the system?

*Data base type.* What type of data base structure is used? Most systems use a form of a relational data base structure.

*Product support.* Is product support, such as an "800" number, available? At what cost? Are there in-house experts to assist users?

*Report writing.* Does the system have a user friendly report writer? How easy is it to generate reports? Do you need to use the programming language?

*Compiler.* Can the system be compiled (converted to machine language) to increase processing speed? How fast is the package?

*Interface.* Can the DBMS interface easily with other systems? Can it import and export information without causing the users to consider changing employers if not professions?

Exhibit 6.3  Flat File versus Relational Data Base Structures

*Flat File*

| Lastname | First | Sex | Age | SS# | Location Code | Address1 | Address2 | City | State | Zip | Phone |
|---|---|---|---|---|---|---|---|---|---|---|---|
| Cash | Brett | M | 34 | 317454589 | Corp | 5 State Ave | Floor 6 | Albany | NY | 12232 | 443-1612 |
| Hoham | Hal | M | 62 | 455679876 | Corp | 5 State Ave | Floor 6 | Albany | NY | 12232 | 443-1612 |
| Anderson | Cathy | F | 29 | 211345678 | Corp | 5 State Ave | Floor 6 | Albany | NY | 12232 | 443-1612 |
| Piper | Bonnie | F | 44 | 456835609 | Plant1 | 12 Grey St. | Bldg. 4 | Newark | NJ | 23145 | 324-6969 |
| Beard | Rebecca | F | 53 | 987668971 | Corp | 5 State Ave | Floor 6 | Albany | NY | 12232 | 443-1612 |
| Who | Doc | M | 35 | 121548679 | Plant1 | 12 Grey St. | Bldg. 4 | Newark | NJ | 23145 | 324-6969 |
| Nelson | Meg | F | 33 | 345765432 | Corp | 5 State Ave | Floor 6 | Albany | NY | 12232 | 443-8767 |

*Relational*

*Table 1: Personal Information*

| Lastname | First | Sex | Age | SS# | Location Code |
|---|---|---|---|---|---|
| Cash | Brett | M | 34 | 317454589 | Corp |
| Hoham | Hal | M | 62 | 455679876 | Corp |
| Anderson | Cathy | F | 29 | 211345678 | Corp |
| Piper | Bonnie | F | 44 | 456835609 | Plant1 |
| Beard | Rebecca | F | 53 | 987668971 | Corp |
| Who | Doc | M | 35 | 121548679 | Plant1 |
| Nelson | Meg | F | 33 | 345765432 | Corp |

*Table 2: Work Location*

| Location Code | Address1 | Address2 | City | State | Zip | Phone |
|---|---|---|---|---|---|---|
| Corp | 5 State Ave. | Floor 6 | Albany | NY | 12232 | 443-1612 |
| Plant1 | 12 Grey St. | Bldg. 4 | Newark | NJ | 23145 | 324-6969 |

*Note:* Notice that in the flat file, eighty-four items of information are kept and many data elements are repeated. For example, the work address information is the same for all Corp employees, but since this is a flat file, the information must be repeated each time to allow it to be associated with each employee. In the relational example, the redundancy is eliminated and only fifty-six items of information need to be kept, a 33.3 percent reduction in data storage. By using the location code (the relational factor) the work address of any employee can still be determined.

167

*Applications generator.* Does the system have an applications generator? As mentioned earlier, applications generators actually assist the user in writing the program code needed to generate a given application. They are especially helpful to new users.

## Distributed Processing and Data Bases

The advent of networks and large computer systems tied together by telecommunications technology has created additional design issues for HRIS managers. These relate to (1) whether the processing of employee data will be done centrally or shared among a number of remote sites, and (2) where the data base(s) is to reside. These are both hardware and software issues.

The first issue pertains to whether remote sites (e.g., plants, field offices, divisions) will process/manipulate employee data or simply extract data that have been processed at a central facility. For example, some systems are designed such that each site processes HR information and sends fully or partially processed data to a central system. Individual units are responsible for inputting and maintaining information about their employees and only transmit certain key data elements to the central facility. When cross-unit reports are requested, each unit processes "its" information and submits the transformed data to the central facility for final processing and report generation. This is termed a **distributed processing** system. HRISs do not need to be either centralized or distributed but can vary in their degree of decentralization. Completely decentralized systems have no central processing, and all processing takes place at the local level.

The trend is toward greater decentralization of HRISs. Many organizations seek to push information management and decision making lower in the organization, and distributed systems are one way to implement this strategy. Such an approach can enhance support for the system and build the overall level of computer skills of the HR staff. On the other hand, more user training, coordination, integration, and sophisticated processing equipment are required with distributed systems. Remember, selecting a processing mode is as much a strategic policy decision as an operational one.

The second major design issue is the location of the data base. The options range from a single, centralized data base to a design in which data are maintained in a fragmented fashion at a variety of sites. There are four options. First, the data can be completely centralized, with all records kept at a single location. Remote sites receive information from the central computer and may do some local processing; however, the sites do not maintain employee records. The second type of data base design involves locating a core set of data items in a centralized location, with detailed records kept at remote sites. For example, the corporate mainframe might keep an abstract of each employee record, while the detailed historical employment record is kept at the local level. When corporate staff need specific information on a given employee, the local HRISs are polled by the mainframe and the detailed data are uploaded as required. The third type of design involves duplicating the complete data base at each site. Each location is capable of any and all analyses. This design requires comparable processing equipment at each site and may lead to increased costs and difficulty in maintaining the integrity of the multiple data bases. The final type of data base design requires no centralization. Each site maintains complete records of the employees associated with that site. The separate systems are connected in a network, and if summary reports are required each site is polled and information collected for these reports.

The choice of data base design will depend on the sophistication of the HR department and the software selected for the HRIS. An organization new to HRISs may not want to choose a distributed data base because it requires greater user sophistication and coordination. Issues such as security and data integrity become more difficult with distributed data bases. Also, the software required to support distributed data bases is more complicated and may not be cost-effective for many organizations.

## Information Security

Employee information is among the most sensitive data kept by the organization. Managing the confidentiality of employee information has legal, ethical, and strategic business impact. Legally, the company must protect the privacy of employees and can be held liable for inappropriate release of information about workers. Ethically, the firm must ensure that confidential information (e.g., health data, drug test results, wage garnishments) remains confidential to protect employees. Strategically, the HRIS contains information on staffing levels, the distribution of employees across divisions, succession planning, and other information that could be of great interest to competitors.

Information security in the context of HRISs has three components. The first is the physical security of the data and the system. The second is access security to information in the system. Procedural security and compliance with information privacy regulations is the final component. Each of these issues is examined below.

*Physical Security*    The physical security of the system is perhaps the easiest to ensure. The concern here is with the theft or destruction of data or equipment. The HRIS administrator can undertake a variety of measures to enhance the security of the system. Restricting access to the system is one of the easiest ways to reduce opportunities for theft and/or damage. In large installations involving mainframe systems, the computing center is often a secure site where only authorized personnel are allowed entry. In smaller installations, however, it may not be possible to restrict entry since the system is often in an office setting where employees, vendors, job applicants, and others come and go frequently. When possible, place the HRIS or terminal in a location away from office traffic. Also, secure backup copies of the data base and software in a separate location to avoid a catastrophic loss of the system (e.g., by fire, weather, vandalism).

Be careful to protect the system from disgruntled current or former employees. For example, a recently fired employee who worked in a large mainframe computer site got "revenge" on her former employer by causing a major failure to the system. She returned to the computer center to "clean out her desk" and say good-bye to co-workers. She carried a rather large briefcase and made sure to stop in the tape library, by the disk storage units, and by the tape drives. Unfortunately for the company, she had a large iron bar wrapped in wire and connected to several dry-cell batteries in the briefcase. The large electromagnet radiated a magnetic field large enough to scramble tapes and jumble disk drive units. In another organization, a staff member changed large amounts of data in the system and altered the formulas used to compute paychecks. In still another case, an employee who anticipated being fired unleashed a "virus" into the system that not only damaged the HRIS data base but also infected the general ledger.

These examples point out the importance of backing up the data base (e.g., onto tape or removable disks) on a regular basis and keeping these archive copies in a separate and secure location. They also point out the need to manage the employee separation process strictly, especially where employees who have access to information systems are concerned.

*Access Security*    The second security issue, access security, refers to controlling entry into the system and individual portions of the data base. Most modern systems have multilevel password protection. For example, at Level 1 (the lowest level), authorized users can only view part of the data base. At Level 2, users can view portions of the data and change those portions. At Level 3, users can view and change any data in the data base. A good policy is to use a "need to know" rule; that is, individuals should only have access to those portions of the data base they need to do their job. Passwords should be changed on a regular basis and the importance of security should be impressed on all users. The most important task in maintaining the integrity of the security system is the constant monitoring and updating of passwords, authorized users, and staff compliance with security standards. A related security issue concerns data change authorizations or **edit controls**. These are procedural and management controls built into the system's operation to ensure that changes in the HRIS data base are proper and authorized. For example, how do you verify that changes in pay rates for individual employees were legitimately authorized? This is a financial control issue as well as an HRIS security issue. One approach to this problem is the dual authorization system used by The State of New Jersey. In the New Jersey Personnel Management Information System (PMIS), authorized HR users have access to a variety of personnel information and can alter selected items of information (an extensive set of data entry checks are built in). Critical or sensitive data items (e.g., pay grade classification) can be changed only by users with higher levels of clearance in conjunction with a member of the PMIS staff. That is, it takes two individuals to alter sensitive information. Although such a procedure is somewhat cumbersome, it does reduce the opportunity for unauthorized changes.

A second access issue deals with the telecommunications capabilities common in modern systems. Because these capabilities provide another entrance to the system and the potential for unauthorized access, they are potentially troublesome from a security standpoint. Networks, in particular, provide a host of new entry points for vandals, hackers, and unauthorized users. Techniques for limiting telecommunication access include automatic log-off after repeated log-on attempts, call-back systems that limit users to authorized phone numbers, passwords, and simply turning off the system when it is not in active use. When considering a system, be careful to evaluate critically the telecommunications security provisions of the package.

***Procedural Security and Compliance with Regulations*** The final security issue is procedural security and compliance with state and federal regulations. Procedural security refers to establishing a set of security policies and operational practices. These procedures should be in written form and distributed to all employees in contact with the system. Practices range from procedures for backing up data, to prohibitions on sharing passwords, to policy statements on releasing employee information. Legal issues involving information systems and information privacy are complex and beyond the scope of this book.[15] However, you should be aware of several general principles.

In 1973, the federal Department of Health Education and Welfare (HEW) established the Code of Fair Information Practice Principles.[16] These principles apply to information systems in general and definitely to HRISs:

> No personal data record-keeping system the very existence of which is secret, should be established or maintained.

> Individuals should be able to find out what data are kept about them, how they are collected, and how they are used.

> A mechanism should be provided to allow individuals to prevent information collected for one purpose from being used for another purpose.

> A mechanism should be provided to allow incorrect information to be challenged and corrected.

> There should be limits on the disclosure of information to outside parties. Confidentiality of the information must be maintained.

> The organization collecting the information assumes the responsibility for its reliability and must take precautions against misuse. The organization is responsible for the currency and accuracy of the data and the security of the system.

In addition to these guidelines, the Privacy Act of 1974 regulates the release of employment-related information stored in federal information systems. Many states have also enacted laws to protect the privacy of individuals. Organizations are well advised to consider the HEW guidelines, Privacy Act provisions, and state regulations when establishing their policies for system use and security.

## Data Integrity

The eventual usefulness and effectiveness of the system will depend on accurate and timely data. Probably the single greatest operational concern for HRIS managers is maintaining the integrity and accuracy of the data base.

Several techniques can be employed to verify the accuracy of information and to catch errors before they appear embarrassingly in output documents.

Data inaccuracy can come from three sources: (1) the data were entered inaccurately; (2) the system somehow changed the data to become inaccurate; or (3) the data have become outdated (e.g., the number of dependents for an employee has changed). Input inaccuracy results from incorrect entering of data, inaccurate data supplied to the entry operator or entry system, or intentional incorrect entering of data. Many data entry errors of the first type are caught by the "rules" in the software. For example, if employee gender is to be entered as "M" or "F" and the operator enters an "N," the system will indicate to the user that the entry for gender is incorrect and ask for a correction. This eliminates most keystroke input errors. However, this type of error detection will not be able to determine if a male employee was entered into the system as a female or if the input data provided are inaccurate (e.g., an employee profile form lists a male employee as a female). These kinds of errors are best corrected with the use of turnaround documents. Turnaround documents are output reports that are used to verify the accuracy of the information in the system. For example, an employee may complete a benefits election form that serves as input for the HRIS. Soon thereafter, he or she receives a summary of his or her benefit elections that can be checked for errors. Such turnaround documents are typically included in an HRIS. Exhibit 6.4 presents a turnaround document for benefits election. The edit checks noted previously can help minimize intentional "errors."

Another potential source of input inaccuracy can occur when data are transferred from another system. Downloading information from one system to another is never an easy task; however, it is relatively easy to determine if the data have been transferred correctly. If you plan to use information from another system, use the following steps:

1. Determine the data elements to transfer.
2. Estimate the amount of time it will take to make and verify the transfer.
3. Double the estimate in Step 2.

The second major source of data error is manipulation of the data after they have been entered. This type of error can be difficult to detect and quite damaging since it often affects a large number of records. Fortunately, when detected, the errors are easily corrected. For example, in determining

**Exhibit 6.4**  Benefits Election Turnaround Document

---

Empire Corporation
Employee Benefits Verification Form

This form contains a summary of your selections under
our flexible benefits system.  Please check the
information below and indicate any corrections beside
the item.  If all the information is correct, keep
the form for your records.  If any corrections are
required, return the form to Human Resources, BA 325.
If you have any questions, call the benefits
coordinator at ext. 4941.

**Employee Name:**  GRETCHEN HOHAM

**Social Security Number:** 317-59-4823   **Age:** 37

**Marital Status:** MARRIED                **# Dependents:** 2

**Insurance Elections:**

  **Dependent Coverage:** NOT ELECTED

  **Medical Insurance:** BLUE CROSS, PLAN A1-IND

  **Dental Insurance:**  BLUE CROSS, PLAN D1-IND

  **Supplemental Health:** NOT ELECTED

**Additional Vacation Days Elected:** 5

**401(k) Additional Monthly Contribution:** $300.00

**Benefit Credits Not Used:** 1500

---

years of service, the total number of hours worked by an employee might
be divided by the number of work-hours in a year (8 hours × 5 days ×
52 weeks = 2,080). However, if a calculation error is made and employee
hours are divided by 208.0 hours, an error that would impact virtually all
employees would be made. Once detected, however, such an error can be
quickly eliminated. A good way to avoid these errors is to have calculations
or data transformation formulas checked by more than one staff member.

The final type of data error occurs as data become outdated. HRIS information has a life span that ranges from weeks (e.g., current project assignment) to virtually forever (e.g., race of the employee). As data are designated for inclusion in the HRIS, the life expectancy of each element should be determined and provisions made for updating the information as required.

## Data Base Size and Employee History

A critical question that arises during the design/acquisition phase is, How much data will we need to keep in the system? A second and equally important issue is, How much data will we need to store over time? Will the system be able to handle the volume of data in one year? five years? Long-term data retention and access is a necessity for HRISs. Federal legislation ranging from OSHA to ERISA as well as many other regulations require organizations to retain information for long periods of time. Increasing litigation against employers also makes the availability of accurate data critical for an adequate legal defense. For example, the HR department may be required to reconstruct the composition of a project team assigned to a government contract five years ago because of the exposure of team members to a toxic substance. Without good archival data in computer-readable form, such a task would take an enormous amount of time and entail considerable expense.

The HRIS must be designed to support the retrieval of any information that may reasonably be required. As data storage costs continue to decline, it may be possible to keep all employee data on-line. Today, however, attempting to retain all employee information on-line will quickly overwhelm virtually any system. As a result, decisions must be made about how much on-line storage the system should have and about which data elements should be kept on-line and which should be archived.

The most common approach to determining which data to keep on-line and which to archive is to rate each data element in terms of how critical it is for daily or weekly HR operations. Those elements rated most critical should be included in the on-line system. Using commonly accepted methods (see Walker[17]) for estimating the amount of space required for a single record and multiplying that by the number of records, an estimate of the minimum amount of space required can be calculated. A good rule of thumb is to take this estimate and increase it by 50 percent, since you will almost surely find that some of the "less critical" data are actually necessary. In general, buy as much on-line storage as you can afford.

The amount of data stored by the organization will increase dramatically over time. It is critical that archival data be stored in a secure location. This usually means away from the work site to ensure that a catastrophic event does not wipe out years of records. Many large organizations have safe repositories or contract with firms to provide such storage. The choice of storage site is less important than keeping the data physically secure. In any case, the HRIS data base should be considered in the organization's data backup planning.

## Summary

This chapter focused on issues related to the design/acquisition of HRISs. The options available to users as they move from the needs analysis to the design/acquisition phase were reviewed. Each option, along with its advantages and disadvantages, was described. The structure and content of the request for proposals was also discussed. Finally, several technical issues that should be kept in mind during the design/acquisition process were reviewed. Chapter 7 focuses on the next step in acquiring the HRIS—system implementation.

## Discussion Questions

1. Compare and contrast the advantages of microcomputer-based systems and mainframe systems. When is each type of system best?
2. What are the key questions you would ask a vendor making a presentation of an HRIS to your firm?
3. What security procedures would you implement to reduce the chance of theft or damage to a microcomputer-based HRIS?
4. What is a turnaround document? Why is it important for data integrity?
5. How much data should you keep in an HRIS? How would you decide which elements to keep on-line?
6. What policies would you establish to balance the employee's rights to privacy with the employer's need to have easy access to information about employees?

## Notes

1. Payroll/HRIS systems are discussed in Chapter 10. See also the "Option 3: Use an External Service" section later in this chapter.

2. N. J. Mathys, H. LaVan, and G. Nogal, "Issues in Purchasing and Implementing HRIS Software," *Personnel Administrator* (August 1984): 92.
3. R:Base for DOS is available from Microrim, Inc., P.O. Box 97022, Redmond, WA 97022.
4. Revelation™ is available from Revelation Technologies, Inc., Two Park Avenue, New York, NY 10016.
5. S. K. Corson, "Installing an HRIS at DRAVO Corp.," *Computers in Personnel* (Fall 1986): 13–20.
6. *Personnel Journal*, P.O. Box 2440, Costa Mesa, CA 92626.
7. *Computers in Personnel*, Auerbach Publishers, Inc., One Penn Plaza, New York, NY 10119.
8. D. Mahal, ed., *HR/PC: Personnel Computing for Human Resource Professionals* (Marina Del Rey, CA: DGM Associates).
9. Human Resource Systems Professionals, P.O. Box 801646, Dallas, TX 75380-1646.
10. Mathys, LaVan, and Nogal, "Issues in HRIS Software," 92.
11. Lotus 1-2-3 is available from Lotus Development Corporation, 55 Wheeler Street, Cambridge, MA 02138.
12. L. M. Plantamura, "Choosing an HRIS Vendor," *Personnel Administrator* (November 1985): 18–22.
13. K. C. Laudon and J. P. Laudon, *Management Information Systems* (New York: Macmillan, 1988), 749.
14. A. F. Cardenas, *Database Management Systems*, 2nd ed. (Boston: Allyn and Bacon, 1985), 745.
15. For further readings on security, privacy, and information systems, see P. J. Donohue, "Linking Personnel Computers with Mainframe," *Personnel* (November–December 1984): 43–47; L. Hoffman, *Modern Methods for Computer Security and Privacy* (Englewood Cliffs, NJ: Prentice-Hall, 1979); K. C. Laudon, *Dossier Society: Value Choices in the Design of National Information Systems* (New York: Columbia University Press, 1986); J. Ledvinka, *Federal Regulation of Personnel and Human Resource Management*, 2nd ed. (Boston: PWS–KENT Publishing, 1989); P. L. Tom, *Managing Information as a Corporate Resource* (Glenview, IL: Scott, Foresman, 1987), 322.
16. Privacy Protection Study Commission, *Personal Privacy in an Information Society* (Washington, DC: U.S. Government Printing Office, 1977).
17. A. J. Walker, *HRIS Development: A Project Team Guide to Building an Effective Personnel Information System* (New York: Van Nostrand Reinhold, 1982), 243.

# 7

# HRIS Implementation: How Do I Make This Thing Work?

T his chapter deals with the most serious problem faced in designing, developing, and using an HRIS—how to get people to use it properly and, more important, to keep using it over time. The major problem faced by any organization when implementing new technology or, for that matter, any change that affects the way employees do their jobs is to overcome employees' resistance to changing their work behaviors. The worst mistake a company can make in implementing an HRIS is to wait until it arrives on their doorstep to inform employees that it will be used tomorrow. Successful implementation of an HRIS depends on the involvement of everyone affected by the new system, collectively called stakeholders, at the very beginning of the planning stages and needs analysis for the system. A number of ideas for implementing a new or reautomated HRIS were discussed in Chapter 4. This chapter complements that discussion but focuses more on the behavioral issues involved in implementing and maintaining the new HR system.

A general model of planned change, called action-research, and two more specific approaches to the implementation of change, particularly in terms of the impact on the psychological and social processes of the stakeholders, are first discussed. Next, organization development and organizational change literature as well as recent HRIS literature are examined to find models and principles that apply to implementing and maintaining the HRIS. In examining these models and the literature, the focus is on practical suggestions for the successful implementation and maintenance of the HRIS.

## Models of Change Processes

The rapid spread and acquisition of computer technology for human resources operations has led to major changes in the operation of the HR function in the organization. These changes, however, are not limited to the HR department. They affect numerous employees in a variety of ways. The employees affected by the HRIS are called stakeholders in the system and, as you will see later in this chapter, each employee or group of employees has differing expectations and skills regarding the HRIS. Although this complicates the implementation process, it can be handled as long as the principles of change are understood and applied during the implementation and maintenance phase of the systems development process. However, as each model of change is discussed, keep in mind that implementing an HRIS creates different expectations for different employees and that these differences complicate the implementation and maintenance process.

Change is pervasive in our society, affecting all aspects of our lives. Societal changes are reflected in our work lives, and organizations must respond to these changes. In fact, an organization's ability to respond to these changes is related to its survival.[1] In opposition to this need for organizations to change is the basic human need to resist change. In trying to bring about positive changes in organizational functioning, such as by computerizing the HR function, managers are often frustrated by employees' resistance to the change. For example, in attempting to implement a new HRIS in a health insurance firm, we were frustrated by the unwillingness of one HR department employee, who kept avoiding our attempts to secure the EEO codes for racial information on employees. When we investigated this problem further, we found that this employee was afraid she was going to lose her job once the HRIS was implemented.

This resistance to change is understandable and has been well documented in the organizational change literature.[2] Suggesting a change to employees implies that the way they currently perform their jobs is somehow inadequate. Thus, changes in the workplace may be perceived as negative feedback on current job performance, a basic fact the project team must recognize in implementing an HRIS. However, there are ways to deal with change that make it less threatening. Many organizations have developed the capability to respond to change using planned change, or **organization development (OD)**.[3] Underlying these OD approaches are some basic models of how changes affect the individual psychological responses and social relationships of employees.

In this section, three different approaches to planned change are discussed: (1) a general model of planned change called action-research OD, (2) a three-stage description of individual change processes, and (3) an approach that shows the effects of technological change on the social relationships and structure of the workplace. These three approaches have been chosen because of their demonstrated usefulness in previous planned change work and because they apply to the behavioral problems of implementing and maintaining an HRIS. It should be emphasized, however, that these are not alternative ways of handling HRIS implementation. They are complementary and can be used in combination. However, the project team should choose some perspective to guide them during the implementation and maintenance phase as opposed to operating without a plan. Any one of these three approaches alone or in some combination can accomplish that objective.

### Action-Research Organization Development

*Purpose of Models*    Before explaining this general model of how to manage planned change, it is first important to understand the function of using models in implementing a new HRIS. Models provide a guide, or perspective, for those involved in managing the implementation process—namely, the HRIS project team. They help the team plan an orderly implementation and prepare them for the barriers and problems that will certainly occur during the implementation and maintenance phase. Attempting to manage this phase of the systems development process without a specific plan will likely lead to major problems, perhaps failure.

*Action-Research Approach*    The action-research model is the best general perspective to use in any planned change effort.[4] Although this model could be used for the entire systems development process as depicted in Exhibit 4.3, beginning with needs analysis and ending with implementation and maintenance, the focus in this chapter is on its application to the implementation and maintenance phase.

The action-research model involves taking action to implement change and collecting data to evaluate that action. The total model is based on the interlocking of the research processes of data collection, analysis, and evaluation and the management action processes of planning, directing, and implementing change. An entire cycle or loop within the action-research framework involves six steps: (1) initial data collection and analysis; (2) feedback of results; (3) action planning; (4) implementing planned changes; (5) data collection and analysis to evaluate the changes; and (6) feedback and action planning.

***Action-Research Cycle***   This cycle is depicted in Exhibit 7.1. Within the HRIS project, the initial data collection step involves the needs analysis phase. But remember there can be multiple data collections in the needs analysis. For example, the first step may be data collection through structured interviews with potential users of the HRIS. The next step involves

**Exhibit 7.1**   The Action-Research Cycle

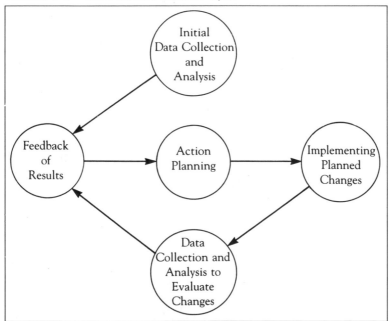

the feedback of results to the project team, followed by the project team's action planning. At this point, the project team, on the basis of the results from the structured interviews, may do a number of things. They may plan more data collection through surveys or questionnaires; they may proceed to obtain management approval; or they may proceed to write an initial request for proposal (RFP). In any case, this action planning will involve design and development plans that will be implemented in the next step of the action-research cycle.

During the implementation of these planned actions or changes, further data collection, analysis, and evaluation of the changes would be done. These results are then fed back to the project team, which begins the cycle again. This cycle can be repeated within the HRIS project, and it could be repeated within any phase of the systems development process described in Chapter 4. For example, this cycle could be repeated within the implementation and maintenance phase as different task or activity milestones are reached. Thus, the project team can more effectively manage the implementation of the new HRIS.

**Action-Research Cycle and Project Management**    The action-research approach is compatible with project management techniques. The action-research cycle can be repeated for different tasks or milestones within the total HRIS development process by combining it with project management techniques such as PERT and **CPM (Critical Path Method)**.[5] A complete discussion of these techniques is beyond the purposes of this book.

These techniques are easy to understand and use within the context of HRIS implementation. They consist of establishing goals and timetables for the tasks and activities to be accomplished within the HRIS project. After the tasks and activities are identified (e.g., training new operators or completing documentation for users), specific start and end dates can be assigned to each task and activity. From this information, a graphic presentation, usually a chart, is prepared so that the HRIS project team can monitor and manage the implementation and maintenance phase. For an example of this technique, a Gantt chart to be used in the needs analysis phase, see Exhibit 5.3.

This recommendation for using a Gantt chart within the action-research perspective is similar to suggestions made by Walker.[6] During conversion and implementation, he recommends that a plan that contains a detailed, step-by-step guide to the entire implementation phase be developed. Using the action-research cycle of planning, research, feedback, and planning within this plan as well as project management techniques will help ensure the new HRIS is successfully implemented in the firm.

## Lewin's Three-Stage Model

The most frequently cited and discussed description of the personal psychological processes involved in organizational change is based on the work of Kurt Lewin, a social psychologist.[7] Using the concept of force-field analysis, as depicted in Exhibit 7.2, all organizational change is conceptualized as

**Exhibit 7.2**   Force-Field Analysis for Implementing HRIS

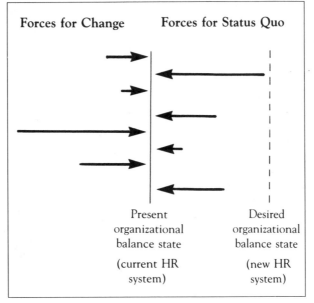

forces toward and against movement to some equilibrium state. The arrows in Exhibit 7.2 represent the number and strength of the factors for both change and maintenance of the status quo in the organization. The length of the arrow indicates the amount of force for each factor. If the algebraic sum of the forces for change and status quo are equal, a state of equilibrium exists and no change will take place, a situation pictured in Exhibit 7.2. If the forces for change were to increase, for example, if a new and cost-effective technology became available, the total force for change would disrupt the equilibrium state, attempting to move it to the right in Exhibit 7.2.

Assuming the desired organizational balance state in Exhibit 7.2 to be a new or reautomated HRIS, the increased forces for change could be any of the various factors, such as new technology and legislative changes, discussed in Chapter 3. The forces for the status quo could be employee resistance to change and disruption of the current operating system of the firm. As Lewin cautions, increasing the forces for change without decreasing the forces for the status quo to move to the desired organizational balance state will create tension and conflict in the organization.[8] That is, forcing the acquisition and implementation of a new HRIS by management order, increasing force for change, is likely to be resented and resisted by employees. Reaching the desired organizational balance state by decreasing the forces for the status quo is preferable to applying more force, particularly through management orders.

Most forces for change are rational and legitimate and usually based on technological, economic, or production factors. As stated at the beginning of this book, improving both the timeliness and accuracy of HR information is a desirable goal from an economic and production perspective. Most forces opposing legitimate change are irrational social and psychological ones based on employees' perceptions. Employees may perceive that they will be replaced by a machine or not be able to work with their colleagues anymore. Although these initial perceptions are often incorrect (i.e., the company has no intention of substituting machines for personnel or shifting staff from one area to another), they represent the real feelings and fears of the employees and must be treated seriously.

In order to reduce the forces for the status quo in the most efficient manner, Lewin describes the implementation of organizational change as going through three phases: unfreezing, changing, and refreezing. Each of these three phases is described with reference to moving to a desired organizational balance state of a new or reautomated HRIS as seen in Exhibit 7.2.

*Unfreezing*    The first phase of unfreezing involves reducing the power of the forces that are keeping the organization at its present state. As the term implies, something must be unfrozen or thawed before it can be reshaped and changed. This something is the behavior of the employees. As discussed earlier in this chapter, the major concern of implementation and maintenance of a new HRIS is changing the behaviors of the employees (the end users) of the system. In this first state of unfreezing, these behavioral changes are accomplished by providing information and new experiences that disconfirm the employees' current beliefs or show old behaviors to be inappropriate. Thus, information about the newly proposed HRIS, particularly information comparing new system capabilities to the current HR system, should be widely distributed. A public relations campaign to all affected employees via the various communications media of the firm should accompany any proposed change to a new HRIS. These communications should emphasize the value of adopting the new behaviors within the organization.

Employees should be given an opportunity for hands-on experience with the proposed new system. Vendor "demo" packages as well as planned seminars demonstrating the new system should be made available to employees. Because the affected employees are the critical ingredient in the success of the implementation and continued maintenance of the new HRIS, their active involvement is crucial during the unfreezing, changing, and refreezing stages. Remember that the focus of change is on the employees' behavior. Thus, the focus of the unfreezing stage must be on behavior. Information aimed at changing attitudes and values is fine, but it must be linked to behavioral change.

**Changing**   During this phase of the change process, values, attitudes, and behaviors are reshaped. This means developing new ways of operating in the firm. During the implementation of any new HRIS, both the old and new system usually operate in parallel for a period of time. This is necessary because the new system is still in a testing mode and could completely **crash** or fail at any time. The old system thus runs in parallel as the operating and backup system for the new HRIS. This is the time when the stakeholders of the new system can have firsthand experience with it. They can practice new work behaviors with the new HRIS without any fear of mistakes since the old (current) HR system is still operational.

During this phase, employees should be encouraged to experiment with the new system, without fear of being somehow punished if they do something wrong. They will, in fact, do many things wrong! But they must be allowed to make these mistakes at this point rather than when the new system comes on-line completely. Remember that stakeholders' attitudes and behaviors are changing at this time, and they should be given the freedom to change in a nonpunitive environment. Most important, stakeholders should have an opportunity to see and personally experience the advantages of the new HRIS over the current HR system. For example, HR department employees should be permitted to use the report writer to create both standard and ad hoc reports. If the firm is converting from a manual HR system, this report-writer function in the new HRIS should convince employees that changing is a good idea.

*Refreezing*     This phase involves the stabilization of change at the new balance or equilibrium point. Thus, in Exhibit 7.2, once the desired organization state is reached the goal is to stay there. This is done by influencing work-group norms, changing management policy, or altering the organizational structure in some cases. For example, it may be necessary to create a new position (HRIS manager) or an entire new section (HRIS) within the HR department. Because each organization will be different, it is impossible to prescribe specific actions to refreeze the changes. However, one common element in the refreezing of changes to accommodate the new HRIS is that the organizational reward system must be modified to positively reinforce or value the new employee behaviors necessary to continue to maintain and use the new HRIS. This may mean, for example, that the people involved in using the new system will have their jobs evaluated for changes in classification and wages or salary adjustments. This could involve increasing the pay scale for clerical employees, who are now expected to be the front-line operators of the new HRIS. If the reward system is not changed, behaviors and attitudes to support the use and maintenance of the new HRIS will not refreeze and the system will fail.

## Sociotechnical Systems Approach

Another important and well-established approach from the literature on organizational change and development is the sociotechnical systems approach.[9] This approach, as its name indicates, deals with the interrelationship of the social and technical systems in the organization. The social system involves the pattern of relationships both within and between work groups. Thus it can involve any interaction from two-person to large, multiple-group meetings, and it can involve both work and friendship relationships. The technical system involves the various machinery and equipment that are used to get work done. Because the development of a new HRIS is primarily a technological change, this approach seems the most logical one to use in implementing and maintaining a new HRIS.

*Dependence Relationship*     Establishing a high degree of interaction and dependence between the social and technical systems underlies the goal of the sociotechnical approach to organizational design and change.[10] Its goal is to design and implement the total system, in this case the new or reautomated HRIS, such that the individual employees' social psychological needs are met and the materials and machinery are used in the optimal economic way. Thus, it is apparent that any change in the technical system will have a direct effect on changing the social system, a fact that must be considered when implementing the new HRIS.

If, for example, the new HRIS requires that all the computer workstations must be centrally located because of physical and fiscal restraints, the current social structure will be altered because all operators (e.g., secretaries) will need to be in that one location. On the other hand, if the new workstations are microcomputers, the operators may be located in individual offices instead of working together in one location, like a secretarial pool. In both these scenarios, there is a change. Clearly, this technological change will result in changes in social interaction. The project team should be aware of these changes when implementing the new HRIS.

When using a sociotechnical system perspective to implement and maintain the new HRIS, it is important to recognize that the functions of employees and machines are not being equated. In considering the fit between individuals and machines, the relationship is a complementary one.[11] This means the employees and the machines must complement each other in their functioning. Although the new HRIS is capable of making many functions easier, it cannot replace the human functions. This fact is often downplayed in new system acquisition and implementation, particularly by vendors. A cardinal rule to remember is that the new HRIS will do many things for you, but it will not do your job completely.

**Implications**   The real heart of the sociotechnical approach is understanding this high degree of dependence between employees and machines (social and technical systems) in terms of implications for organization and task design. Central to this perspective in terms of task and organization design change is that any work activity can be altered by either its behavioral or technological components. Implementation and maintenance of the new HRIS will alter work activities and, thus, the tasks employees complete and the organization of the work itself. The new HRIS may require both new-position descriptions as well as changes in reporting requirements for employees. Some employees may find their jobs changed significantly, while others may be part of the new section within the HR department or report to a new boss.

Using this sociotechnical systems approach means the HRIS project team can anticipate in advance the need for both work and organizational changes. This should lead them to ask pertinent questions *before* beginning the implementation process: How will this new technology affect the day-to-day relationships of employees? How will it affect the relationships between the HR department and other departments? How will it change the work flow, particularly reports? How will those changes impact the social relationships of the employees? These are the kinds of questions that must be considered when implementing a new HRIS using a sociotechnical perspective.

*Integration*   Before proceeding to the next section of this chapter, it is important to emphasize that the action-research model, Lewin's three-stage approach, and the sociotechnical approach are not in conflict and can be used jointly. Considering each one should help guide the implementation and maintenance phase better than using a haphazard approach. However, the HRIS project team need not use all three. The team should decide in advance what approach they want to use, since this will guide the HRIS project for the next one to two years during implementation and maintenance activities.

## Stakeholders in the HRIS

As mentioned in the introduction to this chapter, a number of people will be directly affected by the implementation of a new or reautomated HRIS in the company. These people are called **stakeholders** because they all have a "stake" in seeing the system run smoothly. However, each group of stakeholders has different criteria on which it will judge whether the system is operating properly and whether it is meeting expectations. These different stakeholders and their differing expectations and criteria for the HRIS are identified in Exhibit 7.3.

As can be seen, different people have different stakes in the HRIS. Only a sample of the expectations and criteria these stakeholders have of the HRIS is listed in Exhibit 7.3. The discussion there on the potential users included in the needs analysis also applies to implementation. The important point of Exhibit 7.3 for the implementation and maintenance of the new HRIS is that the different stakeholders want different things from the HRIS, and in some cases these criteria are in conflict. For example, the elegance of the system the designer wants may work against the ease of use the HR user desires.

**Exhibit 7.3**    Differing Expectations and Criteria of Stakeholders
in the HRIS

| *Stakeholder* | *Expectations/Criteria* |
|---|---|
| System designer | Is the system elegant?<br>Was the system challenging to design?<br>Is the system enjoyable to maintain? |
| HR user | Is the system easy to use?<br>Is the system well documented?<br>Does it provide timely information? |
| Manager | Does the system aid in managing?<br>Does it reduce administrative paperwork?<br>Are reports accurate and timely? |
| Employees | Will my personal information be kept private?<br>Is my personal information accurate?<br>Will the system control me? |
| System operator | Is the system easy to operate?<br>Is the technical documentation adequate?<br>Is the system easy to maintain? |

It is important to recognize these differences during the unfreezing, changing, and refreezing stages of implementation. This is one of the reasons the HRIS project team should remain active for at least six months to a year after the initial implementation of the new system. Further, using the action-research general model of planned change discussed earlier in the chapter, all of these various stakeholders should be used as data sources to evaluate both implementation and maintenance of the new HRIS. Using the cycle of data collection, feedback, and action planning prescribed by this general model will ensure that the necessary adjustments are made to the HRIS during implementation to ensure its eventual success as a well-maintained management tool.

## Advice from the Professional Literature

In this final section, the advice on implementing and maintaining the new HRIS from the professional literature is summarized. According to Horsfield,

**Exhibit 7.4** Implementation and Maintenance Advice

---

### Organization Development Literature

1. Top management support is desirable, but a neutral position is acceptable.
2. Commitment to a specific OD approach is desirable for the change to be successful.
3. Change begins at the lower levels of the organization.
4. Diagnosis and recognition of change must occur at all levels of the organization.
5. Intervention, usually with an outside consultant, is necessary.
6. Change occurs in the three stages described by Lewin.
7. Invention and commitment through employee participation are critical to change.
8. Experimentation and search behaviors must be allowed.
9. Learning comes after experimentation and feedback on the proper new procedure on the job.
10. Reinforcement through changes in the reward system is critical for change and acceptance of the change.
11. Structural and interpersonal subsystems changes must reinforce each other.
12. Internal change leaders must be identified and used in the change process.
13. Changes to one part of the organization must be reflected in changes to other parts to support the changes.
14. Continue the action-research cycle to be certain the changes become permanent.

---

implementation "consists of training, reorganization, and conversion from the existing system—manual or computerized—to the new system.[12]" Walker, as discussed earlier, recommends a detailed, step-by-step guide for the implementation of the HRIS.[13] Much more detailed advice is available in the literature and will be covered in this section.

In doing this, the prescriptions from the more general, science-based literature on planned organizational change will be combined with the more specific, practice-based literature on implementing an HRIS.

**Exhibit 7.4**  *continued*

---

### HRIS Literature

1. Top management support is critical.
2. Use a specific technique, like prototyping or piggybacking, during implementation.
3. User involvement is necessary for implementation.
4. Expect resistance to change and conflicts over work assignments and system priorities, particularly by the MIS department.
5. Make a detailed plan with a realistic timetable, then double the time required.
6. Develop a change checklist to monitor implementation.
7. Determine and provide training.

8. Recognize the psychological differences between system designers and users.
9. Organizational forces, particularly politics, must be dealt with to succeed.

10. Documentation, both user and operator, is critical for successfully implementing and maintaining of the HRIS.
11. Have regular meetings of users and system designers.
12. Change policies and procedures for the entire organization to accommodate the new HRIS.
13. Determine rules for access, security, and certification on the new system.

14. Audit the new system periodically for maintenance.

---

*Source:* The list from the OD literature is based on the work of L. Greiner, "Patterns of Organizational Change," *Harvard Business Review* 45 (1967): 119–130; M. Beer and E. Huse, "A Systems Approach to Organization Development," *Journal of Applied Behavioral Science* 8 (1972): 79–101; and K. Sperling, "Getting OD to Really Work," *Innovation* 26 (1971): 39–45. The list from the HRIS literature is based on a variety of sources that are cited in the text discussion of this exhibit.

Exhibit 7.4 contains a parallel listing of recommendations from these two literatures. This exhibit shows the similarity of recommended advice from both literatures. Because of the overlap in these two literatures, various topics are collapsed within one heading even though numerous references

192 7: HRIS Implementation: How Do I Make This Thing Work?

to the published literature are supplied. In this way, implementation and maintenance are discussed against a rich background of supplemental literature.

Because the major concern of this book is to provide guidance for companies implementing a new HRIS, only the advice from the HRIS literature in Exhibit 7.4 is covered below. Those interested in the more general and theoretical OD literature can consult the references provided.

## Top Management Support

This is the most common factor that underlies successful changes to a new HRIS. Remember, this involves not only initial support for the project during the needs analysis phase but continued support through the implementation and maintenance phase. Top management should be made aware that the entire systems development process is a lengthy one. In an examination of the literature on implementing operations research, management science, and management information systems, Lee lists top management support as the most important element in implementing a new HRIS.[14]

## Using a Specific Technique

This advice to use a specific model in implementing the new HRIS comes from both literatures. Using action-research and program management techniques such as PERT and CPM have been recommended in this book. Prototyping and **piggybacking** are both techniques for introducing the new system while maintaining the old system in the *parallel systems* phase of implementation.[15] By having both the new and the old systems operable at the same time, employees can experiment with the new system without fear of completely destroying the old system.

## User Involvement and Participation

In the discussion on needs analysis in Chapter 4 and on stakeholders in this chapter, the importance of employee participation in implementation has been stressed. This advice is repeated throughout the HRIS literature.[16] It is patently obvious that the new HRIS system will not be implemented or maintained without the participation of the people affected by it. There are many stories of problems with industrial robots that resulted from a lack of employee participation in implementing the new technology. All of the stakeholders described earlier in this chapter must be allowed to participate in implementing the new HRIS.

## Resistance to Change and Conflict

Points 4 and 8 are combined in this suggestion. In a survey of HRIS users by Mathys, LaVan, and Nogal, they found that 76 percent of the respondents felt that the major problem in implementation was the resistance to change and the conflict between the HR and MIS departments over work assignments and system priorities.[17] Lee spells this out further when he discusses the psychological difference between system designer and system user, a point made in Exhibit 7.3 regarding the differing criteria of stakeholders in the system.[18] Lee claims the systems designer has a problem-solving style that is characterized as quantitative, explicit, and analytic, while the problem-solving style of HR professionals and managers is qualitative, implicit, and intuitive. Whether this simplistic differentiation is adequate is not relevant for this book. What is relevant is that the MIS and HR departments will likely be in conflict over the implementation and maintenance of the new HRIS. The HRIS team or senior management must handle this conflict directly, both through high levels of participation by members of both departments in the implementation and maintenance of the new HRIS and by frequent meeting of these departments, as is recommended in Point 11.

## Detailed Plan and Checklist

Points 5 and 6 address the same need for tight project management control by the HRIS team.[19] The ideal way to do this is by developing a Gantt chart that is used not only by the HRIS project team but also by all managers, including top management, that are affected by the implementation of the new HRIS. This means, of course, that progress reports on the goals and timetables for the tasks and activities in the Gantt chart must be sent to these same managers, including top management. As a caveat, top management will quickly lose interest after the new HRIS technology (hardware and software) is delivered. These periodic progress reports are a means of keeping them informed and maintaining their support for the project.

## Determine and Provide Training

This is one of the most important parts of a successful implementation and maintenance phase of an HRIS, and numerous authors have emphasized the need for it.[20] Perhaps the most important advice in terms of training on the new HRIS is that different stakeholders have different training needs, and these must be determined first by the project team. That is, it is not sufficient to use training provided by the vendor for all employees. It is clear that HR professionals, system operators and designers from MIS, and managers all have differing expectations of the new system. Thus, they all have differing training needs, and the successful implementation and maintenance of the new HRIS depends on this training.

## Dealing with Organizational Forces and Politics

This point (9) is also related to Point 12. The HR function is a subsystem of the entire organizational system. The organizational system also contains other subsystems, such as marketing, finance, and accounting. Changing the HR subsystem by introducing a new HRIS will impact all the other subsystems connected to it. As an example, refer to the discussion of the HRIS-payroll interface in Chapter 10. Not only are there going to be organizational and job design changes, that is, new authority-reporting lines and new task responsibilities, created by the introduction of a new HRIS, but there will be tremendous politics that must be handled. The introduction of the new HRIS must not become a power struggle between the HR and MIS departments. There must be a significant intervention, usually by upper management, to convince these two departments to work together to implement a new HRIS that will benefit all employees. Alternately, the new HRIS can simply be placed in one department, thus removing the issue from argument. This one department should be the HR department, for all the reasons detailed throughout this book. All departments or stakeholder groups that feel threatened by the new system must be dealt with. One of the best ways to do this, as discussed above, is to have all parties affected by the HRIS fully participate during the implementation phase.

## Create Documentation for the New System

Documentation of the new system during implementation is critical but is often an overlooked or dreaded aspect of the new system. Employees would much rather "do" the new HRIS system than write about it. The HRIS project team must recognize this fact. However, in terms of successful implementation and maintenance of the new HRIS, documentation is probably the one aspect that will make it a viable operating system over time.[21]

It is crucial that documentation be created for both the technical support group and the systems users. What needs to be documented? In an ideal situation, the answer is "everything." However, most situations are not ideal. First and foremost, the new software or hardware from the vendor needs to be documented as you customize it for your firm. This is the start of what has been identified as **homegrown documentation**.[22] Homegrown documentation must be developed since the installation of almost any new HRIS software will require customizing for the individual firm. The vendor documentation is never completely sufficient. Second, all new procedures developed by users of the new HRIS need to be carefully and completely recorded. One idea, which has worked for numerous companies, is to have employees who interact with the new system maintain a diary of those experiences. These diaries contain suggestions and ideas for dealing with the new system. These can be collected and placed in a central place for all users of the system. Remember to collect these from *all* stakeholders of the new HRIS.

Finally, well-developed and documented rules for access, security, and certification of users of the new system, as listed in Point 13, must be determined. These rules also need to be part of the official policies and procedures of the firm and need to be circulated with top management approval. These rules, particularly those that involve security, will be of vital interest to all the employees, one of the most important stakeholder groups. Further, the certification must make it clear what training and experience are necessary before anyone uses the HRIS. The security system must be established so that individuals can only access those data elements and reports that are necessary to do their jobs. Most HRIS software has features that allow the firm to customize these aspects for their individual use. However, it is crucial that this customization be made a part of the documentation.

## Auditing the New System

It has been argued that the new system be audited every 500 days after it has been implemented to make sure it is working correctly.[23] That is, specific checklists should be developed to evaluate whether the new HRIS is meeting expectations. These expectations were first developed in the needs analysis, modified and refined through the design and development phase, and now form the basis for evaluation via formal audit in this phase of the systems development process. This is the data collection and evaluation step in the action-research cycle that provides feedback to the HRIS project team for their future action planning.

You may want to follow a 500 day schedule or audit more frequently, depending on your situation and project management plan. However, it is crucial that this audit activity be built into the project management plan. Without this audit activity, the system will soon fall into disuse or misuse. Auditing keeps the system current and corrects errors in its use. For long-term maintenance, this audit should be continued for as long as the new system is on-line. This is the data collection phase of the action-research model. It will, at some point in time, tell you when the system is becoming obsolete and when you will need to initiate a new system development cycle.

## Summary

In this chapter, the theoretical and empirical literature on planned change in OD and the practitioner literature on HRIS implementation and maintenance have been merged to provide advice for the implementation and maintenance phase of the system development process. The importance of three perspectives from the behavioral literature—action-research OD, Lewin's three-stage model, and sociotechnical systems OD—during the implementation of a new HRIS was emphasized. More important, the use of project management tools by the HRIS project team to manage the implementation and maintenance of the new HRIS was stressed. With the past few chapters, this chapter should provide clear guidelines to designing, acquiring, and using a new HRIS.

## Discussion Questions

1. Why is it important to have a perspective or approach like the ones discussed in this chapter when implementing the HRIS?

2. Why would people resist the implementation of a new HRIS that could make their jobs easier?

3. Why should the action-research cycle be continually repeated during the implementation and maintenance phase of the HRIS development process?
4. How would the recommendations from Chapter 4 on systems implementation fit with those in this chapter on behavioral issues in implementing and maintaining an HRIS?
5. What are the implications of having multiple stakeholders during the implementation and maintenance of an HRIS?
6. Develop a checklist of specific dos and don'ts for implementing and maintaining an HRIS from the advice in Exhibit 7.4. Prioritize your list in terms of importance.

# Notes

1. M. Beer, "The Technology of Organizational Development," in M. D. Dunnette, ed., *Handbook of Industrial and Organizational Psychology* (Chicago: Rand McNally, 1976), 937–993.
2. L. Coch and J. R. P. French, Jr., "Overcoming Resistance to Change," *Human Relations* 1 (1948): 512–553.
3. Beer, "Technology of Organizational Development"; W. L. French and C. H. Bell, Jr., *Organization Development*, 2nd ed. (Englewood Cliffs, NJ: Prentice-Hall, 1978).
4. M. A. Frohman, M. Sashkin, and M. J. Kavanagh, "Action-Research as Applied to Organization Development," *Organization and Administrative Sciences* 7 (1976): 129–161.
5. For good explanations of these techniques, see W. S. Davis, *Systems Analysis and Design: A Structured Approach* (Reading, MA: Addison-Wesley, 1983); and J. D. Wiest and J. Levy, *A Management Guide to PERT/CPM* (Englewood Cliffs, NJ: Prentice-Hall, 1969).
6. A. J. Walker, *HRIS Development: A Project Team Guide to Building an Effective Personnel Information System* (New York: Van Nostrand Reinhold, 1982): 57.
7. K. Lewin, *Field Theory in Social Science* (New York: Harper and Row, 1951).
8. Lewin, *Field Theory*.
9. R. Cooper and M. Foster, "Sociotechnical Systems," *American Psychologist* 26 (1971): 467–474.
10. Cooper and Foster, "Sociotechnical Systems," 467.
11. Ibid., 470.
12. D. Horsfield, "Homegrown Documentation," *Computers in Personnel* (Summer 1987): 51.
13. Walker, *HRIS Development*, 150–164.

14. A. S. Lee, "What Human Resource Planning and the Research on OR/MS/MIS Can Learn from Each Other," *Human Resource Planning* 9 (1986): 59–68.
15. M. P. Martin, "The Human Connection in System Design: Part VI. Designing Systems for Change," *Journal of Systems Management* (July 1987): 14–18; M. P. Martin, "The Human Connection in Systems Design: Part VII. Prototypes for User Training," *Journal of Systems Management* (July 1988): 19–22.
16. For example, see N. J. Mathys, H. LaVan, and G. Nogal, "Issues in Purchasing and Implementing HRIS Software," *Personnel Administrator* (August 1984): 91–97; R. J. Balicki, "Teamwork Makes the System Fit," *Infosystems* 30 (1983): 36–49; V. R. Ceriello, "The Human Resources Management System: Part I," *Personnel Journal* 61 (1982): 764–767.
17. Mathys, LaVan, and Nogal, "Issues in Purchasing."
18. Lee, "Human Resource Planning."
19. Walker, *HRIS Development*; Martin, "The Human Connection: Part VI," 53.
20. Balicki, "Teamwork Makes the System Fit"; Ceriello, "Human Resources Management"; L. M. Plantamura, "Basic Training for a New HRIS," *HRSP Review* (Fall 1987): 23–25; E. Whitkin, "Training for Computer Literacy," *HRSP Review* (Spring 1988): 21–25; C. H. Fay, "Educating Old and New HR Managers," *Computers in Personnel* (Summer 1988): 20–25; C. Smith and J. W. Boudreau, "Education: Masters of the HR Universe," *Computers in Personnel* (Summer 1987): 35–39; H. G. Gueutal, S. I. Tannenbaum, and M. J. Kavanagh, "Where to Go for an HRIS Education," *Computers in Personnel* (Spring 1988): 22–25.
21. T. S. Eason and E. D. Eason, "HRIS Documentation: A Road Map to Application and Maintenance," *Computers in Personnel* (Fall 1988): 38–40.
22. Horsfield, "Homegrown Documentation," 49–51.
23. L. G. Need, "The Importance of Being Audited," *Computers in Personnel* (Spring 1988): 60–62.

# III
# HRIS Applications

# 8

# HRIS
# Applications I

I n Chapters 8 and 9 several computer applications designed to support the
human resources function are discussed. Some of the data requirements,
reports, analyses, and interpretations of various applications are examined.
The applications are addressed according to the major HR subfunctions
listed in Chapter 1 (Exhibit 1.4).

## HR Subfunctions

In Chapter 1 the HR function was said to consist of six major subfunctions.
Exhibit 8.1 shows the subfunctions and lists three common activities that
are representative of each. For additional information about each of the HR
subfunctions, refer to the specific sources cited within each HRIS application.

Our categories of subfunctions are somewhat arbitrary. Each organization will perform many of the activities noted in Exhibit 8.1 but may cluster
them differently. For example, in Exhibit 8.1 labor relations planning is
listed under Planning, and health and safety under Quality of Work Life.

Some companies might have a subfunction called Labor Relations that is responsible for both these activities.

In fact, HR subfunctions, regardless of categorization, are highly interdependent. Performance management and career development contribute to or detract from organizational preparedness and thus greatly influence HR planning. Compensation should be tied to performance

**Exhibit 8.1**   HR Subfunctions and Typical Activities

| *Subfunction* | *Typical Activities* |
| --- | --- |
| Planning<br>(Chapter 8) | Personnel and succession planning<br>Labor relations planning<br>Targeted analysis |
| Staffing/Employment<br>(Chapter 8) | Recruitment<br>Selecting<br>EEO/AA |
| Training and Career Development<br>(Chapter 8) | Training administration<br>Career development<br>Training needs analysis |
| Performance Management<br>(Chapter 9) | Performance appraisal<br>Time and attendance<br>Grievance |
| Compensation and Benefits<br>(Chapter 9) | Compensation<br>Benefits<br>Compliance |
| Quality of Work Life<br>(Chapter 9) | Health and safety<br>Employee assistance programs<br>Child-care programs |

management. Adequacy of recruitment and stringency of selection criteria will influence training needs. Subfunctions overlap and the boundaries can be drawn in many ways. Nonetheless, most HR departments operate along functional lines, and the six subfunctions used in this book are not atypical. In Chapters 8 and 9 some computer applications designed to support each of the six subfunctions are explored.

In this chapter, computer applications that deal with planning, staffing/employment, and training and career development are addressed. Performance management, compensation and benefits, and quality of work life applications are considered in Chapter 9. Some applications support more than one subfunction. For example, a position control application may support the planning subfunction as well as the staffing/employment subfunction. However, to avoid redundancy, detailed information is presented only in one section.

## The Applications: What Is Presented?

As the proliferation of computers within the HR function continues, additional applications are constantly being developed. It is impossible to present examples of or even to discuss each possible type of application. Instead, a few illustrative applications from each of the major subfunctions are highlighted, and other applications that support each subfunction are noted. Additional sources of information for the other applications can be found in the Notes at the end of the chapter.

As discussed in Chapter 2, the most common applications currently used are those that support the compensation and benefits and the staffing/employment subfunctions. Human resource planning is one of the most critical yet undersupported subfunctions. Therefore, more examples of applications for these subfunctions than for the others are provided.

As noted throughout the book, there are many types of applications. Some applications are part of a comprehensive HRIS, while others are independent of a comprehensive system. These stand-alone applications may perform activities normally part of a comprehensive system (e.g., EEO analysis) or may address unique needs not normally part of a "standard" HRIS (e.g., training registration support). Stand-alone applications may be used by companies as a supplement to their HRIS or by companies without a comprehensive HRIS but with a specific need for the application. Both stand-alone and integrated applications are considered in Chapters 8 and 9.

Another distinction across applications is whether they are primarily EDP-, MIS-, or DSS-type applications. This distinction was discussed in detail in Chapter 1. To date, most applications have tended to be predominantly EDP- or MIS-oriented, with far fewer DSS-type applications. In Chapters 8 and 9, applications from the entire spectrum are discussed.

Examples of screens, data fields, and simple reports (EDP-type) are provided. Some suggested analyses and more complex management reports (MIS-type) are also shown. Because DSSs tend to be most complex and customized, fewer examples exist. However, what can be done with DSSs or "what-if" analyses is shown in a few instances.

The examples provided are based on applications in operation at a variety of companies, vendor products, prototypes, and our suggestions. In many cases, the example is a combination of applications to illustrate what can or should be done to support specific HR activities. Where appropriate, how the application can be used and what advantages it presents are explained.

For an application to be effective, the necessary data must be available (or at least attainable), accurate, and up-to-date. The examples presented assume data availability and integrity. Although basic data requirements for each application are presented, it is assumed that each organization may have special data needs.

## Human Resource Planning Applications

The first HR subfunction is planning. Human resource planning (HRP) is a critical component of effective HR management. Through HRP, the HR function attempts to support the company's strategic direction by analyzing jobs and people; scanning the environment to assess potential changes; forecasting future personnel supplies and needs; assessing the impact of potential HR programs, policies, and strategies; and planning, implementing, and evaluating HR actions based on the above. In other words, HRP attempts to identify and implement appropriate activities to ensure that the HR function is supporting the company's direction. This is done through a process of data collection, analysis, and evaluation. [1]

Larger companies are more likely to employ HR planners and to use formalized HRP systems. Because HRP is related to business strategy, the users of HRP information are likely to be HR executives and senior managers. For this reason, HRP applications are more likely than applications for other subfunctions to take the form of decision support tools. A DSS for HRP should allow decision makers to determine the implications and feasibility of various options for meeting future staffing needs. Exhibit 8.2 identifies some of the HRIS applications that can support HRP. In the next section some specific HRP applications are discussed in more detail.

**Exhibit 8.2**    Common HRIS Applications to Support HRP

---

*Labor Relations Planning*    Labor costs continue to rise, and preparing for labor negotiations is a critical planning activity. A DSS application in this area should help planners consider trade-offs and costs of various potential labor agreements.

*Personnel Planning*    Personnel planning involves forecasting future personnel supply and demand based on past conditions, external events (e.g., labor market, competition), and internal policies (e.g., recruitment). A personnel planning application might use Markov analysis to project supply and demand and could allow decision makers to vary their assumptions (e.g., future turnover rate) to conduct "what-if" analyses.

*Organizational Charting*    Organizational charts show the reporting relationships within an organization. These can be useful as part of the planning process, focusing on issues such as span of control. Organizational charting applications provide graphic output of the company's jobs.

*Turnover Analysis*    Turnover analyses examine the extent and nature of turnover throughout the organization. They are designed to identify problem areas and are useful for formulating targeted solutions.[2]

*Succession Planning*    This refers to the identification of short-term backups for jobs (sometimes called replacement planning) and/or the process of longer-term management successions. Often this includes identifying and tracking "high-potential" employees. Succession planning is designed to allow the organization to have smoother transitions and fewer shortages by developing and recruiting employees for future positions.

*Other Targeted Analyses*    To identify and evaluate other HR issues and needs, targeted analyses may be conducted. For example, if a corporate relocation is being considered, a targeted analysis might be developed to assess the implications of various options. Surveys and other forms of data collection may be used and specific analyses developed based on the data collected and assumptions of key decision makers.[3]

---

## Context

The HRP process at one large diversified company consists of four major components: (1) environmental scanning, (2) business plan analysis, (3) personnel planning, and (4) program and policy review. Environmental scanning refers to reviewing external conditions to identify opportunities and threats related to the company's human resources (refer to Exhibit 3.4). For example, What does the labor market look like, and what changes are projected? Will there be any technological changes that may influence labor productivity? What is the legal environment like with regard to labor law interpretations? Business plan analysis refers to examining the company's business plans. Will the company be growing or retrenching? Will there be new products, markets, and so on? This analysis is done to identify company direction and areas of potential HR intervention. Personnel planning (often referred to as "manpower planning") attempts to forecast future human resource supply and demand and reconcile any imbalance between them. Program and policy review is a detailed examination of HR programs and policies to determine if they are addressing organizational needs. Together, these four components are designed to identify critical HR issues that should be addressed to support the strategic direction of the organization.

Two computer applications designed to support the HRP process, with a particular focus on personnel planning, are presented in this chapter: (1) work force profile review and (2) work force dynamics reporting, analysis, and decision support. These applications are designed to provide summary information about the number and type of employees currently in the organization, to track how employees have moved into, through, and out of the company, and to project future work force supply and demand based on previous trends.

## HRP Application 1: Work Force Profile Review

To assess future supply and demand, the current work force statistics must first be examined. A work force profile review takes a "snapshot" of the current work force.

### *Data Requirements*

The data required to perform a work force profile review are the key employee demographic data elements (e.g., age) and the key organizational data elements (e.g., job class). Some of the key data elements that may be used are listed below:

Employee age                    Wage level
Job information (level, title)    Function (e.g. marketing)

Division
Performance ratings
Position code
Promotability rating
Willingness to relocate
FTE or Full Time Equivalents
(ratio of scheduled hours
to hours in a full week)

Length of service (LOS)
EEO category
Status (full-time,
part-time, on leave)
Experience
Overtime
Union status

## Reports

A series of simple reports can be used to describe the profile of the work force. These may be developed as standard reports, although the HR analyst attempting to understand the nuances of work force demographics would probably use several iterations of ad hoc queries to supplement the standard reports.

For example, a standard report might show the average age and length of service of employees for each division of the company. If concerns about aging workers emerge, ad hoc queries can go deeper. One query could be used to list the average employee age by function and job type. Which age groups might be of greatest concern? The age bands of over 55 and less than 30 tend to show the highest turnover rates, because of retirement and job change, respectively. A report can be developed to examine those age bands by function and job type to anticipate possible problem areas. This information can be used to target recruiting efforts or to develop other programs to alleviate future personnel concerns.

Some of the key questions that should be addressed by the HRIS to support work force profile review are listed in Exhibit 8.3. In addition to these questions, the work force profile review could also consider issues of gender and race trends, performance trends, and skill mix. All of these issues will impact on planning future staffing levels.

## Interpretations

The purpose of a work force profile review is to examine the makeup of the work force to identify factors that can affect the way the company's human resources support its strategic direction. Using the HRIS to answer the types of questions noted in Exhibit 8.3 helps identify current problem areas and anticipate future problems or potential opportunities. HR executives and

**Exhibit 8.3**    Sample Work Force Profile Questions

Which units have age profiles showing more than 20% of employees under the age of 30? Which show age profiles of more than 25% over 55?

Which units show age profiles with more than 60% in the 35–49 age bands, with few younger or older employees? Which units, if any, have age profiles that will present problems in replacement staffing? Why?

Which units show gaps in length of service (LOS) profiles that may indicate replacement problems for the future? Which units have the greatest concentration of employees with less than five years of service? Which units have the greatest concentration of employees with more than thirty years of service?

Which units and levels have the highest overall level of education? Which show the lowest? Is the profile of educational levels among different salary grades within technical functions acceptable?

Which units demonstrate large discrepancies (or negative correlations) between education level and salary grade?

Which units have insufficient numbers of promotable people? Too many promotable people? What is the relationship between promotability and performance?

Which units rely predominantly on part-timers or employees that average less than .5 FTE?

key decision makers will consider how to deal with these problems and opportunities as the next step in the planning process. When interpreting the results of the work force profile review, decision makers must be sure to consider external events (environmental review) and company direction (business plan analysis). These issues are addressed further at the conclusion of the HRP section.

## HRP Application 2: Work Force Dynamics Reporting and Analysis

While a work force profile review focuses on the makeup of the current work force, a work force dynamics analysis focuses on employee movements over a period of time. If a work force profile is the equivalent of a snapshot, then work force dynamics are analogous to a videotape. Work force dynamics can be used in simple reports and can be integrated as part of a DSS to project what the work force will look like in the future. The DSS should also enable decision makers to conduct "what-if" analyses to assess the effects of proposed programmatic or policy changes on the makeup of the work force in the future.

## Data Requirements

To be able to examine work force dynamics, the organization must have historical data regarding employee movements through the organization. In particular, each promotion, demotion, transfer, and exit (turnover, retirement, etc.) should be recorded and maintained. Because some analyses will need to be categorized by function, job type, division, and/or time frame, these key data elements must be associated with each employee movement. In addition, the DSS requires average salary and benefit costs for each job class, anticipated growth (or decline) rate, and anticipated salary growth rates. If a detailed turnover analysis is needed, turnover reason (i.e., fired, retired, illness or death, voluntary), length of service, and performance ratings will also be useful.

## Reports

As with the work force profiles review, a series of simple reports can provide insights into the company's work force dynamics trends. Some of the key reports that can be used to support a work force dynamics analysis are listed in Exhibit 8.4. Exhibit 8.5 illustrates an analysis of a company's annual turnover by division.[4]

## Analysis

While work force dynamics reports illustrate past trends, they do not show what the work force will look like in the future and how changes in dynamics may affect the work force. A prototype DSS, based on Markov analysis, that uses previous work force dynamics information to project future labor supply is described below. This application also allows a comparison of supply with anticipated demand, estimates labor costs, and allows decision makers to change assumptions or anticipate policy changes and to assess what would happen if those changes were to occur.

**Exhibit 8.4**   Sample Work Force Dynamics Reports

---

Number of new hires by unit (or job type).

Number of new non–entry-level hires by unit (i.e., above a certain grade level).

Number of lateral transfers by division, unit, and function.

Performance ratings of those receiving lateral transfers (to determine if laterals are being used for development or dumping).

Age and LOS of those receiving lateral transfers by division (to point out divisions where there may be promotion blockages).

Number of demotions/downgrades by function (or job type).

Performance ratings of those receiving downgrades.

Promotions by division, department, and position.

Supervisory promotions versus hires for each division (to identify extent of promotion from within).

Number of promotions from job A to job B (to determine if official career paths are being followed; dual paths; etc.).

Number of turnovers by unit (or job class) broken down by reason, LOS, age, and performance of turnovers by unit and job type (to determine who is being lost and where).

---

*Note:*   Most of these reports should also be run comparing the current year's movements with the previous year's movements to identify trends. In addition, these reports can be run before and after policy changes to assess the effects of the changes.

**Work Force Dynamics DSS**   This prototype system was developed using Lotus 1-2-3, a microcomputer-based spreadsheet package. The company name and data are fictitious. For those familiar with Lotus 1-2-3, the system is based on one large spreadsheet, with macros—stored keystrokes that are used to automate operations, dramatically reducing the number of keystrokes necessary to perform complex or repetitive actions—to simplify data entry, navigation, analysis, and reporting. Microcomputer spreadsheet applications are being used at organizations such as Houston Lighting and Power Company and the U.S. Navy to support personnel flow analyses.[5] Users enter information about the baseline year and the forecast year, expected inflation rates (percent annual salary increases), anticipated divisional or company

**Exhibit 8.5**    Turnover Analysis

| Annual Turnover Analysis — 1/89–12/89 | | | | | |
|---|---|---|---|---|---|
| | | | Divisions | | |
| | Year | Home | East | West | International |
| *Categories of Turnover* | | | | | |
| Percentage voluntary | | | | | |
| Exempt | 89 | 10.5 | 5.4 | 14.1 | 17.8 |
| | 88 | 0.0 | 3.1 | 17.2 | 12.5 |
| Nonexempt | 89 | 10.9 | 14.5 | 20.2 | 7.1 |
| | 88 | 10.5 | 13.2 | 20.8 | 6.6 |
| Percentage involuntary | | | | | |
| Exempt | 89 | 5.2 | 3.2 | 0.5 | 0.0 |
| | 88 | 2.1 | 0.0 | 1.1 | 0.0 |
| Nonexempt | 89 | 3.0 | 1.9 | 6.0 | 4.2 |
| | 88 | 3.6 | 1.2 | 6.7 | 2.2 |
| *Profile of People Leaving the Company* | | | | | |
| Average performance | 89 | 2.7 | 2.4 | 2.2 | 2.5 |
| | 88 | 2.7 | 2.2 | 2.5 | 2.8 |
| Average % pay increase | 89 | 3.7 | 4.2 | 5.9 | 4.4 |
| | 88 | 4.2 | 4.8 | 5.8 | 3.5 |
| Average LOS | 89 | 5.0 | 13.2 | 2.2 | 7.6 |
| | 88 | 5.4 | 13.9 | 2.6 | 5.2 |

*Source:* Adapted from J. Verdin and J. Lapointe, "Performance Measurement Decision Evaluation Cost Models Using Human Resource Data," *HRSP Review* 3(3) (Fall 1987): 7–10. Used with permission.

growth rate (as generated by top management or bottom-up estimates), and head count data (see Exhibit 8.6). These estimates can be changed to compare different scenarios, and company growth rate can be manipulated to vary from year to year.

**Exhibit 8.6**   Sample Data Entry Screen

Empire Corporation
Division: Beer/Wine/Liquor

Directions
1. Please input the year you would like to forecast

Forecast year:        1990
Transition matrix year:   1987
Initial head count:      1986

2. Input expected inflation rate for forecasted year as decimal!

Inflation rate:         5.00%

3. Enter "Projected" growth rate using 1987 as a baseline!

Projected growth:       111.58%

4. Enter the head count data for the year shown (with or without hires)!

! page down to enter head count data

The system contains current average salary and benefit costs for each job class. These can be easily updated. In addition, the system requires data on the number of people who stayed in the same job class, were promoted, demoted, and left the company. These too can be easily updated. The system converts these numbers into a historical transition matrix on which future projects are based. Exhibit 8.7 shows a sample transition matrix. Subsequent data manipulations are based on a form of Markov analysis. As mentioned in Chapter 3, Markov analysis is used to track past patterns of personnel movements and to project these patterns into the future. Markov analysis is based on matrix algebra and the underlying mathematical components are somewhat complex. However, as a technique it is very straightforward to use. As with any technique, certain requirements must be met. In this case, one requirement is a sufficiently large number of employees in each job class to establish stable transition estimates. Anyone considering developing an

**Exhibit 8.7** Sample Transition Matrix

Empire Corporation
Beer/Wine/Liquor Division

Historical Transition Information
(1986–1987)

|  | Unskilled | Semiskilled | Skilled | Prof/Tech | Managerial |
|---|---|---|---|---|---|
| Retention rate | 55.99% | 73.13% | 69.32% | 72.18% | 70.86% |
| Demotion rate |  |  | 1.02% | 0.75% |  |
| Promotion rates |  |  |  |  |  |
| To semiskilled | 20.93% |  |  |  |  |
| To skilled | 7.82% | 12.40% |  |  |  |
| To prof/tech | 0.25% | 1.03% | 5.11% |  |  |
| To managerial | 0.38% | 1.55% | 6.95% | 12.30% |  |
| Turnover | 14.63% | 11.89% | 17.59% | 15.04% | 29.14% |

application based on an employee flow model should examine some of the technical references on this topic.[6]

Based on data provided by the user, and incorporating certain assumptions, the application generates a series of screen reports that illustrate what the work force will look like in the future. Exhibit 8.8 is an attrition report based on a simple flow model. This shows the shortages and excesses that would occur in the various job classes, based on past trends, should the organization not hire anyone else.

Naturally, organizations do hire people. To support personnel planning, this application can project demand ("target demand") based on anticipated division growth (or decline) rates and can compute the number of hires necessary to meet that demand. In addition, the user can decide if the organization will hire to meet target demand in all job classes and whether it is willing to lay off employees should supply exceed demand. Exhibit 8.9 shows a report of this analysis. This particular analysis was based on the assumptions that fewer unskilled workers will be hired (projected hires) than were determined from target demands (which would require increases in labor productivity), that no layoffs were allowed for unskilled, semiskilled, and skilled groups, and that the number of managers was reduced by the excess supply identified each year. This report also projects labor costs both with and without benefits. The user can see which job classes will requi₋e the heaviest hiring efforts and how the current promotion and turnover patterns will influence the work force in subsequent years.

Decision support systems should be flexible and should allow the user to vary assumptions and perform "what-if" analyses. This versatility is what makes DSSs so valuable. In this system the user can manipulate several variables individually or simultaneously and can assess the implications of these changes. Exhibit 8.10 shows an adjusted transition matrix that could be used to perform comparative analyses. In this case the analyst changed the matrix based on the previous analysis, input from decision makers and consideration of labor agreements. These changes are noted at the bottom of Exhibit 8 10. This matrix would provide results that might then trigger other what-if analyses. These analyses are useful for decision makers trying to make policy and program decisions. They can stimulate thinking and resolve questions such as, Should we change our promotional policies? Encourage faster or slower promotions? If faster, how will we develop people to fill these positions? Are we promoting sufficiently from within? If not, why not? Where should we heighten our recruiting efforts? Do we need to

**Exhibit 8.8** Simple Flow Projection: Attrition Report

Empire Corporation
Beer/Wine/Liquor Division

Attrition Report
(no hires or reductions)

Simple Flow Model Without Replacement

|  | 1989 | | 1990 | | 1991 | |
|---|---|---|---|---|---|---|
|  | Shortage | Excess | Shortage | Excess | Shortage | Excess |
| Unskilled | 389.70 |  | 589.75 |  | 680.93 |  |
| Semiskilled |  | 48.26 |  | 16.76 | 39.79 |  |
| Skilled | 40.52 |  | 78.70 |  | 114.42 |  |
| Prof/Tech | 55.25 |  | 89.72 |  | 110.93 |  |
| Managerial |  | 14.84 |  | 22.01 |  | 23.15 |

Note: This set of projections is based on estimated transition rates from 1986–1987, assuming no hires or reductions. Through 1990, there is an excess of employees at the managerial and semiskilled levels and shortages in the other groups. However, by 1991, there will be shortages in all groups except managerial, where there will be an excess. Attrition will eliminate the excesses in the semiskilled group by 1991.

215

**Exhibit 8.9** Manpower Analysis

Empire Corporation
Beer/Wine/Liquor Division

| Year: 1989 | Beginning Head Count | + Projected Hires 1 | = Projected Ending Head Count | Deviation from Target Demand | Total Salary Costs | Total Salary Costs with Fringe Benefits |
|---|---|---|---|---|---|---|
| Unskilled | 521.66 | 308.05 | 829.71 | -3.96% | $8,990,757 | $11,490,187 |
| Semiskilled | 461.53 | 12.77 | 474.30 | 0.00% | $7,425,402 | $9,838,658 |
| Skilled | 493.28 | 26.92 | 520.20 | 0.00% | $11,612,423 | $15,595,484 |
| Prof/Tech | 257.35 | 44.57 | 301.92 | 0.00% | $7,928,569 | $10,862,139 |
| Managerial | 222.43 | -4.15 | 218.28 | 0.00% | $7,347,959 | $10,176,924 |
| Totals | 1956.26 | 388.15 | 2344.41 | | $43,305,110 | $57,963,393 |

| Year: 1990 | Beginning Head Count | + Projected Hires 1 | = Projected Ending Head Count | Deviation from Target Demand | Total Salary Costs | Total Salary Costs with Fringe Benefits |
|---|---|---|---|---|---|---|
| Unskilled | 511.01 | 309.84 | 820.85 | -4.03% | $9,339,484 | $11,935,861 |
| Semiskilled | 465.51 | 4.03 | 469.54 | 0.00% | $7,718,506 | $10,227,020 |
| Skilled | 500.47 | 14.51 | 514.98 | 0.00% | $12,070,801 | $16,211,086 |
| Prof/Tech | 262.41 | 36.48 | 298.89 | 0.00% | $8,241,534 | $11,290,902 |
| Managerial | 226.88 | -10.79 | 216.09 | 0.00% | $7,638,015 | $10,578,651 |
| Totals | 1966.29 | 354.07 | 2320.37 | | $45,008,341 | $60,243,520 |

| Year: 1991 | Beginning Head Count | + Projected Hires 1 | = Projected Ending Head Count | Deviation from Target Demand | Total Salary Costs | Total Salary Costs with Fringe Benefits |
|---|---|---|---|---|---|---|
| Unskilled | 505.55 | 291.64 | 797.20 | -3.91% | $9,523,847 | $12,171,476 |
| Semiskilled | 460.76 | 0.00 | 460.76 | 1.17% | $7,952,878 | $10,537,563 |
| Skilled | 495.41 | 4.11 | 499.52 | 0.00% | $12,293,816 | $16,510,595 |
| Prof/Tech | 259.78 | 30.14 | 289.92 | 0.00% | $8,393,801 | $11,499,508 |
| Managerial | 224.61 | -15.00 | 209.60 | 0.00% | $7,779,121 | $10,774,082 |
| Totals | 1946.12 | 310.89 | 2257.01 | | $45,943,462 | $61,493,223 |

Assumptions:

Based on the assumption that the beer/wine/liquor industry will be declining over the next few years, only 90% of target hires in the unskilled group were hired.

Since there is a no-layoff policy for the unskilled, semiskilled, and skilled groups in the Beer/Wine/Liquor Division, there is no reduction in work force at the semiskilled level in 1991.

Since the division has an excess of managers in 1989-1991, the managerial work force is reduced by the excess supply in each year.

217

**Exhibit 8.10** Adjusted Transition Matrix for 1988–1991

|  | Unskilled[a] | Semiskilled[b] | Skilled[c] | Prof/Tech | Managerial |
|---|---|---|---|---|---|
| Retention rate | 61.59% | 70.20% | 69.33% | 75.79% | 70.86% |
| Demotion rate |  |  | 1.02% | 0.75% |  |
| Promotion rates |  |  |  |  |  |
| To semiskilled | 15.33% |  |  |  |  |
| To skilled | 7.82% | 15.33% |  |  |  |
| To prof/tech | 0.25% | 1.03% | 5.11% |  |  |
| To managerial | 0.38% | 1.55% | 6.95% | 8.42% |  |
| Turnover | 14.63% | 11.89% | 17.59% | 15.04% | 29.14% |

[a]The retention rate for the unskilled level was increased by 10% to 61.59%. As a result, the promotional rate from the unskilled level to the semiskilled level declined to 15.33%, a rate that is still in compliance with the union agreement.

[b]The promotional rate for the semiskilled level to the skilled level was increased to 15.33% in order to comply with the current union contract. Therefore, the retention rate at the semiskilled level was decreased to 70.20%.

[c]Because of the projected excess of managers, the promotion rate of the prof/tech group was reduced from 12.30% to 8.42%.

reduce turnover? In which job classes? Is it worth the money to reduce turnover? Other decision support analyses could be developed that could help decision makers decide whether to close or relocate a plant, speculate on the impact of salary increases, or examine cross-divisional transfers. A DSS can be an effective tool to support the HRP process. However, it *does not* make decisions. The key to using any planning tools, whether a profile report, a dynamics report, or a dynamics analysis, is in the interpretation and use by decision makers.

## Interpretations

Human resource planning is the process of identifying and implementing appropriate activities to ensure that the HR function is supporting the company's direction. This requires data collection, analysis, and evaluation. Planning applications are useful because they summarize information. They can be used to identify gaps and surpluses (e.g., too many middle managers), evaluate policy compliance (e.g., Are we promoting from within?), and determine the implications of implementing new programs (e.g., What is the effect of our turnover reduction program?).

However, the information they convey has significance only in context. Other factors that might be considered when interpreting the data from HRIS applications include external data such as area unemployment rates, economic forecasts, labor market statistics, legal changes, and technological advancements that might affect labor productivity. Internal data, such as business plans, attitude surveys, and other studies should also be considered.

In sum, while HRP applications generally provide quantitative information, other sources of information must be considered as part of the qualitative interpretation process. Questions such as, Which functions have the greatest potential for technical competency problems? Which new jobs cannot be staffed sufficiently from within? How will training and development programs need to be changed to meet changing needs? or Is the current HR function appropriately staffed and structured to support the company's strategic direction? are critical interpretive questions. Reports and analyses help decision makers address these types of questions. In fact, the questions are almost impossible to answer without the necessary data. But answering them clearly involves more than any report or analysis can provide. That is the qualitative element to human resource planning.

The employment/staffing HR subfunction and some of the applications used in that area are examined next.

## Employment/Staffing Applications

The employment/staffing subfunction encompasses identifying, attracting, and selecting prospective employees within budgetary and legal guidelines as well as maintaining pertinent employee data over time. Although the importance of a strategic focus, as exemplified by the HRP applications, has been emphasized, any HR department that fails to provide quality employment services will not meet its customers' needs. Failure to recruit, select, and identify employees legally and cost-effectively can be disastrous. It is a matter of attending to the basics.

Fortunately, a variety of computer applications are designed to support the employment/staffing function (Exhibit 8.11). Because much of the employment/staffing data may originally be collected on applicant-tracking applications, these are discussed briefly. However, the bulk of this section focuses on two categories of applications that help the employment subfunction stay within legal guidelines: EEO applications and AA applications. These applications were selected for several reasons. The heavy record-keeping and reporting requirements associated with legal compliance make these areas very attractive for computerization. They are very labor-intensive areas and mistakes can be quite costly.[7] As a result of the effort involved and the costliness of litigation, computer applications are used by a great many organizations to facilitate EEO and AA compliance.

### Context

In manual systems, everything screams to a halt when EEO reports are due and people have to be pulled from other projects to help accumulate the necessary data. Companies that receive government contracts are required to meet AA guidelines as well. Conducting the analyses to ensure AA compliance is another labor-intensive operation in a manual system. Fortunately, several computer applications that can facilitate the EEO/AA compliance process considerably have been developed. A few of these applications are described below: (1) applicant tracking; (2) EEO applications, including EEO reporting and adverse impact analyses; and (3) AA applications, including eight-factor or weighted analysis and utilization analysis.

**Exhibit 8.11**   Common HRIS Applications to Support Employment/Staffing

*Applicant Tracking*   During the recruiting/selection process a great deal of information is collected. An applicant-tracking system helps maintain information to allow for faster, more accurate information on applicants and to help identify appropriate applicants for specific positions. It may also monitor costs during the process and provide data for subsequent EEO/AA analyses.[8]

*Recruiting Analyses*   Recruiting quality employees is a critical part of the staffing subfunction. A recruiting analysis application evaluates the effectiveness of recruiting efforts to help maximize subsequent recruiting activities.

*Basic Employee Information*   This is the first module in most HRISs and the repository of relevant employee information. A variety of analyses and reports can be developed to support the employment/staffing subfunction. For example, historical employee data can be analyzed to identify trends in staffing patterns. See Chapter 2 and Walker for more information about the basic employee module.[9]

*Equal Employment Opportunity (EEO)*   Several laws require organizations to avoid employment discrimination. As part of this, most organizations are required to file reports to the government regarding the demographics of their work force. An EEO application maintains data on employee demographics, conducts analyses to evaluate legal compliance, helps assess the effectiveness of special programs, and generates reports required by the federal government.

*Position Control*   Position control applications are used to control labor costs by monitoring head count in the organization. A position control application may be based on identification numbers for each position in the organization and is typically tied in to the budget and position requisition infrastructure.

*Scheduling*   These applications perform analyses designed to facilitate the scheduling of personnel. They may be used by unit managers or by centralized management.[10]

*Selection Aids*   There are two types. One assists the decision maker in identifying which candidate to hire. Automated tests and interviewer protocols are examples of these. The second form of selection application is designed to evaluate the effectiveness of the selection process. These may monitor the validity and costs of different selection methods.

*Affirmative Action (AA)*   Government contractors and, in some circumstances, many other companies are required to engage in AA efforts for protected classes (e.g., minorities, women) that go beyond equal employment opportunities. Applications to support AA can, among other features, analyze whether women and minorities are underutilized within an organization.

## Employment/Staffing Application 1: Applicant Tracking

Some applicant-tracking applications are stand-alone systems, maintaining a separate data base of applicants apart from the HRIS. Others are a module of the HRIS. As noted in Exhibit 8.11, applicant-tracking applications can support several activities. They can be used to streamline the administrative components of hiring by maintaining invitation schedules, routing status, applicant status (e.g., second interview, rejected), and position requisitions and by generating letters to applicants. They can be used to identify in-house candidates as potential applicants for openings or to suggest that applicants apply for another job opening.

An applicant-tracking system may also collect information that can be used to evaluate the recruiting program. By maintaining records of recruiting sources (e.g., walk-in, newspaper, etc.), a company can assess the effectiveness of various recruiting media. By recording which college recruiter identified each new trainee and by tracking the subsequent performance of the trainees, a company can determine which interviewers have been most effective in selecting the best employees. Finally, an applicant-tracking system can collect information that is used in EEO and AA analyses.

Exhibit 8.12 shows a form used to collect applicant flow data. As you will see shortly, this type of data must be maintained to be able to conduct certain compliance tests. Applicant data can be maintained manually, using forms such as the one in Exhibit 8.12, but the retrieval and analysis process becomes extremely time-consuming. In addition, manual data maintenance does not reduce the administrative components of applicant tracking (e.g., scheduling), nor does it readily allow for analyses of recruiting effectiveness. For these reasons many organizations are developing or acquiring computerized applicant-tracking applications.

## Employment/Staffing Application 2: EEO Reporting and Adverse Impact Analysis

Title VII of the Civil Rights Act of 1964 is the most prominent of several laws, executive acts, and judicial interpretations that prohibit organizations from discriminating against protected classes of employees. As part of the compliance process, many organizations are required to file reports that

**Exhibit 8.12**  Applicant Recording Form

## Applicant Flow

Period Covered ___January___

| Applicant Name | Check Appropriate Column | | | | | | | Job Title Applied for | Job Group | Referral Source | Status and/or Disposition |
|---|---|---|---|---|---|---|---|---|---|---|---|
| | Race | | | | | Sex | | | | | |
| | Caucasian | Black | Oriental | American Indian | Hispanic | Male | Female | | | | |
| Michaels, Jill | ✓ | | | | | | ✓ | Marketing Rep | 10 | 2 | 4 |
| Denson, John | ✓ | | | | | ✓ | | Marketing Rep | 10 | 2 | 5 |
| | | | | | | | | | | | |
| | | | | | | | | | | | |
| | | | | | | | | | | | |
| | | | | | | | | | | | |
| | | | | | | | | | | | |

<u>Status/Disposition:</u>
1. Another applicant chosen
2. No suitable opening/file
3. Declined offer to interview
4. Declined job offer
5. Hired
6. Other

<u>Referral Source:</u>
1. Walk-in
2. Advertisement
3. Employment agency
4. Employee referral
5. File search
6. Other

223

reveal their employment patterns with federal agencies. In addition, larger organizations are required to conduct analyses demonstrating that they have not discriminated unfairly against legally protected classes of employees in their employment practices, as discussed in Chapter 3.[11] The data maintenance, manipulation, analysis, and reporting functions associated with these activities can be supported by an HRIS. However, it is important to remember that the data that are collected and analyzed as part of this process are "discoverable" in case of a complaint against the organization. Therefore, the organization must not only be prepared to collect and analyze employment data but also to rectify problems that have been identified.

## Data Requirements

To conduct the necessary analyses and to develop the necessary reports, several data elements must be maintained. Applicant information, including the number and type of applicants for each job, must be recorded. Recording the race and gender of each applicant can be touchy since hiring decisions cannot be based on race or gender. There are several established EEO categories into which each applicant/employee should be classified. Gender categories are obvious: male or female. There are five EEO ethnic categories:

1. White
2. Black
3. Hispanic
4. Asian or Pacific Islander
5. American or Alaskan Native

Veterans' status and handicap code may also be required for compliance with other legal guidelines.

To this point the focus has been on job applicant data. Applicant information is only a small part of the data that must be maintained. Organizations are subject to legal scrutiny if they have substantially different rates of selection in hiring, promotion, or other employment decisions that operate to the disadvantage of members of a race, gender, or ethnic group.[12] This is referred to as **adverse impact**. Organizations must be able to demonstrate that their employment system does not have adverse impact or they must be able to provide a legitimate, bona fide reason why adverse impact is acceptable.[13] Therefore, every promotion, demotion, and termination (i.e., each personnel action) must be recorded. Again, this information can be maintained manually, but for all but the smallest companies the subsequent compilation, analysis, and mandated report preparation of manually maintained data is a major work effort.

Job information must also be maintained. There are nine standard EEO job categories into which each job may be placed:

1. Officials and managers
2. Professionals
3. Technicians
4. Sales workers
5. Office and clerical
6. Craft workers (skilled)
7. Operatives (semiskilled)
8. Laborers (unskilled)
9. Service workers

In addition, organizations can establish job groups. Each job group is made up of job titles with similar work content, similar compensation, and similar opportunities for advancement.[14] Typically, job groups will be made up of jobs from within one EEO job category, although there may be several job groups for each EEO job category. Because job groups are the basic unit for several analyses, they must be maintained in addition to EEO job category codes.

## EEO Reporting

Organizations are required to file several reports regarding the gender and ethnic makeup of their employees. An example of part of an EEO-1 report is shown in Exhibit 8.13. Ideally, these data are maintained in the HRIS during the year and a standard, production report that summarizes the data necessary for the EEO-1 can be produced. In addition, EEO detail reports specifying gender and ethnic distributions for various departments, job types, and so on can be used to examine EEO trends.

## Adverse Impact Analysis

As noted above, adverse impact is said to occur when an organization has substantially different rates of selection in hiring, promotion, or other

**Exhibit 8.13** Portion of an EEO-1 Report

## Section D—Employment Data

Employment at this establishment—Report all permanent full-time or part-time employees including apprentices and on-the-job trainees unless specifically excluded as set forth in the instructions. Enter the appropriate figures on all lines and in all columns. Blank spaces will be considered zeros.

### Number of Employees

| Job Categories | | Overall Totals (Sum of Columns B-K) A | Male | | | | | | Female | | | | |
|---|---|---|---|---|---|---|---|---|---|---|---|---|---|
| | | | White (Not of Hispanic Origin) B | Black (Not of Hispanic Origin) C | Hispanic D | Asian or Pacific Islander E | American Indian or Alaskan Native F | White (Not of Hispanic Origin) G | Black (Not of Hispanic Origin) H | Hispanic I | Asian or Pacific Islander J | American Indian or Alaskan Native K |
| Officials and managers | 1 | 2,528 | 1,342 | 9 | 5 | 5 | 2 | 1,118 | 23 | 11 | 9 | 4 |
| Professionals | 2 | 232 | 87 | 1 | 2 | 1 | | 133 | 3 | | 5 | |
| Technicians | 3 | 138 | 88 | 1 | 2 | 4 | 1 | 40 | | | 2 | |

226

| Job Category | Line | Male | | | | | | Female | | | | | |
|---|---|---|---|---|---|---|---|---|---|---|---|---|---|
| Sales workers | 4 | 57 | 26 | 1 | | 15 | 1 | 29 | | | | 104 | 26 |
| Office and clerical | 5 | 6,733 | 760 | 65 | 15 | 15 | 1 | 5,418 | 254 | 75 | 1 | | |
| Craft workers (skilled) | 6 | 10 | 10 | | | | | | | | | | |
| Operatives (semiskilled) | 7 | 76 | 55 | 2 | 2 | 5 | | 10 | 2 | | | | |
| Laborers (unskilled) | 8 | 1 | 1 | | | | | | | | | | |
| Service workers | 9 | 142 | 103 | 9 | 2 | 30 | 4 | 26 | 2 | | | | |
| TOTAL | 10 | 9,917 | 2,472 | 88 | 28 | 30 | 4 | 6,774 | 282 | 89 | | 120 | 30 |
| Total employment reported in previous EEO-1 report | 11 | 8,197 | 2,059 | 74 | 18 | 16 | | 5,693 | 211 | 49 | | 55 | 22 |

*(The trainees below should also be included in the figures for the appropriate occupational categories above)*

| Formal on-the-job trainees | | Male | | | | | | Female | | | | | |
|---|---|---|---|---|---|---|---|---|---|---|---|---|---|
| White collar | 12 | 94 | 30 | | | | | 54 | 9 | 1 | | | |
| Production | 13 | | | | | | | | | | | | |

employment decisions that operate to the disadvantage of members of a race, gender, or ethnic group. How different is *substantially different?* Several methods have been proposed:[15]

1. *Intuition.* If the difference offends a judge's subjective notion of fairness.

2. *Four-fifths rule.* If the ratio of the discriminated-against group's selection ratio to the selection ratio of the group most likely to be hired or selected is less than four-fifths.

3. *Ninety-five percent confidence interval.* If the differences between the selection ratios is one that, statistically speaking, would not be expected to occur by chance alone more than 5 percent of the time.

4. *Two or three standard deviation rule.* If one selection ratio exceeds the other selection ratio by more than two or three standard deviations (a statistical comparison).[16]

For the most part the four-fifths rule has been the standard for determining adverse impact.[17] However, it is important to realize that the four-fifths rule is simply a rule of thumb or guideline—it is not a law. Regardless, most organizations will assess their selection rates (e.g., the percent of applicants hired, the percent of employees promoted) and will calculate the impact ratio. Exhibit 8.14 illustrates the steps involved in these calculations comparing promotion rates among males and females.

Exhibit 8.15 is an analysis from a microcomputer-based adverse impact application. The example shown is an analysis of minority and nonminority hiring rates. The necessary data elements (i.e., the number of minority and nonminority applicants and hires) are supplied by the company's applicant-tracking system. Similar analyses are conducted for promotion decisions and termination decisions and comparing males and females. The data elements needed for the promotion and termination analyses are maintained by and tabulated from the company's mainframe-based HRIS.

Each analysis must be performed for every job group. In this organization, job groups correspond to the standard EEO categories.

This adverse impact computer application computes the selection rate for all minorities and compares it to the selection rate for the group most likely to be hired or selected, usually a nonminority group. The application evaluates the four-fifths rule and issues a warning for each job group that violates the rule. In addition, for those categories whose impact ratio fails

**Exhibit 8.14**   Calculating Impact Ratio to Assess Adverse Impact

---

Example: Promotion Decisions for Males and Females

### Data from HRIS

Number of people in job group (by gender) at beginning of AA planning period:

Male:      60
Female:   20

Number of promotions from job group (by gender) during AA planning period:

Male:      20
Female:    4

### Compute Rate of Selection

Number of promotions divided by number of potential promotees:

$$\frac{20 \text{ male promotions}}{60 \text{ potential male promotees}} = .33$$

$$\frac{4 \text{ female promotions}}{20 \text{ potential female promotees}} = .20$$

### Compute Impact Ratio

$$\frac{.20 \text{ female rate}}{.33 \text{ male rate}} = .61$$

### Is There Adverse Impact?

If impact ratio is less than .80 (4/5), then adverse impact exists.

---

to reach 80 percent, it computes the number of minorities that should be expected to be promoted.

# Exhibit 8.15 Adverse Impact Analysis Microcomputer Application

10-Mar-89

Minority Adverse Impact Studies
Affiliate:
Date:

***Appl/Hire***

| Jb gr # | Job Group Name | Blac Appl | Hisp Appl | Asian Appl | Am In Appl | Min Appl | Min Hired | Min % Hire | Tot Non Min App | Tot Non Min Hir | Non Min % Hire | 80 % Rule | | Exp | Actl | Dif | # SD | | |
|---|---|---|---|---|---|---|---|---|---|---|---|---|---|---|---|---|---|---|---|
| | | | | | | | | | | | | | | Only if Under 80% | | | | | |
| 1 | | 28 | 9 | 15 | 5 | 57 | 13 | 22.81% | 95 | 14 | 17.74% | 155.0% | OK | | | | | | |
| 2 | | 11 | 1 | 1 | 3 | 16 | 1 | 6.25% | 31 | 11 | 35.48% | 18.0% | Warning | 4.1 | 1.0 | 3.1 | 2.18 | * | ** |
| 3 | | 20 | 4 | 9 | 12 | 45 | 5 | 11.11% | 63 | 11 | 17.46% | 64.0% | Warning | 6.7 | 5.0 | 1.7 | 0.92 | * | |
| 4 | | 10 | 2 | 2 | 2 | 16 | 4 | 25.00% | 55 | 15 | 27.27% | 92.0% | OK | | | | | | |
| 5 | | 3 | 1 | | 2 | 6 | 3 | 50.00% | 30 | 11 | 36.67% | 136.0% | OK | | | | | | |
| 6 | | 14 | 4 | 6 | 3 | 27 | 1 | 3.70% | 180 | 20 | 11.11% | 33.0% | Warning | 2.7 | 1.0 | 1.7 | 1.19 | * | |
| 7 | | 1 | 1 | 1 | | 2 | | 0.00% | 2 | 1 | 50.00% | 0.0% | Warning | 0.5 | 0.0 | 0.5 | 1.15 | | |
| 8 | | 3 | | 2 | | 6 | | 0.00% | 14 | 6 | 42.86% | 0.0% | Warning | 1.8 | 0.0 | 1.8 | 1.92 | * | |
| 9 | | | 1 | 1 | | 1 | | 0.00% | 3 | 1 | 33.33% | 0.0% | Warning | 0.3 | 0.0 | 0.3 | 0.67 | | |
| 10 | | 1 | | | | 1 | | 0.00% | 3 | 2 | 0.00% | 0.0% | Warning | | | | | | |
| 11 | | | | | | 0 | | 0.00% | | | 0.00% | 0.0% | OK | | | | | | |
| 12 | | | | | | 0 | | 0.00% | | | 0.00% | 0.0% | OK | | | | | | |
| 13 | | | | | | 0 | | 0.00% | | | 0.00% | 0.0% | OK | | | | | | |
| 14 | | | | | | 0 | | 0.00% | | | 0.00% | 0.0% | OK | | | | | | |
| 15 | | | | | | 0 | | 0.00% | | | 0.00% | 0.0% | OK | | | | | | |
| 16 | | | | | | 0 | | 0.00% | | | 0.00% | 0.0% | OK | | | | | | |
| 17 | | | | | | 0 | | 0.00% | | | 0.00% | 0.0% | OK | | | | | | |
| 18 | | | | | | 0 | | 0.00% | | | 0.00% | 0.0% | OK | | | | | | |
| 19 | | | | | | 0 | | 0.00% | | | 0.00% | 0.0% | OK | | | | | | |
| 20 | | | | | | 0 | | 0.00% | | | 0.00% | 0.0% | OK | | | | | | |
| Total | | 91 | 22 | 37 | 27 | 177 | 27 | 15.25% | 473 | 92 | 19.45% | 78.0% | Warning | 32.4 | 27.0 | 5.4 | 1.23 | * | |

* There may be adverse impact in this job group. Validate all transactions!!
** The number of standard deviations is two or more and may indicate discrimination.

The expected number is based on the selection rate among all applicants regardless of ethnicity, multiplied by the number of minority applicants. Using Job Group 2 in Exhibit 8.15 as an example, there were 47 applicants (16 minorities and 31 nonminorities) and 12 hires (1 minority and 11 non-minorities), yielding an overall selection rate of .256. Taking the number of minority applicants (16) and multiplying that by the overall selection rate (.256) yields the expected number of minority hires (4.1). Next, the system computes the difference between the number of expected and actual minority hires and calculates the number of standard deviations between expected and actual practices. Warning messages based on the computed standard deviations are printed at the bottom of the application.

It is easy to see how computer applications that support EEO compliance pay for themselves many times over. Using a manual system, extraordinary amounts of time must be spent in maintaining and tabulating the necessary data and conducting all the necessary analyses for ethnic and gender comparisons, for promotions, hiring, and termination decisions, across nine or more job groups.

### Interpretations

Organizations can use EEO reports and adverse impact analyses to assess their compliance with employment laws and to target corrective actions when necessary. Organizations that are found to have adverse impact have only a few alternatives. They can eliminate the unequal impact through adjustments to the selection process (e.g., adjusting test scores, etc.) or by establishing an affirmative action goal, or they must demonstrate the validity of their selection procedures.[18]

# Employment/Staffing Application 3: Affirmative Action Analyses

Many organizations engage in voluntary affirmative action practices. All government contractors, as well as any organizations that have been found to have illegal hiring practices, are *required* to engage in AA practices. There are many nuances in the AA guidelines. However, as they apply to government contractors, AA refers to increasing hiring and staffing for groups that are underrepresented in the employer's work force. Re-vised Order No. 4, issued by the Office of Federal Contract Compliance Pro-grams (OFCCP), outlines the required and suggested steps that federal contractors are to take regarding affirmative action. Ledvinka notes that Revised Order No. 4 can be divided into three major components of AA planning:

1. Conduct a *utilization analysis*, a comparison of employment of women and minorities in the employer's work force with the availability of women and minorities in the labor market.

2. Establish *goals and timetables* to eliminate any instances of under-utilization of women and minorities in the employer's work force.

3. Plan *action steps* to be taken by management as means of reducing underutilization and thus attaining goals and timetables.[19]

In the following section, two computer applications designed to facilitate the AA planning process, (1) eight-factor analysis and (2) utilization analysis, are described.

## Data Requirements

The data elements needed for EEO reporting are needed for AA analyses as well. In fact, some of the data that feed the eight-factor and utilization analyses come straight from the EEO reports via the company's HRIS.

In addition, labor market information will be needed. Jobs may need to be clustered into standard occupational categories to allow for comparisons with census data (see Exhibit 8.16). Relevant data are usually available from external data sources (e.g., some vendors sell downloadable data bases), although the courts may debate the appropriateness of the particular external data selected.

Sometimes separate AA plans are constructed for different sets of employees. AA planning groups may be based on divisions, facilities, or geographic locations. If separate groups are used, then plan codes must also be established and maintained.

**Exhibit 8.16**  Census Comparable Codes and Incumbent Job Titles

Example Affirmative Action Plan
Census Comparable Codes and Incumbent Job Titles
by Plan and Job Group

Plan:          (0001)  Example Reports

Job Group:    ( 03)  Mid-Level Managers

| Census Code | Census Description | Job Title |
|---|---|---|
| 008 | Personnel & Labor Relations Managers | MANAGER EMPLOYEE SERVICES |
| 013 | Managers, Marketing, Advertising & P | MANAGER ADVERTISING<br>MANAGER MARKETING<br>MANAGER PRICING<br>MANAGER PUBLIC RELATIONS<br>MANAGER PUBLICITY<br>MANAGER SALES SUPPORT |
| 019 | Managers & Administrators, N.E.C., S | MANAGER ACCOUNTS<br>MANAGER BUSINESS PLANNING<br>MANAGER CONTRACTS<br>MANAGER CUSTOMER SERVICES<br>MANAGER CUSTOMER SUPPORT<br>MANAGER DEVELOPMENT<br>MANAGER FINANCIAL SERVICES<br>MANAGER OPERATIONS<br>MANAGER PRODUCT DEV<br>MANAGER PRODUCT LINES<br>MANAGER RESEARCH<br>MANAGER CORP PLANNING<br>MANAGER REGIONAL<br>MANAGER SPECIAL SERVICES<br>MANAGER INSURANCE SECURITY |
| 023 | Accountants & Auditors | ACCOUNTANT<br>FINANCIAL ANALYST |
| 027 | Personnel, Training & Labor Relation | MANAGER TRAINING<br>SUPERVISOR LABOR RELATIONS |
| 034 | Business & Promotion Agents | PUBLICITY AGENT |
| 064 | Computer Systems Analysts & Scientists | SYSTEMS ADMINISTRATOR |
| 065 | Operations & Systems Researchers & A | MANAGER MIS<br>MANAGER SYSTEMS DEV |
| 243 | Supervisors & Proprietors, Sales , S | SALES SUPERVISOR<br>SUPERVISOR SUPPORT |
| 254 | Real Estate Sales Occupations | MANAGER REAL ESTATE |

*Source:*  This is an example from CAAPS, a microcomputer-based HR software package of Criterion Incorporated, Valley Ranch, 9425 MacArthur Blvd., Irving, TX 75063. Reprinted with permission.

## Eight-Factor Analysis

An eight-factor or weighted-factor analysis is designed to determine the availability of women and minorities in the labor market. It is called an eight-factor analysis because Revised Order No. 4 identified eight factors that must be considered in determining labor availability. Some of the factors pertain to the external recruiting market, and others pertain to the internal labor market. An eight-factor analysis should be conducted for each job group (e.g., clerical) and each AA plan group (e.g., each geographic labor market). Exhibit 8.17 contains a report from a microcomputer-based eight-factor analysis. The eight factors that must be considered are in the first column and include unemployment conditions (Factor 2) and promotability considerations (Factor 6). The second and third columns note the percentages of minorities and women that fall into each category.

The third and fourth columns contain factor weights. Weights indicating their relative importance must be assigned to each factor such that each column totals to 100 percent. Although the OFCCP provides specific weights that may be inserted, the agency does not require that they be used. An organization must *consider* each factor but can weight it as they see fit.

The fifth and sixth columns are based on the first four columns and yield weighted availability estimates. These estimates are used as part of the subsequent utilization analysis.

## Utilization Analysis

Exhibit 8.18 shows a microcomputer-based utilization analysis. A utilization analysis compares the percentage of women or minorities within a job group with the percentage of women or minorities available in the labor market. When underutilization exists, the system notes it, computes an 80 percent rule analysis, and, based on anticipated work force size and labor market availability, computes a hiring goal for the plan year. The system also computes the number of standard deviations between the actual and the availability percentages.

The first and third columns show the job group under consideration and the group title, respectively. The second column is the EEO job code under which the job group falls. The fourth, fifth, and sixth columns are the total number of employees in the job group, broken down into nonminorities and minorities. These data come from the company's HRIS. The remaining columns report the comparisons noted above.

# Exhibit 8.17  Eight Factor or Weighted Factor Analysis

Availability Factor Computation Form

Job Group Name  Clerical  
Job Group #  1          Year  1989/1990

Notes:          State of _____      Statistics

| Statistics | Total Min. % | Total Fem. % | Value Weight Min. % | Value Weight Fem. % | Weighted Factor Tot. Min. | Weighted Factor Tot. Fem. | Comments |
|---|---|---|---|---|---|---|---|
| 1.a. Minority population of labor area surrounding facility | 15.7% | N/A | 10.0% | N/A | 1.6% | N/A | |
| b. Availability of women seeking employment in labor or recruitment area of contractor | N/A | 48.1% | N/A | 10.0% | N/A | 4.8% | |
| 2. Percent of unemployment in the specified labor or recruitment area | 23.8% | 35.0% | 10.0% | 10.0% | 2.4% | 3.5% | |
| 3. Percentage of minorities and females in total work force in the specified labor area | 13.0% | 44.4% | 15.0% | 15.0% | 2.0% | 6.7% | |
| 4. Percentage of availability of minorities or females with the requisite skills in the specified labor area | 13.7% | 80.3% | 30.0% | 30.0% | 4.1% | 24.1% | |
| 5. Availability of minorities or females having requisite skills in an area in which the contractor can reasonably recruit | 13.7% | 80.3% | 30.0% | 30.0% | 4.1% | 24.1% | |
| 6. Percentage of minorities or females promotable and transferable within the contractor's organization in the specified labor area | 0.0% | 0.0% | 0.0% | 0.0% | 0.0% | 0.0% | |
| 7. Estimate of existence of training institutions for the requisite skills required for minorities or females | 15.7% | 48.1% | 5.0% | 5.0% | 0.8% | 2.4% | |
| 8. Estimate of training efforts the contractor is reasonably able to undertake to make sure the job group is available to minorities or females | 0.0% | 0.0% | 0.0% | 0.0% | 0.0% | 0.0% | |
| Weighted Availability | | | 100.0% | 100.0% | 14.9% | 65.6% | |
| Actual Availability | | | | | 14.9% | 80.3% | |

235

# Exhibit 8.18 Utilization Analysis

Utilization Analysis

Date: 1988/1989 Plan Year

Goals

Date: 1988/1989 Plan Year

| JG # | EEO Code | Job Group Title | No. Emp | No. NP | No. Min | % Per JG | % Avail | Under-Utilized | 80% Rule | Anticp. Wk Force | % Goal | # Goal | # SD* |
|---|---|---|---|---|---|---|---|---|---|---|---|---|---|
| 1 | O&C | Clerical | 30 | 18 | 12 | 40.0% | 14.9% | No | | 30 | | | |
| 2 | O&C | Senior Clerical | 21 | 18 | 3 | 14.3% | 13.7% | No | | 21 | | | |
| 3 | O&C | Supervisory | 0 | 0 | | 0.0% | | | | | 0 | | |
| 4 | SW | Service Workers | 0 | 0 | | 0.0% | | | | | 0 | | |
| 5 | O&C | Teller | 3 | 1 | 2 | 66.7% | 19.2% | No | | 3 | | | |
| 6 | O&C | Senior Teller | 23 | 19 | 4 | 17.4% | 19.2% | No | | 23 | | | |
| 7 | O&C | Secretary | 4 | 4 | | 0.0% | 12.0% | No | | 4 | | | |
| 8 | O&C | Senior Secretary | 0 | 0 | | 0.0% | | | | 0 | | | |
| 9 | PROF | Professional | 0 | 0 | | 0.0% | | | | 0 | | | |
| 10 | SLS | Sales | 0 | 0 | | 0.0% | | | | 0 | | | |
| 11 | O&C | Senior Management | 0 | 0 | | 0.0% | | | | 0 | | | |
| 12 | OPER | Operatives | 0 | 0 | | 0.0% | | | | 0 | | | |
| 13 | TECH | Technical | 0 | 0 | | 0.0% | | | | 0 | | | |
| 14 | O&M | Branch Officers | 0 | 0 | | 0.0% | | | | 0 | | | |
| 15 | O&M | Sr Branch Officers | 0 | 0 | | 0.0% | | | | 0 | | | |
| 16 | O&M | Loan Officers | 0 | 0 | | 0.0% | | | | 0 | | | |
| 17 | O&M | Sr Loan Officers | 0 | 0 | | 0.0% | | | | 0 | | | |
| 18 | O&M | Entry Management | 23 | 21 | 2 | 8.7% | 9.2% | No | | 23 | | | |
| 19 | O&M | Middle Management | 10 | 9 | 1 | 10.0% | 9.2% | No | | 10 | | | |
| 20 | O&M | Senior Management | 8 | 8 | | 0.0% | 11.6% | Yes | 0.0% | 8 | 11.6% | 1 | 1.02 |
| TOT | | | 122 | 98 | 24 | 19.7% | | | | | | | |

*Two or more standard deviations may be an indication of discrimination.

236

An availability analysis and a utilization analysis should be conducted for minorities and women, for each job group, and for each geographic location or AA plan. At the risk of belaboring the point, the data collection, maintenance, reporting, and analyses associated with these tasks are quite time-intensive without the assistance of computer applications.

## *Interpretations*

Some organizations take affirmative action guidelines seriously, believing in the principle. Others simply view AA as another hoop the organization must jump through. Regardless of their philosophical perspective, many organizations are required to collect the data and complete the AA analyses noted above. The computer applications highlighted here provide information about the availability and utilization of women and minorities in the organization. They yield information necessary to develop AA goals, time tables, and action steps. To evaluate the longer-term implications of preferential treatment on organizational demographics, Markov or other personnel flow analyses can be conducted as well.[20]

# Training and Career Development Applications

Training and career development are often contained within the same subfunction of the HR department since they both deal with the growth or development of the employees. In fact, in some companies this program is called employee development. Training and career development are crucial to maintaining a committed work force that will ensure the viability of the organization into the future. However, the training and career development activities within a firm are usually treated differently. Training is usually seen, and spoken of, as something that is needed—some deficiency in a skill or knowledge area that is necessary to do a particular job. Career development is usually seen as a more uplifting process, as in, "I'm not learning to operate a keyboard; I'm engaged in career development." Although this distinction may seem trivial to some, it is important to the employees.

For the purposes of this book, because both career development and training involve the process of learning, they are treated as comprising the employee development program in the HR department. Learning is a life-long process, and training and career development can keep this process flourishing. Given this perspective, we wholeheartedly agree with this recent statement: "Policy makers on corporate boards and in Congress, managers and employees, agree that training [employee development] is what it takes to keep the American work force skilled and knowledgeable."[21]

From a management perspective, training and career development are critical activities. Internal development of employees, through training or career development, enhances the HRP program discussed earlier in this chapter by preparing employees with the new skills needed for internal transfers or promotions. Management also needs to know the costs of training and its effectiveness. Are they really getting their money's worth? The entire administration of training and career development through needs analysis, training and career development programs, and evaluation needs careful monitoring. Finally, does an enhanced, or different, approach to training or career development lead to increased individual performance and, thus, improved organizational productivity? Training and career development can be tied to the performance management system discussed in Chapter 9. Regardless of the performance level of the individual, most employees want to know where they are going in the company, and this means their performance appraisal must be tied to career development.

Although training and career development can be seen as part of the same process within the organization, they are treated separately here, as seen in Exhibit 8.19, because the computer applications are usually independent although they may be contained within the same HRIS module. In fact, in the managerial and HR literature, these two activities are usually treated separately.[22] Regardless of whether training and career development are part of the same process or are considered separately, HR professionals should treat them as parts of the overall process of full utilization of employees, recognizing that both activities are concerned with developing the potential of the individual for the value added to the organization as well as the value added to his or her individual feelings of worth.

As with the other HR programs in this chapter and Chapter 9, only a few of the applications listed in Exhibit 8.19 will be covered in depth here. However, all of the applications listed do exist in some form. For more information about a specific application, contact a software vendor and request the information on a specific application.[23] You should be able to be quite specific in your request if you have followed the recommendations on needs analysis in Chapter 5.

**Exhibit 8.19** HRIS Applications in Training and Career Development
Programs

---

### Training

*Training Administration.* As the importance of training increases, the need to
monitor it and its costs becomes more important. A system to determine who
needs training, who has had training, and the costs of training must be used.

*Training Needs.* There must be a way to evaluate the training needs of
employees in the organization as well as of those coming into the organization.
This application should be capable of generating lists of employees needing
specific training programs within the firm.

*Formal Education Needs.* This would have the same capability as the training
needs application but for training outside the firm (e.g., certification courses
or advanced degrees).

*Training Evaluation.* This application should be capable of determining the
utility, in costs and benefits, of any training program. This would mean the
identification and development of ways of measuring costs and benefits. This
application would be particularly useful for vendor-provided or contracted
training programs.

*Computer-Based Training.* This application involves any training program
that incorporates computers for the delivery of instructional materials. This
does not include training that only requires the use of computers (e.g.,
accounting or sales mathematics). This is used most often as a replacement
for paper-based training such as textbooks or assigned readings.[24]

### Career Development

*Career Profile.* This would be a listing of all the previous work experience,
for both the current firm and other firms, for each employee. It would also
include all in-service and formal education as well as specific skills linked to
the organization's master list of specific skills. This would also be useful as an
employee turnaround document. An example of a report for employees with
computer science degrees is contained in Exhibit 8.22.

*Future Development.* This would be an application listing all planned training
for a specified future period of time. Most firms use one year, since this
coincides with both the annual performance appraisal period and the typical
HRP cycle.

*Career Planning.* This is a highly sophisticated application that would allow
individual employees to assess their career opportunities within the firm. It is
interactive and closely tied to the performance appraisal module.

# Training and Career Development
# Application 1: Training Administration

Training administration is probably the most widely used application of those listed in Exhibit 8.19. It serves as an accounting tool for monitoring the entire employee development program. It is frequently combined with the career profile application to give a complete picture of the employees' past history of training and experience. This information is also recorded in the employees' skills bank for use in the HR planning program.

## Data Requirements

The data required for the training administration application are employee identification information from the employee master file, work experience, in-service and formal training experience, and information on training programs. Some of the key data elements are listed below:

| | |
|---|---|
| Employee ID | Training course class lists |
| Current job | Training course location |
| Previous jobs with firm | Training course cost |
| Other work experience | Formal education experience |
| Education reimbursement | Skills acquired |
| Course title | Certifications |
| Educational degrees | Education completed |
| Apprenticeships | Training course evaluations |

Depending on the organization, there may be other company-specific data elements. For example, there may be specific requirements for a period of formal on-the-job training, as is the case for air traffic controllers. Or there may be a formal requirement for an annual check of specific skills, acquired through in-service training, as is the case with registered nurses. However, the list above should provide the guidance necessary to customize any application for a specific organization.

Most software packages, whether they are stand-alone applications or a comprehensive HRIS, will have data entry screens to help the user build this application. An example of such a screen from the HR-1 microcomputer-based HRIS is presented in Exhibit 8.20. Note that there is an instruction to press the F5 key to view this screen as well as instructions on how to enter formal education. Although this screen is only an example from the HR-1 user's manual, it gives you an idea of how a software application should work.

**Exhibit 8.20** A Data Entry Screen for Formal Education

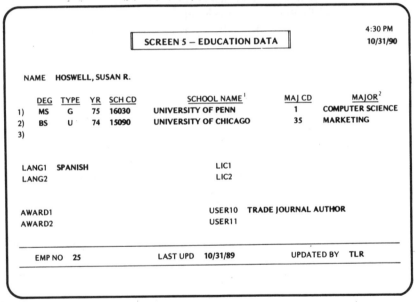

PRESS

to view this screen

[1] SCHOOL1, SCHOOL2, and SCHOOL3 are retrieved from the school table upon entering a valid school code.

[2] MAJOR1, MAJOR2, and MAJOR3 are retrieved from the major table upon entering a valid major code.

*Source:* This exhibit is an example from HR-1, a microcomputer-based HR software package of Revelation Technologies, Inc., 2 Park Ave., New York, NY 10016.

## Reports

A variety of reports that are useful to employees, the HR department, and management are available from this HRIS application. A number of standard reports come with any software package purchased, but you should anticipate a number of ad hoc reports depending on specific information needed at a given time. Employee development is a major cost of maintaining a committed and productive work force. Thus, this HRIS application will receive considerable use in any assessment of costs of the HR function. However, and this point must be emphasized, this is a cost that management often seems completely certain will pay off. It is up to the HR professional to utilize this application properly to assure management they are correct. This application, like the others, is only as good as the user makes it.

The reports in Exhibit 8.21 are examples of the kinds of standard reports that would be expected in this HRIS application. The first three reports can be done on individual employees, or summary reports can be done across all employees. An example of a summary report for education history of employees is contained in Exhibit 8.22. This report provides a listing of all employees who have majored in computer science in one of their educational degree programs. In addition, this report provides their job titles and department names. Thus, if a manager was seeking individuals with a computer science background to serve on a project team, this would be an efficient way to identify these employees. In a similar manner, summary reports on job history and training could also be done to identify employees with specific skills or experiences.

The first three reports generated for individual employees can also be used as turnaround documents for employees to verify. Frequently, employees will take courses without informing the company. This use of the turnaround document system enables management to identify skills and experiences that may be useful to the firm. The career profile reports for individual employees can be combined across all employees to help identify needed skills for internal transfers and promotions. A good example of this occurred in a regional supermarket chain. The chain had recently acquired a floral business and intended to move it inside one of their larger stores. They had anticipated hiring someone from the labor market to manage the business. However, upon checking their career profile report file, they found a current employee who had previously managed a floral shop. The internal transfer of this employee saved the company money, and the employee was quite pleased with the promotion.

**Exhibit 8.21    Training Administration Report Examples**

*Employee Job History.* This report summarizes the job history of a single employee and is usually concerned only with jobs held within the company. This can be used as a turnaround document for verification by employees.

*Employee Training Report.* This report is similar to the job history report, but it contains all formal training, whether in-service or outside the company, that the employee has had while employed for the firm.

*Career Profile.* This report is done for each employee. It contains the information in the job history and training reports. However, it also includes education level achieved, formal diplomas and certification, previous employment history, and skills acquired as a result of these experiences.

*Training Course Report.* This report includes information on every training course sponsored by the company. This includes costs, attendees, contractor (if used), skills intended by course content, evaluation data, and demographic data on employees. The demographic data, such as gender, age, salary, and job title, are important for management control and EEO reporting.

The training course report is particularly important to the HR department and line management for several reasons. First, it allows for the evaluation of the cost-effectiveness of the training courses, assuming the evaluation data are accurate. Second, it allows for comparisons between alternative training courses or programs. This is particularly important for firms that use external vendors or consultants for training. Finally, it can be used for EEO audits and compliance reviews. In most firms, training is used to enhance the employee's skills for the next-level position. As such, entrance to a training program is covered by the EEO regulations discussed in Chapter 3. As part of the annual internal audit (the EEO-1 report) of compliance, this report will be most useful.

As mentioned, in addition to standard reports, ad hoc reports will always be needed in this application. For example, the training manager may want to know how many courses in a six-course sequence all male and female employees have taken. Or, a production supervisor may want a summary report of required in-service courses taken by her fifteen employees. This application should be capable of these types of ad hoc inquiries.

**Exhibit 8.22**  Education History Report

```
                             Mainframe Micros, Inc.
          Major Report for Employees with Major Code = 1 : Computer Science

Emp No  Name                School                 Degree  Type  Yr  Job Title

25      Hoswell, Susan R.   University of Penn      BS      U     74  Sr Programmer Analyst
22      Jensen, Harry R.    Brown University        BS      U     73  Sales Representative I
1       Perry, Stephen G.   St Mary's College       BS      G     82  President
3       Rosenthal, Andrew   Harvard University      MBA     G     83  VP Marketing
31      Shedigant, Irina    Univ of Calif-Berkeley  MS      G     85  Programming Supervisor

5 Records processed
```

*Source:*  This exhibit is an example from HR-1, a microcomputer-based HR software package of Revelation Technologies, Inc., 2 Park Ave., New York, NY 10016. Reproduced by permission.

244

## Training and Career Development Application 2: Career Planning

The career planning application is particularly important to the company for two main reasons. First, it can be used for internal movement of employees, thus avoiding the more costly route of external hiring for all positions. Second, it allows the employee to see exactly where he or she can expect to progress within the company. It can chart a path for employees to follow that could include training and job experiences necessary to reach their career goal. This should improve employee morale and motivation, leading to more committed, longer-term employees.

### Data Requirements

The career planning application uses much of the same data as the training administration application. However, this application also requires the skills, experience, and educational-level requirements for all positions beyond entry level in the company. As such, it is a difficult application to develop. Some firms create the career planning application with a specific career field. If this application is to be used properly, it must also have a list of current job openings in the company. Such an application is examined in the next section.

### Reports

Obviously, the career planning application should be capable of generating an individual report for each employee. This report would include a summary of the individual's skills, experience, and training to date. Using these data, the application should add to the report the career path or paths for the individual based on his or her input of a specific career goal. In a specific example of this type of application and report, General Electric has created what they call their Computing People Project.[25] This interactive HRIS application is used by employees who are in jobs requiring computer skills.

This application will generate a list of companywide openings for employees with computing skills as well as a listing of accessible computer people in the company, all done on a personal computer workstation. Thus, this application can be used by individual employees looking for job changes and career advancement within GE, and it can also be used by managers looking for employees with computer skills. This enables GE to retain a higher percentage of computing personnel, a human resource they consider quite valuable.

Another example of a similar application is Jobmatch, which is used by Citibank for its nonprofessional employees. This application matches available employees to available jobs through profiles of task similarities. Employees and their supervisors respond to a list of job tasks in terms of how frequently the employee has done the task. Employees may also respond to the same list of tasks in terms of their preference for their next job. These job candidate profiles are then input to an automated candidate file. This file is matched with a file containing available positions with task-profile data. An example of the type of report generated from the automated matching is contained in Exhibit 8.23. As can be seen, John Q. Staffmember, a grade 07 teller seeking another job, has been matched with three open positions— window clerk, reconcilement/bookkeeper, and payroll audit clerk. Based on this information, John can now apply for these positions and, after the appropriate screening and interviewing, may find himself in a new position that he had input in selecting. Regarding Jobmatch's use, Sheibar, the Personnel Manager, Finance Division, of Citibank, N.A., states: "We've discovered that it's not the ultimate answer to nonprofessional selection and placement at Citibank, but nonetheless, a system with great potential."[26]

## Training and Career Development Application 3: Training Evaluation

Perhaps the most common complaint in the human resources and management literature is that training evaluation is either done poorly or not at all. The training evaluation application is concerned with the evaluation

**Exhibit 8.23**  Sample Report from Jobmatch

```
            Jobmatch        Personnel Relations - Staffing       Date    5/19/90    Page  0001

** Candidate Matched to Requisitions **                   Distribute to                          PS

Options  -- Same Group Only:  No              Grades 07 to 9    Minimum Salary  319C

Candidate: Staffmember   John    Q    Pers No: 0190025 Grade 07 Tellers
Banking Group: 001 Consumer Services Group  Performance Rating: F  Employment Date:  1/15/80

Special Qualification:  Prefer Wall St Assignment

- - S c o r e s - - -
Overall Specific Generic  Reqn  Grade  Position                 Missing Specific Tasks

81.32  74.73  87.91      0446   07   Window Clerk                 02 24 44 70 71
75.44  68.14  82.74      0681   09   Reconcilement/Bookkeeper     44 47
73.21  65.82  80.60      0355   08   Payroll Audit Clerk          02 44 48 71
                         Same as above 0356

*** 003 Matches Printed ***
```

*Source:*  P. Sheibar, "A Simple Selection System Called 'Jobmatch,'" *Personnel Journal* (January 1979): 53.  Reproduced by permission.

247

of training and, in some instances, the evaluation of what happens when training requirements or applicant qualifications are altered.

## Data Requirements

This application includes the same data elements as the training administration application. However, to develop a DSS in this application, additional data elements might include training outcome measures such as exam scores, trainer evaluations, and job performance changes after training, and information on the training participants, such as educational level. This latter information allows for the determination of whether the course is appropriate for employees differing in job experience, skill, or educational level. This can prove to be quite valuable information in terms of maximizing the dollar return in employee job performance by sending the appropriate employees to the appropriate training program.

## Reports

The most obvious report is one that evaluates individual training programs on a cost-benefit ratio. Using the training evaluation outcome measures and cost per employee, this application should be capable of generating this ratio. Further, if training outcome measures can be standardized across all training programs, this application should be capable of generating a report contrasting the costs-benefit ratio for all company-sponsored training programs. Obviously, this report will be valuable to the training manager in selecting future training programs to sponsor. It should also help the personnel director justify annual budget requests.

## DSS

This application can also contain a decision support system capable of answering "what-if" questions about training employees in certain programs.

9. A. Walker, *HRIS Development: A Project Team Guide to Building an Effective Personnel System* (New York: Van Nostrand Reinhold, 1982), 26.

10. See T. J. Holloran and J. E. Byrn, "United Airlines Station Manpower Planning System," *Interfaces* (1986): 39–50; R. A. Blau, "Multishift Personnel Scheduling with a Microcomputer," *Personnel Administrator* 31 (1985): 43–58.

11. This area is extremely technical and requires a detailed understanding of labor law and industrial psychology. In this section a flavor of the complexity of EEO/AA is provided and some EEO/AA concerns the HRIS must address are illustrated. For a more detailed analysis of these and other personnel law topics, see J. Ledvinka, *Federal Regulation of Personnel and Human Resource Management* (Boston: PWS-KENT, 1982).

12. Ledvinka, *Federal Regulation*, 102.

13. Ibid., 105.

14. Revised Order No. 4, 41 Code of Federal Regulations, Part 60, at Sec 2.11 (b) (1979).

15. Ledvinka, *Federal Regulation*, 102.

16. The two or three standard deviation rule is an extension of the Hazelwood case. See Ledvinka, *Federal Regulation*, 102.

17. This is based on the *Uniform Guidelines on Employee Selection Procedures*, 29 Code of Federal Regulations, Part 1607, and on several court rulings.

18. Ledvinka, *Federal Regulation*, 109.

19. Ibid., 124–125.

20. For an example, see J. Ledvinka, "Technical Implications of Equal Employment Law for Manpower Planning," *Personnel Psychology* 28 (1975): 299–323.

21. D. E. Kirrane, "Training: HR's Number One Priority," *Personnel Administrator* 33 (December 1988): 70–74.

22. For a review of training, see I. L. Goldstein, *Training in Organizations: Needs Assessment, Development, and Evaluation*, 2nd ed. (Monterey, CA: Brooks/Cole, 1986). For information on career development, see D. T. Hall and Associates, eds., *Career Development in Organizations* (San Francisco: Jossey-Bass, 1986).

23. For a list of many vendors, see (AA), R. Frantzreb, *The Personnel Software Census* (Roseville, CA: Advanced Personnel Systems, 1988).

24. For a discussion of computer-based training, see B. Storms, "Follower-Led Computer-Based Training," *Computers in Personnel* 1 (Summer 1987): 25–29; J. W. Toigo, "Don't Dismiss CBT," *Computers in Personnel* 3 (Winter 1989): 41–45.

25. J. L. Craig, "GE's Electronic Corporate Ladder," *Datamation* (April 1986): 117–120.

26. P. Sheibar, "A Simple Selection System Called 'Jobmatch,'" *Personnel Journal* (January 1979): 26–53.

Naturally, this DSS would have to have a statistical or mathematical model based on empirical research. The United States Air Force Human Resources Laboratory has developed such a DSS, which they call the Technical Training Impact Model (TTIM).[27] This DSS is designed to be used when making decisions about Air Force initial skills training courses. The TTIM uses student input variables such as aptitude, reading level, academic motivation, age, and educational preparation along with course content and training outcome variables. Through empirical research, the relationships among these variables are identified. Thus, a decision maker can determine what will happen to training outcomes, such as quality of training performance, if the students' initial aptitude level is changed. For the military, this is an important "what-if" question since enlistment standards are based on initial aptitude level. Although this DSS has not yet been made fully operational by the Air Force, its potential is obvious.

## Summary: Training and Development

This section has covered several specific applications in the HR area called employee development. Because of expected changes in the work force, the importance of this area is going to grow. Reacting to U.S. Department of Labor projections for the year 2000, the American Society of Personnel Administration identified education, training, and retraining as one of the five basic areas in which the most change is expected.[28] If this is so, applications within this area of employee development will be on the rise in the future.

## Summary

In this chapter HRIS applications associated with each of three major HR subfunctions—planning, staffing/employment, and training and career development—were reviewed. Planning applications include work force profile reviews and work force dynamics reporting and analysis. Employment and staffing applications are among the most common HRIS uses, especially in the area of EEO reporting and affirmative action planning. The third major set of applications concerns training and development. Training administration and career planning were discussed. Finally, training evaluation was reviewed, including a discussion of a DSS for training evaluation used by the Air Force. In Chapter 9 applications for three other subfunctions—compensation and benefits, performance evaluation, and quality of work life—are examined.

## Discussion Questions

1. How can compliance with state and federal EEO regulations be facilitated with an HRIS application? How would you cost-justify one of these applications?

2. Which reports do you believe would be most useful in work force planning? Why?

3. What data elements are needed to develop an application to conduct turnover analysis? Would this same data set be useful for any other applications?

4. How can a training manager use an HRIS to improve services to employees and improve the effectiveness of the training subfunction?

5. What are the advantages to employees of HRIS applications directed at career planning? What advantages are there for the organization?

## Notes

1. For more detailed information on the HRP function, see the following readings: E. H. Burack, *Creative Human Resource Planning and Applications: A Strategic Approach* (Englewood Cliffs, NJ: Prentice-Hall, 1988); W. J. Rothwell and H. C. Kazanas, *Strategic Human Resources Planning and Management* (Englewood Cliffs, NJ: Prentice-Hall, 1988); the classic book in the area, J. W. Walker, *Human Resource Planning* (New York: McGraw-Hill, 1980); B. E. Heiken, J. W. Randell, and R. N. Lear, "The Strategic Implications of HR Planning," *Computers in Personnel* (1987): 17–23 discusses HRP projects at a subsidiary of Equitable and at a division of Chase Manhattan.

2. There is a large body of literature dealing with employee turnover. For an example of how turnover analysis fits into a microcomputer-based HR analysis

system, see R. L. Wilson, "Deployment of a Microcomputer Based HRMS as a Distributed Information System: Policy Management Implications and Impact," in R. J. Niehaus, ed., *Strategic Human Resource Planning Applications* (New York: Plenum Press, 1987), 231–250. Other sources on turnover include W. H. Mobley, R. W. Griffith, H. H. Hard, and B. M. Maglino, "Review and Conceptual Analysis of Employee Turnover Process," *Psychological Bulletin* 16 (3) (1979): 493–522; C. E. Michaels and P. E. Specter, "Cause of Employee Turnover," *Journal of Applied Psychology* 67 (1) (1982): 53–59; T. E. Hall, "How to Estimate Employee Turnover Costs," *Personnel* (July–August 1981): 57–61.

3. For an example of a relocation analysis model, see J. Verdin and J. R. Lapointe, "Measurements II: Case Study of a Decision Evaluation Cost Model Using HR Data," *HRSP Review* (Winter 1987): 9–13, 32–33; for a demonstration of the use of a staffing model to project/support a facility shutdown or work force reduction, see R. C. Enderle, "HRIS Models for Staffing," *Personnel Journal* (1987): 73–79.

4. This report is based on a similar one shown in J. Verdin and J. Lapointe, "Performance Measurement Decision Evaluation Costs Models Using Human Resource Data," *HRSP Review* (Fall 1987): 9.

5. For the Navy example, see E. S. Bres, R. J. Niehaus, F. J. Sharkey, and C. L. Weber, "Use of Personnel Flow Models for Analysis of Large Scale Work Force Changes," in R. J. Niehaus, ed., *Strategic Human Resource Planning Applications* (New York: Plenum Press, 1987), 157–167; for the power company example, see D. N. Bulla and P. M. Scott, "Manpower Requirements Forecasting: A Case Example," in R. J. Niehaus, ed., *Strategic Human Resource Planning Applications* (New York: Plenum Press, 1987), 145–155.

6. Technical information can be found in R. C. Grinold and K. T. Marsh, *Manpower Planning Models* (New York: North Holland, 1977), although book requires mathematical proficiency to understand; also see T. A. Bar and P. Cournoyer, "Analyzing Human Resource Flows: Uses and Limita of the Markov Model," in T. A. Kochan and T. A. Barocci, *Human Re Management and Industrial Relations* (Boston: Little, Brown, 1985), 19 for a clear example of a simple microcomputer flow analysis, see A. S. G. E. Biles, "A Microcomputer Model for Human Resource Planning, *Resource Planning* 11 (1988): 293–315.

7. For example, see R. S. Schuler, *Personnel and Human Resource Manag* Paul: West, 1987), 22.

8. For a discussion on developing an applicant-tracking system, see "Developing Requirements for an Applicant Tracking System," *H* (Fall 1988): 22–24, 44–48; and E. Witkin, "Developing Req' an Applicant Tracking System: Part II," *HRSP Review* (V 19–23.

27. M. D. Mumford, F. D. Harding, E. A. Fleishman, and J. L. Weeks, *An Empirical System for Assessing the Impact of Aptitude Requirements on Air Force Initial Skills Training* (Brooks Air Force Base, TX: AFHRL-TR-86-19, Air Force Human Resources Laboratory, 1987).
28. C. D. Bower and J. J. Hallet, "Issues Management at ASPA," *Personnel Administrator* 34 (January 1989): 40–43.

# 9

## HRIS
## Applications II

T his chapter is a continuation of Chapter 8. However, for easier reading
and referencing, HRIS applications are discussed in two separate chapters. Given all the vendors and software available, an entire book could
be devoted to applications.[1] However, the purpose of these two applications
chapters is to explore several specific HRIS applications in depth to demonstrate the power of a computer-based human resources system and to whet
your appetite to try one.

In this second applications chapter, the last three HR subfunctions
contained in Exhibit 1.4—performance management, compensation and
benefits, and quality of work life (QWL)—will be the focus. Since QWL is
an emerging and changing subfunction, fewer applications are available for
it. Thus, this subfunction will not be explored in as much depth as the other
two. However, do not interpret this to mean that QWL is less important.

## Compensation and Benefits Applications

No matter what size the firm, managing compensation and benefits is always
an important activity. The compensation package is a competitive tool. It

can be used to attract and retain employees with critical job skills, enhance motivation, and improve the quality of work life for employees. In terms of management functions, compensation and benefits is probably the easiest to justify automating. It is highly data intensive and has a direct relationship to the bottom line. All organizations must be concerned with maintaining the competitiveness of their compensation package, controlling payroll costs, and complying with the myriad of compensation laws and regulations.

Exhibit 9.1 lists a number of applications that are commonly used in compensation and benefits management. In this section, four applications, two in compensation and two in benefits, are highlighted. In each area a general application and a specific application are examined. For each application, the general HR task to be accomplished, the reasons for automating it, the data requirements, and the types of reports generated and their interpretation are discussed.[2] Chapter 10 builds on this discussion of compensation and benefits by focusing on a related application—payroll systems.

# Compensation and Benefits Application 1: Job Evaluation and Pricing

Job evaluation is the process of examining jobs to determine their relative worth to the organization. It results in a score for each job that indicates the value of that job. After evaluating the work, the points (score) for each job are compared with wage survey information to determine a price for each position. This results in establishing the pay rate for each job.

In most organizations, especially those with large numbers of positions, job evaluation and pricing is a continual process. Large amounts of information are collected and must be analyzed. This information includes data on a variety of compensable factors for each job (e.g., education required, responsibility, physical risk) as well as large amounts of wage survey information. The amount of information used, along with the analysis required, makes job evaluation and pricing a natural HRIS application.

Computer applications can assist with the job evaluation and pricing process in several ways. Compensation applications can combine and summarize information from job evaluation interviews and studies. Systems can also be used to extract wage survey data from various commercial and government data bases. Finally, the system can aid the compensation manager in balancing job worth, as determined by the score on the job, with labor market pay levels.

**Exhibit 9.1**   Common HRIS Applications in Compensation and Benefits

*Compensation Planning.* This involves modeling the costs associated with compensation and benefits. Such models facilitate "what-if" analyses and budgeting.

*Job Evaluation and Wage Surveys.* Job evaluation is the process of valuing work and determining pay rates. Wage surveys are used to ensure that pay structures reflect market realities. This application is described in more detail later in this chapter.

*Executive Compensation.* Executive compensation refers to the "special" compensation and "perks" given to upper levels of management. Examples include stock options, memberships to social clubs, bonuses, use of company facilities, and discretionary expenses. This entails substantial record keeping both from an organizational control perspective and to comply with tax law.

*Compensation Management.* HRISs are indispensable for compensation management. This can be thought of as a general application in that the system supports a large number of tasks for the compensation manager. A key task in this area is reporting. This application is described in more detail later in this chapter.

*Benefits Communications.* Organizations should notify employees as to their benefits status at least once a year. If pension information is included in this communication, annual notification may be required by law. Benefits statements serve several functions for organizations. This application is more completely described later in this chapter.

*COBRA Compliance.* COBRA is a federal law dealing with the provision of health-care benefits to former employees and their dependents. It requires substantial record keeping and actions on the part of employers to avoid penalties. Specific applications for complying with COBRA are widely used. A discussion of COBRA applications is included later in this chapter.

*Benefits Management.* Benefits management as an HRIS application supports a broad range of benefits activities. It is similar to the compensation management function. Critical here is the ability to respond to requests for information and reports in a timely manner. Modeling is also critical. One task that this module can assist with is discrimination testing. Here the job is to ensure that benefits are equitably distributed between highly compensated employees and all others. Section 89 evaluation is an example of such testing.

## Data Requirements

The data requirements include job evaluation points for each compensable factor on each job, position information on each job (e.g., exempt versus nonexempt, unionized versus nonunionized), the "location" of each job in the organizational structure, the labor market employees are drawn from for each job, and wage survey data for each job.

## Reports

Several reports can be generated from these data, including summaries of job evaluation points by position and pay grade level, comparisons of the ranking of jobs by points with current pay levels, identification of personnel with salary levels that do not fall within revised pay ranges, and graphs of job points by wage survey data. Exhibit 9.2 shows a sample report of current pay grades, points, compensation, and position. Exhibit 9.3 shows a graph of job evaluation points and wage survey results. And Exhibit 9.4 graphs a proposed pay policy in relation to current salary information.

## Interpretation

Compensation applications in this area serve primarily to summarize data and present them in a form useful to decision makers. The report in Exhibit 9.2 simply ranks jobs based on the points determined in the job evaluation. It is useful in organizing the job evaluation information and in identifying discrepancies in salaries based on the points. For example, Data Entry Operator III and Senior Executive Secretary have the same number of points (700), but their current salaries vary by $4,525.00.

Exhibits 9.3 and 9.4 show graphic representations of much of the job evaluation data. Exhibit 9.3 shows the relationship of job evaluation points and wage survey data. The line on the graph shows the best description of the relationship of the external labor market wages to job evaluation points for the jobs reviewed. This graph can be useful in establishing a new pay structure that balances external labor market rates with internal job evaluation points.

Such a pay structure is shown in Exhibit 9.4. Here, there are three lines. The top and bottom lines represent the range of pay at various job point levels. The middle line represents the average pay rate. Inspection of the graph shows that most jobs fall within the new salary structure,

**Exhibit 9.2** Sample Compensation Report

| Grade Level | Points | Job Title | Incumbents | Current Salary |
|---|---|---|---|---|
| 16 | 1800 | Vice President Systems Management | 1 | $74,850.00 |
| 16 | 1600 | Vice President Systems | 1 | $56,716.00 |
| 14 | 1300 | Project Manager | 4 | $44,325.00 |
| 13 | 1200 | Manager, Technical Services | 5 | $43,500.00 |
| 12 | 1100 | Project Leader | 8 | $36,450.00 |
| 11 | 1000 | Lead Programmer/Analyst | 16 | $36,800.00 |
| 11 | 1000 | Lead Systems Analyst | 16 | $34,750.00 |
| 10 | 950 | Supervisor | 5 | $25,550.00 |
| 9 | 900 | Senior Programmer/Analyst | 30 | $28,737.00 |
| 8 | 875 | Programmer/Analyst | 35 | $25,350.00 |
| 8 | 850 | Accounting Manager I | 4 | $29,050.00 |
| 7 | 800 | Controller I | 3 | $25,800.00 |
| 6 | 750 | Account Representative III | 15 | $20,825.00 |
| 6 | 750 | Accountant II | 8 | $19,050.00 |
| 5 | 700 | Auditor | 3 | $17,650.00 |
| 5 | 700 | Data Entry Operator III | 8 | $12,925.00 |
| 5 | 700 | Senior Executive Secretary | 3 | $17,450.00 |
| 5 | 650 | Account Representative II | 19 | $15,200.00 |
| 4 | 625 | Staff Assistant I | 5 | $14,900.00 |
| 3 | 600 | Account Representative I | 23 | $14,050.00 |
| 3 | 500 | Data Entry Operator II | 12 | $13,000.00 |
| 3 | 450 | Clerk III | 12 | $12,125.00 |
| 2 | 400 | Data Entry Operator I | 16 | $11,800.00 |
| 1 | 300 | Computer Librarian | 3 | $ 9,800.00 |
| 1 | 300 | Security Guard | 12 | $10,500.00 |

*Source:* Adapted from *Workbench*, a microcomputer-based HR software package by Criterion Incorporated, Valley Ranch, 9425 N. MacArthur Blvd., Irving, TX 75063. Reprinted with permission.

**Exhibit 9.3**    Pay versus Job Evaluation Points

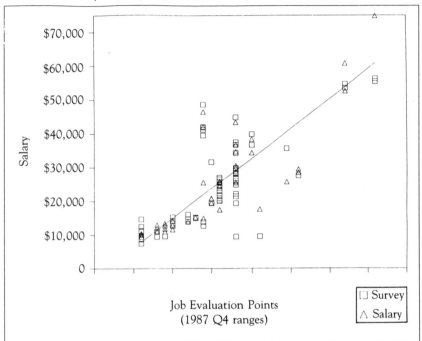

Job Evaluation Points
(1987 Q4 ranges)

☐ Survey
△ Salary

*Note:* This system plots both wage survey data and current salary information on the graph. The regression line is based on job evaluation points and wage survey data. Current salary is not usually shown on this type of graph.

*Source:* From *Workbench,* a microcomputer-based HR software package by Criterion Incorporated, Valley Ranch, 9425 N. MacArthur Blvd., Irving, TX 75063. Reprinted with permission.

although the highest-paid individual (top of graph) is outside the new pay structure. Systems can manipulate and create hypothetical pay range graphs such as this one to model various structures and determine their fit with organizational policy and labor markets.

## Compensation and Benefits Application 2: Compensation Management

Compensation management is one of the most common and general HRIS applications. It can be considered a general application. That is, the HRIS

**Exhibit 9.4**    Pay versus Pay Policy and Wage Survey Results

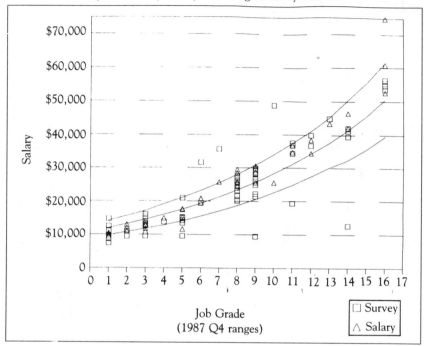

Job Grade
(1987 Q4 ranges)

☐ Survey
△ Salary

*Note:*    This system plots both wage survey data and current salary information on a graph of salary level by job grade. This format is somewhat unusual because only current salary is typically portrayed on this graph.

*Source:*    From *Workbench*, a microcomputer-based HR software package by Criterion Incorporated, Valley Ranch, 9425 N. MacArthur Blvd., Irving, TX 75063. Reprinted with permission.

supports a major function in the organization by facilitating record keeping and generating a variety of standard and ad hoc reports.

Compensation managers deal with many issues and decisions that require timely and accurate information. Government reports must be filed, and requests for information are constant. Significant amounts of time are spent "analyzing" the compensation data and looking for ways to enhance the effectiveness of the compensation function. Compensation applications make sophisticated analysis possible and give the compensation manager the ability to respond to the information demands of the job.

## Data Requirements

The general compensation application requires a large amount of data and needs to interface with the payroll system, benefits applications, and basic employee information module. The list of specific compensation data is lengthy and includes information such as salary, salary basis (e.g., commissions), bonus, premium pay, employee type, date of last raise, hours worked, deductions, and tax status. Because much of this information must be kept on a historical basis, it quickly accumulates.

**Exhibit 9.5**   Compensation Screen Report

```
                    ┌──────────────────────────────────┐
                    │ SCREEN S1—SALARY AND JOB STACKS  │
                    └──────────────────────────────────┘

NAME  AUSTIN, KAREN L.
                                           INC       INC      COMPA    INC
    SALARY DATES      SALARIES    RATE     AMTS      %'s      RATIOS   CODES
         06/01/89    35,200.00      A     6,300.00   21.7      .88      2
         11/30/88    28,900.00      A     2,500.00    9.4     1.25      3
         11/30/87    26,400.00      A     6,400.00   32.0     1.14      2
         01/01/86    20,000.00      A     1,400.00    7.5     1.05      1
         07/01/85    19,600.00      A     4,900.00   35.7      .97      2
         11/01/84    13,700.00      A       700.00    5.3     1.14      2


         JOB DATES   JOB NOS          JOB TITLES              GRADES
         06/01/89    186204    HUMAN RESOURCE MANAGER           18
         11/30/87    144104    PAYROLL SUPERVISOR               14
         07/01/85    114102    PAYROLL ADMINISTRATOR            11
         06/01/84    021002    FILE CLERK II                     2
         11/01/83    011101    FILE CLERK I                      1


    EMP NO  18
```

PRESS
to view this screen

*Source:*   This exhibit is from HR-1, a microcomputer-based HR software package of Revelation Technologies, Incorporated, 2 Park Ave., New York, NY 10016. Reproduced by permission.

## Reports

An almost unlimited number of reports can be generated from compensation data. A number of examples of the types of reports that are commonly generated are presented here. Exhibit 9.5 shows a sample screen report from a widely used microcomputer-based HRIS. This screen shows salary history, raises, position history, and compa ratios for an individual employee. Other reports compare individual compensation level to salary range and may tie this to performance appraisal ratings. Exhibit 9.6 shows such a report generated from the same system that groups employees by performance level. Other reports may list employees due for performance reviews and merit raises. Ad hoc inquiries may list employees within certain pay ranges and break down that information by gender of the employee, thereby allowing pay equity issues to be examined. Reports may also allow analysis of merit raises authorized by supervisors to determine if supervisors are administering raises in a fashion consistent with organizational policy.

## Interpretation

The list of potential reports is virtually endless. The important point is that managers must have this type of information to effectively run a compensation function. If the data are in an HRIS, they can be extracted efficiently and economically. If data are not automated, they still must be obtained, but the costs involved increase significantly and the timeliness decreases significantly.

# Compensation and Benefits Application 3: The Annual Benefits Statement

Most employers offer employees a variety of benefits. The benefits usually include various types of insurance, paid time off, pension, worker's compensation, Social Security, and unemployment insurance coverage. In addition, many employers offer special benefits such as tax sheltered savings plans, discounts on merchandise and services, company cars, and child care subsidies. In fact, a recent survey reported that benefits now account for 39.3 percent of total payroll costs. This makes managing benefits a major concern for most organizations.

Today's complicated benefits systems, such as cafeteria benefits plans, have been made possible in large part by HRIS benefits applications. These systems allow employees to customize their benefits to meet individual needs. Employees are often given a certain number of benefits credits and allowed to spend them on a menu of employer-supplied benefits. These systems require massive amounts of record keeping since the potential benefit combinations are virtually unlimited. Without an HRIS such cafeteria benefits systems would be unmanageable.

Organizations typically provide employees a summary of their benefits elections on an annual basis. These annual benefits statements are a major task for most organizations and serve several functions. First, these statements allow employees to check the correctness of the benefits elections on file with their employer. Second, they provide employees an opportunity to change benefits elections. Third, by providing cost information on the benefits statement, organizations can communicate to employees the value of their total compensation package. Finally, ERISA requires that employees be given an annual statement of their pension accruals. This is often included as a part of the annual benefits summary.

## Data Requirements

As with the compensation applications, the benefits application must interface with the basic employee module and payroll system. In addition, data on benefits elections (e.g., various insurances, level of coverage, optional policies), notification dates, employment history, dependent information, pension and deferred compensation agreements, pension status (e.g., vesting), and miscellaneous benefits (eg., discounts, company car usage, memberships) must be kept.

## Reports

In this application, the primary report is the annual benefits statement. The exact form of the statement will vary based on the benefits package offered by the firm. Exhibits 9.7 and 9.8 present two different samples of benefits statements. Some organizations have taken the annual statement one step further and made it available on demand through computer terminals connected to the HRIS. In this way employees can review their benefits status at any time and make adjustments as needed. Exhibit 9.9 shows a sample from one such interactive system. Other systems actually allow employees to conduct

## Exhibit 9.6   Sample Compensation Report

| Emp-No | Name | Job-Number | Min | Mean |
|---|---|---|---|---|
| 26 | Ryan, Lynette A | 39000 | 5.00 | 6.00 |
| 31 | Sheidgant, Irina | 330000 | 26,000.00 | 28,000.00 |
| 23 | Wong, Kim Loo | 500000 | 23,000.00 | 25,000.00 |
| 24 | Dole, James W | 310000 | 17,000.00 | 19,000.00 |
| 10 | Peaslee, Andrew P | 230000 | 36,000.00 | 40,000.00 |
| 19 | Jauron, Vicki M | 210000 | 50,000.00 | 55,000.00 |
| 35 | McCollum, Ken | 230000 | 36,000.00 | 40,000.00 |
| 9 | Rogers, Kathleen | 160000 | 26,000.00 | 28,000.00 |
| 25 | Hoswell, Susan R | 095050 | 26,000.00 | 33,600.00 |
| 18 | Austin, Karen L | 230000 | 36,000.00 | 40,000.00 |
| 67 | Berry, Sharon C | 333333 | 36,000.00 | 38,000.00 |
| 27 | Cox, Barbara L | 250000 | 40,000.00 | 50,000.00 |
| 12 | Powell, Laura | 800000 | 34,000.00 | 36,000.00 |
| 11 | Martin, Michelle | 310000 | 17,000.00 | 19,000.00 |
| 16 | Roberts, Evelyn | 120000 | 17,000.00 | 19,950.00 |
| 20 | Smith, Joanne P | 18000 | 19,000.00 | 21,000.00 |
| 3 | Rosenthal, Andrew | 333333 | 36,000.00 | 38,000.00 |
| 14 | Richardson, Carol | 500000 | 23,000.00 | 25,000.00 |
| 28 | Korn, Ellen S | 500000 | 23,000.00 | 25,000.00 |
| 18 | Ng, Lawrence | 600000 | 26,000.00 | 29,400.00 |
| 22 | Jensen, Harry R | 120000 | 17,000.00 | 19,950.00 |
| 15 | Bradley, Michael | 310000 | 17,000.00 | 19,000.00 |
| 21 | DeCarlo, John P | 666666 | 5.00 | 6.00 |
| 1 | Perry, Stephen P | 111111 | 74,000.00 | 83,000.00 |
| 2 | Rees, Terri A | 333333 | 36,000.00 | 38,000.00 |
| 4 | Greco, Joan I | 052000 | 32,500.00 | 39,500.00 |
| 8 | Haley, Tom A | 330000 | 26,000.00 | 28,000.00 |
| 7 | Grant, John M | 140000 | 20,000.00 | 21,000.00 |

This report was created with the following LIST command:

```
LIST EMP NAME JOB.NO MIN MID MAX SALARY BREAK-ON PERF.RATING.
MIN HEADING PAGE 'P'                    ---EMPLOYEE COMPENSATION
```

**Exhibit 9.6** *continued*

| Max | Salary | Perf | Compa-Ratio | Percentile |
|---|---|---|---|---|
| 7.00 | 5.75 | | .95 | 37.5 |
| 30,000.00 | 27,000.00 | | .96 | 25.0 |
| 27,000.00 | 24,500.00 | | .98 | 37.5 |
| 21,000.00 | 19,000.00 | | 1.00 | 50.0 |
| 42,000.00 | 41,934.00 | | 1.04 | 98.9 |
| 60,000.00 | 58,000.00 | | 1.05 | 80.0 |
| 42,000.00 | 42,000.00 | | 1.05 | 100.0 |
| | | | | |
| 30,000.00 | 24,000.00 | 1 | .85 | -50.0 |
| 39,000.00 | 29,500.00 | 1 | .87 | 26.9 |
| 42,000.00 | 35,200.00 | 1 | .88 | -19.3 |
| 40,000.00 | 35,000.00 | 1 | .92 | -25.0 |
| 60,000.00 | 53,000.00 | 1 | 1.06 | 65.0 |
| 38,000.00 | 38,800.00 | 1 | 1.07 | 120.0 |
| 21,000.00 | 30,000.00 | 1 | 1.57 | 325.0 |
| | | | | |
| 21,000.00 | 17,400.00 | 2 | .87 | 10.0 |
| 23,000.00 | 22,000.00 | 2 | 1.04 | 75.0 |
| 40,000.00 | 45,890.00 | 2 | 1.20 | 247.2 |
| 27,000.00 | 37,400.00 | 2 | 1.49 | 360.0 |
| 27,000.00 | 37,900.00 | 2 | 1.51 | 372.5 |
| 30,000.00 | 60,000.00 | 2 | 2.04 | 850.0 |
| 21,000.00 | 43,000.00 | 2 | 2.15 | 650.0 |
| | | | | |
| 21,000.00 | 20,100.00 | 3 | 1.05 | 77.5 |
| 7.00 | 9.55 | 3 | 1.59 | 227.5 |
| | | | | |
| 92,000.00 | 85,000.00 | 4 | 1.02 | 61.1 |
| 40,000.00 | 40,000.00 | 4 | 1.05 | 100.0 |
| | | | | |
| 49,500.00 | 40,000.00 | 5 | 1.01 | 44.1 |
| 30,000.00 | 35,000.00 | 5 | 1.25 | 225.0 |
| 23,000.00 | 30,000.00 | 5 | 1.42 | 383.3 |

```
BY PERF. RATING COMPA.RATIO BY COMPA.RATIO PERCENTILE BY-DSND
REPORT AS OF 'D'---                                  EMPCOMP
```

*Source:*   This exhibit is an example from HR-1, a microcomputer-based HR software package of Revelation Technologies, Incorporated, 2 Park Ave., New York, NY 10016. Reproduced by permission.

## Exhibit 9.7    Sample Benefits Statement

### Your Paycheck...Plus, Plus, Plus

Your total compensation is more than just your direct pay. It also includes the benefit programs that you participate in. Your 1986 Personal Benefit Statement outlines the "Plus" to your paycheck "Today's Protection", "Tomorrow's Security" and "Additional Benefits" offered by the Company.

Your estimated compensation for **1989** is

| | |
|---|---|
| Your total annual pay* | $    34,262 |
| Cost of Company paid benefits | $     7,157 |

which include

- Health Care Plan
- Group Life Insurance
- Accidental Death and Dismemberment Insurance
- Long Term Disability Program

- Retirement Program
- Thrift Plan
- Social Security
- Worker's Compensation

Total **1989** compensation                                              $    41,419

*Your total annual pay includes $    **3,162**   for   **18**   vacation days and   **9**   holidays during **1989.**

### Today's Protection

#### If You Need Health Care...
#### Health Care Benefits
You and your family are covered by the KeyCare Plan.

Highlights of the benefits covered under each health care plan are listed below.

| Covered Services* | HMO Plus Plan | Personal Choice Plan | KeyCare Plan | Cost Awareness Plan |
|---|---|---|---|---|
| Inhospital services including semi-private room and board, physician care and miscellaneous hospital services | 100% if approved by HMO Plus physician | 90% of allowable charges after you pay a $100 deductible per confinement | 100% of allowable charges after you pay a $100 deductible per confinement | 100% of allowable charges after you pay a $100 deductible per confinement |
| Outpatient medical care, surgery and treatment for accidental injury | 100% after a co-payment $3 doctors' office $20 outpatient facility | 100% after the deductible $10 doctors' office $30 outpatient facility | 100% after the deductible $10 doctors' office $30 outpatient facility | 100% after the deductible $10 doctors' office $30 outpatient facility |
| Outpatient diagnostic, X-ray and lab services | 100% | 90% | 90% | 90% |
| "Well Baby" care and pre and post-natal care | 100% | 100% | 100% | 100% |
| Routine physical exams | 100% | Not Covered | Not Covered | Not Covered |
| Covered prescription drugs (Out-of-hospital) | $2 co-payment per prescription | $1 deductible per prescription | $1 deductible per prescription | $1 deductible per prescription |
| Out-of-pocket maximum spending limit | $500 per person | $1,000 per person $3,000 per family | $1,000 per person $3,000 per family | $1,000 per person $3,000 per family |

*Different coverage may apply if using providers outside the appropriate network.

#### Dental Benefits

Highlights of your dental plan include:

| Covered Services | HMO Plus Plan | Personal Choice Plan | KeyCare Plan | Cost Awareness Plan |
|---|---|---|---|---|
| Basic services such as periodic oral examinations, cleanings, and X-rays, and additional services including extractions and fillings as medically necessary | 100% | 100% | 100% | 100% |
| Crowns | 60% | 100% | 100% | 100% |
| Periodontic services | 100% | 50% | 50% | 50% |
| Prosthodontic services | 60% | 50% | 50% | 50% |
| Orthodontic services | 50% | 50% | 50% | 50% |
| Lifetime maximum for Orthodontic services | $1,000 per person | $1,000 per person | $1,000 per person | $1,000 per person |
| Calendar year maximum for all other services | $1,000 per person | $1,000 per person | $1,000 per person | $1,000 per person |

## Exhibit 9.7 *continued*

### In Case You Are Disabled...
#### Short Term Disability Benefits
If you are unable to work because of illness or injury, you will receive • • • • • • • • • • • • • • • • • • • • • • • • •   100%
**of your salary for up to 13 weeks, and 50%* for an additional 39 weeks.**
For certain injuries, your Accidental Death and Dismemberment Insurance pays . . . . . . . . . . . . . . . . . . . . . . $   69,000
**\*Unused sick leave days can be applied to increase 50% benefit to 100%.**

#### Long Term Disability Benefits
If you are totally disabled, you may be eligible to receive the following:
From your Long Term Disability Program and primary Social Security . . . . . . . . . . . . . . . . . . . . . . . . $   1,713
From Social Security for each eligible dependent  . . . . . . . . . . . . . . . . . . . . . . . . . . . . . $   420
The maximum family benefit is  . . . . . . . . . . . . . . . . . . . . . . . . . . . . . . . . . . . . . . $   1,260
If you are disabled before age 60, your life insurance benefit of . . . . . . . . . . . . . . . . . . . . . . . $   69,000
continues to age 65.
PLUS your health insurance will be continued.
And, you may receive your Thrift Plan account balance of  . . . . . . . . . . . . . . . . . . . . . . . . . . . $   14,796

### In The Event Of Your Death...
Your survivor may be entitled to the following lump sum benefits:
Group Life Insurance . . . . . . . . . . . . . . . . . . . . . . . . . . . . . . . . . . . . . . . . . . . . $   69,000
Social Security (for an eligible dependent)  . . . . . . . . . . . . . . . . . . . . . . . . . . . . . . . . . $   255
Thrift Plan  . . . . . . . . . . . . . . . . . . . . . . . . . . . . . . . . . . . . . . . . . . . . . . . . $   14,796

Total . . . . . . . . . . . . . . . . . . . . . . . . . . . . . . . . . . . . . . . . . . . . . . . . . . . . $   84,051
And if your death is a result of an accident, the Accidental Death and Dismemberment Insurance benefit
payable is . . . . . . . . . . . . . . . . . . . . . . . . . . . . . . . . . . . . . . . . . . . . . . . . . $   69,000

Your family may also qualify for the following monthly survivor benefits from Social Security:
For each dependent child . . . . . . . . . . . . . . . . . . . . . . . . . . . . . . . . . . . . . . . . . . $   639
For a spouse with dependent child(ren) . . . . . . . . . . . . . . . . . . . . . . . . . . . . . . . . . . . $   1,276
For a spouse age 60 . . . . . . . . . . . . . . . . . . . . . . . . . . . . . . . . . . . . . . . . . . . . . $   638
The maximum family benefit is . . . . . . . . . . . . . . . . . . . . . . . . . . . . . . . . . . . . . . . . $   1,490

**In addition, the following Dependent Life Insurance amounts are payable:**
**To your spouse • • • • • • • • • • • • • • • • • • • • • • • • • • • • • • • • • • • • • • • • • • • • • • •$   10,000**
**For each dependent child • • • • • • • • • • • • • • • • • • • • • • • • • • • • • • • • • • • • • • •$   3,000**

## Tomorrow's Security

### Thrift Plan

As of **12/31/1989**   you have contributed . . . . . . . . . . . . . . . . . . . . . . . . . . . . . . . . . $   9,373
to the thrift plan. Because of the Company's matching contributions to the thrift account and the earnings on all
contributions, the total value of your account is  . . . . . . . . . . . . . . . . . . . . . . . . . . . . . . . $   14,796
(See the chart below for details.)

| Account | as of **Total Value 12/31/1989** |
|---|---|
| Before-tax savings | $   3,272 |
| After-tax savings | $   6,114 |
| Company match | $   5,410 |
| DEC savings | N/A |
| Total | $   14,796 |

For illustrative purposes, the table below shows how your account could grow if you and the Company continue to
contribute $     **2,999**   yearly and the funds earn interest at 7%, 9% and 11%.

| Interest Rate | 7% | 9% | 11% |
|---|---|---|---|
| Estimated Value in 10 years | $   70,541 | $   80,591 | $   92,161 |
| Estimated Value at age 65 | $   367,214 | $   552,381 | $   840,161 |
| Estimated Monthly at age 65 | $   3,338 | $   5,022 | $   7,638 |

**Exhibit 9.7**  *continued*

---

**Retirement Program**

At your normal retirement age of 65 on  **05/01/2018**  you will receive an estimated monthly income from the following:

|  | Lifetime Only Pension | 50% Joint Pension |
|---|---|---|
| Retirement Program | $   1,235 | $   1,097 |
| Social Security | $    803 | $    803 |
| Total | $   2,038 | $   1,900 |

If you are married, your pension benefit will be paid in the 50% Joint form, unless you and your spouse elect otherwise in writing.

Your Group Life Insurance of . . . . . . . . . . . . . . . . . . . . . . . . . . . . . . . . . . . . . . . . . . . . . . $    65,000
will continue. But, this amount will be reduced by $    **6,900**  a year but will not go below . . . . . . . . . $    6,900
Plus, you will be provided with free Medicare Extended Coverage as a supplement to Medicare.

**Additional Benefits**

---

As an employee, you may also take advantage of these valuable Company benefits that are not included above:
- Sick Leave
- Credit Union
- Educational Assistance
- Attendance Bonus Days
- Employees' Association
- Unemployment Compensation

---

*Source:*   Courtesy of Blue Cross and Blue Shield of Virginia as prepared by William M. Mercer-Meidinger-Hansen, Incorporated. Used with permission.

"what-if" analyses to determine the impact of changes in their benefits elections.

## Interpretation

In this case, the interpretation of the output is by the employees who receive the annual benefits statement. The critical issue is the clarity and understandability of the statement. Benefits systems are becoming more complex, as are the statements. For example, the pension portion of the statement may include projections of income at some point in the future under several scenarios (e.g., changes in interest rates, amount of employee contributions, size of annual raise). Even well-educated employees may have difficulty understanding the technical information included in the benefits statement.

## Compensation and Benefits Application 4: COBRA Compliance

COBRA is a major piece of federal legislation that has impacted all employers with twenty or more employees. The intent of the legislation is to extend

## Exhibit 9.8 Sample Benefits Statement

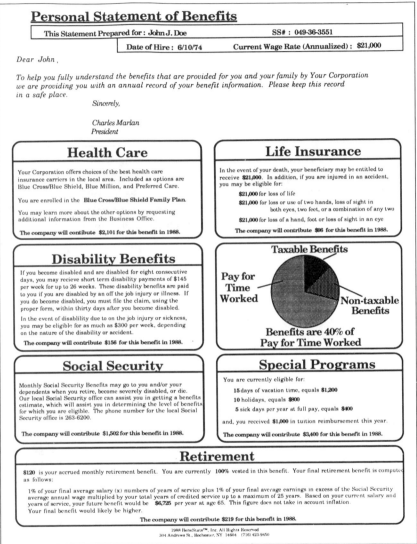

### Personal Statement of Benefits

| This Statement Prepared for : John J. Doe | SS# : 049-36-3551 |
| --- | --- |
| Date of Hire : 6/10/74 | Current Wage Rate (Annualized) : $21,000 |

*Dear John ,*

*To help you fully understand the benefits that are provided for you and your family by Your Corporation we are providing you with an annual record of your benefit information. Please keep this record in a safe place.*

*Sincerely,*

*Charles Marlan*
*President*

#### Health Care

Your Corporation offers choices of the best health care insurance carriers in the local area. Included as options are Blue Cross/Blue Shield, Blue Million, and Preferred Care.

You are enrolled in the **Blue Cross/Blue Shield Family Plan.**

You may learn more about the other options by requesting additional information from the Business Office.

**The company will contribute $2,101 for this benefit in 1988.**

#### Life Insurance

In the event of your death, your beneficiary may be entitled to receive **$21,000.** In addition, if you are injured in an accident, you may be eligible for:

**$21,000** for loss of life
**$21,000** for loss or use of two hands, loss of sight in both eyes, two feet, or a combination of any two
**$21,000** for loss of a hand, foot or loss of sight in an eye

**The company will contribute $96 for this benefit in 1988.**

#### Disability Benefits

If you become disabled and are disabled for eight consecutive days, you may recieve short term disability payments of $145 per week for up to 26 weeks. These disability benefits are paid to you if you are disabled by an off the job injury or illness. If you do become disabled, you must file the claim, using the proper form, within thirty days after you become disabled.

In the event of disablility due to on the job injury or sickness, you may be eligible for as much as $300 per week, depending on the nature of the disability or accident.

**The company will contribute $156 for this benefit in 1988.**

#### Taxable Benefits

Pay for Time Worked

Non-taxable Benefits

**Benefits are 40% of Pay for Time Worked**

#### Social Security

Monthly Social Security Benefits may go to you and/or your dependents when you retire, become severely disabled, or die. Our local Social Security office can assist you in getting a benefits estimate, which will assist you in determining the level of benefits for which you are eligible. The phone number for the local Social Security office is 263-6200.

**The company will contribute $1,502 for this benefit in 1988.**

#### Special Programs

You are currently eligible for:

15 days of vacation time, equals $1,200
10 holidays, equals $800
5 sick days per year at full pay, equals $400

and, you received $1,000 in tuition reimbursement this year.

**The company will contribute $3,400 for this benefit in 1988.**

#### Retirement

**$120** is your accrued monthly retirement benefit. You are currently 100% vested in this benefit. Your final retirement benefit is computed as follows:

1% of your final average salary (x) numbers of years of service plus 1% of your final average earnings in excess of the Social Security average annual wage multiplied by your total years of credited service up to a maximum of 25 years. Based on your current salary and years of service, your future benefit would be **$6,725** per year at age 65. This figure does not take in account inflation. Your final benefit would likely be higher.

**The company will contribute $219 for this benefit in 1988.**

1988 BeneStats™, Inc. All Rights Reserved
304 Andrews St., Rochester, NY 14604 (716) 423-9450

*Source:* This sample benefits statement was produced by BeneStats™, 304 Andrews Street, Rochester, NY 14604. Tel. (716) 423–9450. Reproduced with permission.

**Exhibit 9.9** Screens from an Interactive Benefits Reporting System

Totaling Your Choices

Your 1989 Employer-provided Flexible Credits . . . . . . . . . . . . . . . . . . . . . . . . .$3,000

| | |
|---|---|
| A. Medical Care . . . . . . . . . . . . . . . . . . . . . . . . . . . . . . . . . . . . . . . . . . . . . . . . . . | 459 |
| B. Dental Care . . . . . . . . . . . . . . . . . . . . . . . . . . . . . . . . . . . . . . . . . . . . . . . . . . . | 126 |
| C. Life Insurance . . . . . . . . . . . . . . . . . . . . . . . . . . . . . . . . . . . . . . . . . . . . . . . . . | 45 |
| D. Time Off . . . . . . . . . . . . . . . . . . . . . . . . . . . . . . . . . . . . . . . . . . . . . . . . . . . . . | 342 |
| E. Health Care Reimbursement Account . . . . . . . . . . . . . . . . . . . . . . . . . . . . . . | 2,000 |
| F. Dependent Care Reimbursement Account . . . . . . . . . . . . . . . . . . . . . . . . . . | 0 |

Total Net Cost of Your Choices . . . . . . . . . . . . . . . . . . . . . . . . . . . . . . . . . . . . . . $2,972

Amount to Be Added to Your Savings Fund Plan
Account or Taken as Taxable Cash at the End of 1989 . . . . . . . . . . . . . . . . .   $28

Your Payroll Deduction . . . . . . . . . . . . . . . . . . . . . . . . . . . . . . . . . . . . . . . . . . . .   $0

Please type the letters (A through F) corresponding to your next choice, or type N if you are finished.

---

Before we end, let's estimate how your take-home pay will be affected by the elections you are considering.

| | Before Flexible Selections | After Flexible Selections |
|---|---|---|
| Your Gross Pay (Including Flexible Credits) . . . . . . . . . . . . . . . . . . . . . . . . . . | $30,000 | $33,000 |
| Your Elections Decrease Your Pay by . . . . . | | 5,972 |
| Estimated Federal Income Taxes . . . . . . . . | 5,509 | 4,617 |
| Estimated Social Security Taxes . . . . . . . . . | 2,145 | 1,933 |
| Life Insurance Cost . . . . . . . . . . . . . . . . . . . | 24 | |
| Net Pay . . . . . . . . . . . . . . . . . . . . . . . . . . . . . | $22,322 | $20,478 |
| Difference in Net Pay . . . . . . . . . . . . . . . . . . . . . . . . . . . . . . . . . . . | $1,844 | |

You will spend $5,972 on benefits in 1989. Of that, $3,000 goes to tax-free Flexible Credits and the remaining $2,972 is deducted from your pay. However, your take-home pay is actually decreased by only $1,844 because you're buying your benefits with pretax dollars.

These estimates assume that your pay is your only source of income, that you are single and claim one exemption and no deduction for federal income tax purposes. State and local taxes have not been included. So your actual tax savings could be greater than the amount shown here.

F2 = Continue          F1 = Previous Screen          F3 = Exit

**Exhibit 9.9**  *continued*

1. Your 1989 Employer Flexible Credits . . . . . . . . . . . . . . . . . . . . . . . . . . . . . . . . $3,000

2. Your Flexible Benefit Choices:

A. Medical Coverage:
   American Medical
   For You and Your Children . . . . . . . . . . . . . . . . . . . . . . . . . . . . . . . . . . . . . . . $459

B. Dental Coverage:
   Dental 2
   For You and Your Spouse . . . . . . . . . . . . . . . . . . . . . . . . . . . . . . . . . . . . . . . . $126

C. Life Insurance:
   Life 2 . . . . . . . . . . . . . . . . . . . . . . . . . . . . . . . . . . . . . . . . . . . . . . . . . . . . . . . . $45

D. Flexible Days:
   3 Flexible Days . . . . . . . . . . . . . . . . . . . . . . . . . . . . . . . . . . . . . . . . . . . . . . . $342

E. Health Care Reimbursement Account . . . . . . . . . . . . . . . . . . . . . . . . . . . . . $2,000

F. Dependent Care Reimbursement Account . . . . . . . . . . . . . . . . . . . . . . . . . . $3,000

   Total . . . . . . . . . . . . . . . . . . . . . . . . . . . . . . . . . . . . . . . . . . . . . . . . . . . . . . . . $5,972

3. Your Unused Flexible Credits . . . . . . . . . . . . . . . . . . . . . . . . . . . (1.) − (2.) = $0

4. Your Net Payroll Deduction (if any) . . . . . . . . . . . . . . . . . . . . . . . . . . . . . . . . $2,972

This report will help you with your Flexible Elections.

*Source:* C.I. Harris and S.H. Simon, "Benefits Too Flexible for Pencil and Paper," *Computers in Personnel*, 1 (Summer, 1987): 4–8. (New York: Auerbach Publishers) ©1987 Warren, Gorham & Lamont, Inc. Adapted with permission.

health-care coverage to former employees and their families. While the aim of the legislation is laudable, COBRA has been a major headache for HR departments who must administer it. Failure to comply with COBRA can result in the loss of the deductibility of employee medical insurance by the organization, force "highly compensated" employees to include the value of their insurance benefits in their income for tax purposes, and cause organizations to incur a penalty of $100 per day per affected participant.

Complying with COBRA requires meticulous attention to documenting that the organization has followed the letter of the law. For example, the COBRA administrator must ensure that all eligible former employees and their dependents have been notified of the option of continued coverage, track acceptances and declines of coverage, determine when COBRA coverage has expired (18 to 36 months depending on circumstances), track collections of premiums, and so on. Dates become quite important in determining compliance. As a consequence of the compliance requirements, COBRA applications, either stand-alone packages or as part of the HRIS, are now in place in many organizations.

## Data Requirements

The COBRA application needs to draw information from the basic employee module (e.g., name, address, number and type of dependents), or this information must be included in the data base associated with the application. In addition, a variety of data that are unique to COBRA must be kept. Exhibit 9.10 lists the additional data elements that must be maintained for COBRA compliance.

**Exhibit 9.10**    Unique Data Elements Required for COBRA Compliance

COBRA event (termination, divorce, etc.)

Date of COBRA event

Length of COBRA availability

Date of termination of subsidized benefits

Date of notification

Date by which response must be received

Date of COBRA election

Payment data: Date of last payment

                          Date of next payment

                          Period covered by payment

                          Notices, if any, of overdue payments

Plan involved

Plan coverage summary (options, if any, chosen)

COBRA activity log for each participant

Date of cessation of COBRA coverage due to nonpayment

## Reports

The reports associated with COBRA fall into two groups. The first group includes correspondence with individuals eligible for coverage. The second type are management reports associated with administering COBRA. Letters

**Exhibit 9.11**　COBRA Compliance: Correspondence Generating Screen

```
─────────────── COBRA Correspondence Data ───────────[Ctrl] [F3]

 NAME  JENSON,HARRY

        EVENT DATE  04/10/89        ORIG. EXPIRE DATE  04/10/89
                                    COBRA EXPIRE DATE  10/10/90
     NOTIFIED DATE  04/10/89
 NOTIFICATION SOURCE

         INFORM BY  04/24/89             ELECTION DUE  06/19/89
        INFORMED ON 04/20/89        ELECTION RECEIVED  06/18/89
                                      ELECTION CHOICE  Y
                                         PAYMENT CODE  M   MONTHLY
                                       FIRST DUE DATE  08/02/89

 ───────────────────────────────────────────────────────────────
    COBRA NO  1            LAST UPDATED          UPDATED BY
```

*Source:*　This exhibit is from HR-1, a microcomputer-based HR software package by Revelation Technologies, Incorporated, 2 Park Ave., New York, NY 10016. Reproduced by permission.

include notification of eligibility for coverage, cessation of coverage for nonpayment, expiration of coverage, and so on. Management reports may list individuals currently under the COBRA coverage, expiration dates, dependents covered, and so forth. Exhibit 9.11 presents a COBRA screen from a microcomputer-based HRIS that is used to generate form letters to eligible individuals. Exhibit 9.12 shows a COBRA report generated from the same system.

### Interpretation

Most of the COBRA reports are self-explanatory. For example, a report indicating overdue payments calls for action in terminating participants who have failed to pay premiums within the guidelines established by the organization.

## Performance Management Applications

Although the compensation and benefits subfunction has recently received considerable attention, the area of performance management is just as important. In this area, the concern is with ensuring that employees per-

**Exhibit 9.12** COBRA Beneficiary Plan Report

Empire Corporation
---Active COBRA Beneficiary Report--- May 1989

PAGE 1

| COBRA# | NAME | SOCIAL SEC.# | PLAN CODE | PLAN NAME | COST | FEE | MONTHLY CHG. |
|--------|------|--------------|-----------|-----------|------|-----|--------------|
| 23 | Cash, Scott | 317-47-5968 | BCBS105 | Medical Coverage | 38.75 | 0.77 | 39.52 54.23 |
| | | | DEN656 | Dental—Ind. | 8.75 | 0.18 | 8.93 |
| | | | USL100 | Life—1XSal. | 5.67 | 0.11 | 5.78 |
| 16 | Nelson, C. P. | 555-12-3123 | HMO200 | Medical Coverage | 28.75 | 0.58 | 29.33 49.22 |
| | | | DEN656 | Dental—Fam. | 19.50 | 0.39 | 19.89 |
| 5 | Cook, Raymond | 432-56-7887 | BCBS105 | Medical Coverage | 38.75 | 0.77 | 39.52 110.36 |
| | | | ACC890 | Accident Ins. | 4.50 | 0.09 | 4.59 |
| | | | USL100 | Life—1.5XSal. | 19.50 | 0.39 | 19.50 |
| | | | DIS003 | Disability | 45.83 | 0.92 | 46.75 |

form their jobs as required. As you can see from Exhibit 9.13, the performance management program is quite comprehensive, ranging from individual performance appraisal to the employee grievance program. This breadth is deliberate and indicates our bias that individual (or unit) performance can not be managed only through the performance appraisal program. In fact, the performance appraisal program must be linked with the other parts of performance management to provide a consistent message to the employee.

**Exhibit 9.13**   HRIS Applications in Performance Management

*Performance Appraisal.* This involves the evaluation of employees' job performance against the standards contained in their job description. This information is important for a variety of administrative and motivational purposes and is one of the activities that has a well-developed microcomputer-based application.

*Unit Productivity.* In this application, criteria of unit performance are used to determine whether the unit is performing as expected. In this application, a unit can vary in size from a production work group to an entire division or company. Standardizing unit criteria (e.g., in terms of dollars) allows for comparisons among units.

*Project Management.* This application uses the project management technology discussed in Chapter 7 and makes it into an interactive software. The project manager can use this for project planning as well as project control of single and multiple projects. This can also be used as an input to unit productivity when the project is contained within one unit.

*Time and Attendance.* This application records the time and attendance data for all employees. It is useful for payroll purposes and can be used by line management, particularly in conjunction with the employee discipline program.

*Discipline.* All firms should have a well-documented discipline procedure. This application ensures that any discipline action is recorded as well as guides the line manager through the steps in the discipline procedure. This application requires extremely good security.

*Grievance.* This application explains the grievance procedure to employees in an interactive mode with a terminal. It allows the employee to enter the grievance interactively or indicates the appropriate person to contact to file a grievance. This can be used in both union and nonunion environments.

# Performance Management Application 1: Performance Appraisal

The assessment of individual job performance serves a variety of purposes. For the individual employee, it can be used to determine administrative actions, such as salary increases or promotions, and to help the individual develop better job skills through performance feedback, usually in an appraisal interview with his or her supervisor. It also serves as a monitor for other HR subfunctions. The assumption behind selecting, placing, and training employees is that these HR activities will improve individual job performance. Thus, it can be used to check or, in scientific terms, validate, these activities.[3]

## Data Requirements

The basic data element for this application is the performance measurement of the individual employees. This could be in the form of quantity and quality of units produced, sales records, test scores, or ratings by supervisors and others. Because supervisory ratings are the most common form of performance measure used today, they are used in our examples. Other data elements would be abstracted from the employee core module and would include job title or code, EEO code, supervisor, work unit, annual appraisal anniversary date, and historical performance measures. Other data elements for specific reports could be added by the firm during customization of the application.

## Reports

The assessment of individual performance provides the data for personal, administrative, and management reports, which are listed in Exhibit 9.14. Although there are a variety of methods to measure individual job performance, all the reports in Exhibit 9.14 are based on supervisory ratings on a form with multiple performance dimensions. However, these reports could be produced by using individual job performance data obtained by any performance measurement method. The first of the reports, the performance appraisal administration report, is extremely useful for the HR department. Because it provides information on employees due for their annual performance review, it allows the forms to be mailed to the supervisors in a timely fashion. In most applications, a report by an individual supervisor can also

**Exhibit 9.14** Performance Appraisal Reports

*Performance Appraisal Administration.* This report, typically issued on a monthly basis, shows the annual performance appraisals that are due for the next three months by employee name and supervisor. It also shows the current status of appraisals that are due (e.g., whether complete or not). It could also show appraisals that are under grievance by employees. This report can be summarized on an annual basis.

*Individual Performance Profile.* This is a computer-generated report of an individual employee's job performance based on the performance appraisal system. If the firm uses a supervisor's ratings on multiple aspects of an individual's performance, this profile would show the actual ratings received either in numbers or in a graphic profile.

*Group Performance Report.* This report is based on the individual employee performance data, and "group" represents any meaningful categorization of jobs, organizational unit, or people. For example, there could be a report on all employees within a given job classification or career field; other reports could look at production units. This report contains a variety of descriptive statistics such as means, standard deviations, minimum and maximum scores, and ranges of scores.

*Rater Reports.* In performance appraisal systems with ratings by supervisors or others, this report is used to analyze the ratings of each rater. Comparisons are made with other raters or with historical comparisons of changes over time for the same rater. This would identify raters whose ratings are deviant from those of other raters. This report can also be used as feedback to raters to show them their average ratings compared to those of other raters.

*Rating Instrument Reports.* These reports summarize how the raters are using the various rating categories within the rating form as well as the rating system or scale. These reports could suggest ways in which the rating form could be revised and modified to be used more effectively.

be generated to give supervisors early warning, usually three months, of the appraisals they will have to do. Obviously, this application will also produce a report to the employee indicating when his or her next annual appraisal is due. Finally, as indicated in Exhibit 9.14, this report also allows the determination of delinquent appraisals, thus allowing for follow-up by the HR department or line management, depending on organizational policies.

The second report, the individual performance profile, appears in many HRIS applications, although its format changes with the specific

**Exhibit 9.15**    Individual Job Performance Profile

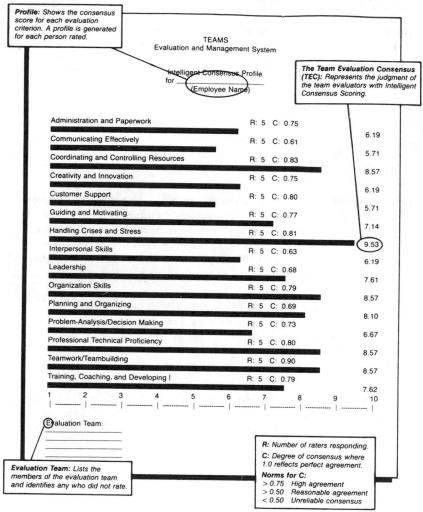

Source:    M.R. Edwards, "An Expert System for Equitable Career Decisions," *Computers in Personnel* 3 (Fall 1988): 44. Adapted with permission.

application.[4] An example of one report from the TEAMS Intelligent Consensus program is presented in Exhibit 9.15. Although this report is based on a team of raters in an expert system designed to help make career decisions, it best illustrates the idea of an individual profile. The value of this profile, for employee counseling and growth, whether arrived at by team consensus as in Exhibit 9.15 or by a single rater, is obvious. It identifies the strengths and weaknesses of the employee and can be used to identify training needs and career progression for the individual employee. In some applications, this individual profile can be enhanced with average profiles from other relevant groups, for example, employees in the same job title or work group. Also, most applications allow for a report showing historical summary data for previous evaluations of this employee. Thus, the individual employee's progress can be followed.

Group performance reports, as discussed in Exhibit 9.14, serve a very useful management purpose in monitoring the performance appraisal system as well as specific groups of employees. For example, lower ratings from one departmental unit relative to all other departments should signal some problems that need investigation and, perhaps, management action. A critical use of this group report is in EEO compliance, particularly in legal defense of promotions or pay raises. Since the performance ratings of all employees can be classified into protected classes under equal employment regulations, it is possible to examine bias against any group by statistical analyses. This report should be a regular part of this application because it provides a monitor of the company's EEO compliance.

In some cases, the work group report that summarizes individual employees' performance can be used as a measure of unit productivity, the second HRIS application in Exhibit 9.14. However, most managers realize that the summation of individual employees' ratings does not completely measure unit productivity. Thus, additional criteria, such as meeting budget and achieving unit goals, are more appropriate and can be combined with summation reports on individual performance. Although HRIS unit productivity application software is usually available, there is usually controversy over what is the best measure of unit productivity.[5]

The last two reports in Exhibit 9.14 are useful for different groups in the firm. The rating instrument reports are used only by the HR department to determine if their rating form is working properly and where revisions are necessary. For example, in one firm a supervisory rating scale with nine rating points was designed and implemented. Upon review of its use, it was found that only seven of the points were being used by raters, and thus the instrument was modified. However, the rater reports in Exhibit 9.14 are typically used by management to identify problems with specific raters. An example of a report on raters is contained in Exhibit 9.16. As can be seen, this report summarizes the ratings given by the same supervisor across all

**Exhibit 9.16**    Performance Ratings by Supervisor Report

| Emp No | Name | Job Title |
|---|---|---|
| 14 | Richardson,Carol | Engineer I |
| 20 | Smith,Joanne P | Payroll Administrator |
| 4 | Greco,Joan I | Attorney II |
| 21 | DeCarlo,John P | Mail Clerk |
| 12 | Powell,Laura | Engineering Manager |
| 18 | Austin,Karen L | Human Resources Manager |
| 25 | Hoswell,Susan R | Sr Programmer Analyst |
| 3 | Rosenthal,Andrew | VP Marketing |
| 17 | Townsend,Leslie J | Project Engineer |
| 28 | Korn,Ellen S | Engineer I |
| 2 | Rees,Terri A | VP Marketing |
| 16 | Roberts,Evelyn | Sales Representative I |
| 1 | Perry,Stephen G | President |
| 11 | Martin,Michelle | Programmer I |
| 67 | Berry,Sharon C | VP Marketing |
| 13 | NG,Lawrence | Engineer II |
| 15 | Bradley,Michael | Programmer I |
| 9 | Rogers,Kathleen | Accounting Supervisor |
| 22 | Jensen,Harry R | Sales Representative I |
| 27 | Cox,Barbara L | Controller |
| 7 | Grant,John M | Accountant I |
| 8 | Haley,Tom A | Programming Supervisor |

employees rated and can be set for any time period. If problem raters are identified, the reasons for the problems can be investigated and corrective action taken, usually training on the rating system. This report enables management to identify quickly raters who consistently rate higher or lower than other raters. Contrast this with a manual system, where a consistently low rater might never be discovered but his or her employees would suffer in promotions or other organizational rewards.

Before leaving the performance appraisal activity, one computer-based application should be mentioned because of its unique qualities. This stand-

**Exhibit 9.16** *continued*

| Department Name | Perf Mgr Name |
|---|---|
| Accounting | 2 Cox,Barbara L |
| Accounting | 2 Cox,Barbara L |
| Corporate | 5 Greco,Joan I |
| Mailroom | 3 Korn,Ellen S |
| Nuclear Research | 1 Perry,Stephen G |
| Payroll | 1 Perry,Stephen G |
| Corporate | 1 Perry,Stephen G |
| Corporate | 2 Perry,Stephen G |
| Hydraulic Engineering | 2 Perry,Stephen G |
| Communications | 2 Perry,Stephen G |
| Corporate | 4 Perry,Stephen G |
| Marketing | 2 Rees,Terri A |
| Special Projects | 4 Rees,Terri A |
| Purchasing | 1 Roberts,Evelyn |
| Marketing | 1 Roberts,Evelyn |
| Thermal Engineering | 2 Roberts,Evelyn |
| Purchasing | 3 Roberts,Evelyn |
| Nuclear Research | 1 Rogers,Kathleen |
| Nuclear Engineering | 2 Rogers,Kathleen |
| Finance | 1 Rosenthal,Andrew |
| Accounting | 5 Townsend,Leslie J |
| Sales Training | 5 Townsend,Leslie J |

*Source:* This exhibit is an example from HR-1, a microcomputer-based HR software package of Revelation Technologies, Incorporated, 2 Park Ave., New York, NY 10016. Reproduced by permission.

alone application, originally called Computerized Performance Appraisal System (ComPAS) and now called Performance Review and Information Standardizing Method (PRISM), runs on IBM PCs and PC-compatible hardware, making it flexible to use.[6] It consists of two components, a rating and a scoring module, which are both used interactively. This means that supervisors enter performance appraisal data directly through a keyboard rather than completing paper forms that must be entered later by HR employees. Another aspect of this application is its computer-based scoring module, which attempts to control for subjective influences by raters and scores rated job performance against the performance feasible in the job rather than ideal performance. That is, it allows the supervisor, again interactively, to specify upper limits to individual job performance while taking account of performance constraints such as faulty equipment or supplies. Although PRISM appears to have the potential to solve performance appraisal problems, there have been no reports of its use in a practical setting.

## Performance Management Application 2: Time and Attendance

This HRIS application is the most favored by line managers, particularly first-level supervisors, since it allows them to monitor the time their employees spend on the job. This is particularly important to management, since, with new cost-estimation procedures, it is apparent that employee absenteeism and tardiness cost employers billions of dollars annually. It seems clear that attendance should be monitored, and attendance tracking by computer seems to be part of the answer.[7] As should be obvious, monitoring employee absence and tardiness has additional importance because of its interface with payroll, a topic discussed more fully in Chapter 10.

### Data Requirements

The basic data elements involve time spent on the job. In some firms, tardiness is monitored by a time clock or badge that is directly linked to the computer; in others, it is monitored by supervisors. Reasons for tardiness, excused or unexcused, must also be entered. Attendance data elements are similar. Each absence record includes start and end date, total time taken, and reason. Typically, data entry for absence and tardiness are combined. Other elements from the employee core module include demographic data such as gender, age, job title or code, EEO code, work unit, anniversary date (for accruals), leave-time accrued, and other personal data depending on the customization in the firm.

### Reports

Reports in this application generally fall into one of three categories: individual, work unit, and analysis. An example of an individual report for employee absences is contained in Exhibit 9.17. Notice that this absence report was run at the end of the calendar year and covers absences for the entire previous year (01/01/90 to 12/31/90). The report indicates the employee's department and includes all information on absences, from time taken to the reason. Note that the third entry under "reason for absence" is tardiness. Thus, the report covers all time off the job. At the bottom, this report also summarizes disciplinary hours, a topic discussed in the next section of this chapter. Finally, notice that this report is an employee turnaround document requiring the employee's signature and date. One can assume the employee is provided an opportunity to dispute this record of absences via the firm's grievance procedure.

What is not included in this individual report is sick and annual leave accruals. These accruals are sometimes reported separately, but they could be combined in this report. Further, since sick and annual leave are usually accrued on a monthly basis, employees are frequently provided monthly accrual reports as turnaround documents that must be signed and returned to the HR department. These employees turnaround reports are important since they can frequently identify disagreements between company and individual employee records early. This can usually lead to informal resolution before a formal grievance action is started.

The second type of report in this application is the unit report. This type of report can summarize absence information for a single department or for any number of departments. The latter type is contained in Exhibit 9.18. As you can see from the top of this report, it summarizes the absence by department for Division 001 of the East Plant for the dates 01/01/90 to 12/31/90. Obviously, the manager of this division was interested in the absence data, particularly the average departmental absence data, so they could be compared with both company and divisional absence averages. Notice especially that the department that exceeds company and divisional averages is marked by an asterisk. Finally, note that this report covers tardiness and disciplinary hours, with the warehouse clearly in the lead on both.

Based on this report, it is likely that the manager would request summary reports for those departments in which there appear to be problems. This application should be able to provide these reports as well as detailed individual reports as in Exhibit 9.17 for each employee. Since the inclusive dates of these reports are specified, it is assumed that this application can provide these reports for any specified set of dates. Most managers do not want to wait until the end of the year to discover they have serious employee attendance problems. As is obvious,

**Exhibit 9.17** Individual Employee Absence Report

```
Date: 12/31/90              XYZ Corporation              Time: 09:31
                         Classified--Confidential
                                 Report 2
                    Individual Employee Absence Record
               For absences between 01/01/90 and 12/31/90

Name: Washington, George
Division: 001  Location: East Plant      Department: 111 Accounting

Absence     Absence     Absence     Absence
Start       Start       End         End        Hours      Reason
Date        Day         Date        Day        Absent     For
                                                           Absence

01/08/90    Monday      01/08/90    Monday      8.00      Sick
01/17/90    Wednesday   01/19/90    Friday     24.00      Sick
03/09/90    Friday      03/09/90    Friday      1.50      Tardy
05/28/90    Monday      05/28/90    Monday      8.00      Holiday
07/04/90    Wednesday   07/04/90    Wednesday   8.00      Holiday
06/18/90    Monday      06/22/90    Friday     40.00      Vacation
```

| Date | Day | Date | Day | Hours | Type |
|---|---|---|---|---|---|
| 07/04/90 | Wednesday | 07/04/90 | Wednesday | 8.00 | Holiday |
| 08/17/90 | Friday | 08/17/90 | Friday | 8.00 | Personal |
| 09/03/90 | Monday | 09/03/90 | Monday | 8.00 | Holiday |
| 09/17/90 | Monday | 09/20/90 | Thursday | 32.00 | Sick |
| 10/02/90 | Tuesday | 10/02/90 | Tuesday | 8.00 | Jury Duty |
| 11/22/90 | Thursday | 11/22/90 | Thursday | 8.00 | Holiday |
| 12/24/90 | Monday | 12/24/90 | Monday | 8.00 | Holiday |
| 12/25/90 | Tuesday | 12/25/90 | Tuesday | 8.00 | Holiday |

Total disciplinary hours from 01/01/90 to 12/31/90:  73.50
Total incidents during this period:  5
Percent one-day Monday/Friday incidents:  60%

Reviewed by: _____  Employee/Date

_____  Manager/Date

Source: E. J. Drumm, "Stolen Moments Recaptured by Attendance Tracking," *Computers in Personnel* 3 (Fall 1988): 15. Reproduced by permission.

**Exhibit 9.18** Report on Departmental Absences

Date: 03/21/90                                                                 Time: 14:25:35

```
                              XYZ Corporation
                           Classified--Confidential
                                  Report 3
                          Departmental Absence Summary
                             Division: 001 East Plant
                     Absence data from 01/01/90 to 12/31/90
```

| Department Name | Sick Hours | Personal Hours | Total Tardy Hours | Unexcused Hours | Disciplinary Hours | Employees in Department | Average Absence Hours |
|---|---|---|---|---|---|---|---|
| Accounting-111* | 184.00 | 36.00 | 5.25 | 8.00 | 233.25 | 6 | 38.875 |
| Warehouse | 500.00 | 50.00 | 25.25 | 75.50 | 650.75 | 25 | 26.030 |
| Manufacturing-Line 3 | 233.00 | 91.50 | 14.25 | 9.50 | 348.35 | 17 | 20.485 |

Average company absence hours:      31.05
Average divisional absence hours:   25.67

* = Department exceeds company and divisional averages

*Source:* Adapted from E. J. Drumm, "Stolen Moments Recaptured by Attendance Tracking," *Computers in Personnel* 3 (Fall 1988): 16. Reproduced by permission.

this computer-based attendance tracking is one positive way to control employee absenteeism costs.

Another way to attempt to control employee absences is through the third type of report, called analysis. This time and attendance application should be capable of computing statistical analyses to identify what types of employees—older or younger, male or female, short- or long-term, and, in particular, those protected by EEO regulations—have the most serious absence records, particularly unexcused. In short, these analysis reports should help the HR and line manager pinpoint the specific group or groups of employees in which absenteeism is a more serious problem. With this information, the reasons and possible solutions to the problem can be investigated.

# Performance Management Application 3: Discipline and Grievance

Discipline and grievance applications are established and used in ways similar to the time and attendance application. Although they are not covered in detail here, this is not meant to deemphasize their importance, since they are critical parts of the performance management subfunction.[8] However, discipline, grievance, time and attendance are frequently combined into a single application since they share common data elements and produce similar reports.[9] Naturally, data on disciplinary actions and grievances would have to be added to the time and attendance application to make them work together.

## *Reports*

Discipline and grievance applications produce reports similar to the ones in the time and attendance application—individual, unit, and analysis. Thus, a report on the disciplinary record of each individual employee can be obtained for any period of time. Likewise, the grievance procedure can be tracked and a record of all grievances filed by an individual employee can be kept. In terms of unit records, an example is given in Exhibit 9.19 that combines disciplinary information as well as attendance information for a single department. As you can see, this is a report on the accounting department (that was in trouble in Exhibit 9.18) at the East Plant from the dates of 01/01/90 to 12/31/90. This annual report shows two employees, G. Washington and J. Adams, who are in the disciplinary process (see the entries under the "disciplinary level" column). In addition, the information

**Exhibit 9.19** Department Report on Grievance and Attendance

Date: 03/21/90

XYZ Corporation

Time: 14.25.35

Classified--Confidential

Report 1

Departmental Attendance Summary

Division: 001 East Plant  Department: 111 Accounting

Absence Data from 01/01/90 to 12/31/90

| Employee Name | Sick Hours | Personal Hours | Total Tardy Hours | Unexcused Hours | Disciplinary Hours | Disciplinary Level | Date of Discipline |
|---|---|---|---|---|---|---|---|
| Washington, George | 64.00 | 8.00 | 1.50 | 0.00 | 73.50 | Probation | 01/12/90 |
| Adams, John | 53.00 | 4.00 | 2.25 | 8.00 | 67.25 | Written | 12/21/89 |
| -------Employees above this line should be in the disciplinary process------- | | | | | | | |
| Jefferson, Thomas | 31.00 | 8.00 | 1.00 | 0.00 | 40.00 | | |
| Madison, James | 24.00 | 4.00 | 0.50 | 0.00 | 28.50 | | |
| Monroe, James | 12.00 | 12.00 | 0.00 | 0.00 | 24.00 | | |
| Adams, John Quincy* | 0.00 | 0.00 | 0.00 | 0.00 | 0.00 | | |
| | | | | | 233.25 | | |

Average company absence hours:     31.05
Average divisional absence hours:  25.67
Average department 111 absence hours: 38.88**

\* = Employee has perfect attendance during time period
\*\* = Department exceeds company and divisional averages

*Source:* Adapted from E. J. Drumm, "Stolen Moments Recaptured by Attendance Tracking," *Computers in Personnel* 3 (Fall 1988): 16. Reproduced by permission.

288

at the bottom of this report provides comparisons to the company and the division as well as identifying one employee who has a perfect attendance record.

Finally, these applications should be capable of the same kinds of analysis reports as were discussed with the time and attendance application. These analysis reports are crucial diagnostic tools for management to uncover problems with employee behavior.

## Summary: Performance Management

In this section the importance of the management of the human resources of the firm has been discussed and demonstrated. The various applications have deliberately been linked together to emphasize our bias that they belong together, particularly in terms of providing tools for line managers in their daily supervisory responsibilities. The specific reports and uses of the applications are only the beginning. The interested reader should examine the Notes at the end of the chapter for more detailed information.

## Quality of Work Life

Quality of work life (QWL) is a general term that has come to refer to any program that leads to an improvement in working conditions. Various authors disagree on its exact definition.[10] In fact, the Work in America Institute, which has been the major proponent of QWL, identified eleven areas that were important for the 1980s.[11] These eleven areas appear to cover every major issue that has arisen in the workplace in the past decade. In spite of this disagreement about what comprises QWL, QWL programs will remain very important. In forecasting the five most important issues for human resources in the future, a panel from the American Society of Personnel Administration named two areas, work and family relationships and employer/employee rights and responsibilities, that fall within the mainstream of the QWL subfunction.[12]

Although QWL is a broadly defined subfunction, it has usually been identified with the following programs: (1) health and safety, (2) employee assistance, (3) child care, (4) quality circles, (5) flextime and job sharing, and (6) a variety of joint union-management programs. Programs in the QWL subfunction are aimed at maintaining and improving employee morale by attending to important and changing issues in the workplace that affect employees' well-being.

## QWL Applications

Because this is an emerging and ever-changing subfunction, it is not easy to identify specific applications. If this area is defined broadly, applications in organization development and survey processing clearly belong. If it is defined more narrowly, the only applications are in the safety and health area. Using these varying definitions, a number of applications are listed in Exhibit 9.20. Some of these applications are available commercially, while others are ones that are necessary in this subfunction. The reference at the

### Exhibit 9.20   HRIS Applications in QWL

*Health and Safety*   This is an important area because of the necessity to comply with the Occupational Safety and Health Act (OSHA). It is also important since safety is critical to a quality work environment. This application can provide reports to individual employees on the history of exposure to toxic materials as well as unit and total company reports for health and safety hazards for both government and management use.*

*Employee Assistance Programs*   This application should maintain confidential records on employees who are involved with EAP programs. It can also generate information for employees about the availability of programs within the firm as well as other community resources.

*Family-Work Integration*   This application could handle any program that attempts to resolve the conflicts that arise between family and work responsibilities. This could include day care and job-sharing programs as well as flextime. The application could coordinate schedules of employees wishing to be involved in such programs to maximize their use. It could also provide information on the programs to employees. And, finally, it could produce reports for management showing the utilization of these programs.

*Survey Processing*   This application generates, distributes, inputs, analyzes, and reports on employee attitude surveys. It can be either mainframe- or microcomputer-based. It is capable of generating a variety of reports for management action planning as well as individual reports for employees.*

*Organization Development*   This application helps in the joint management-employee process of planned change. It usually involves survey feedback and focuses on individual and group (team building) changes. It can provide individual, group, or company profiles of attitudes to be used in organizational change programs.*

---

* See R. Frantzreb, *The Personnel Software Census* (Roseville, CA: Advanced Personnel Systems, 1988).

bottom of Exhibit 9.20 is a good source to check if you are interested in any of the commercially available applications.

Of all the applications in Exhibit 9.20, the most well developed are the attitude survey processing ones. This is interesting, since it would appear that employee attitude surveys should be at the heart of any QWL program. Results from these surveys can be used to identify areas in which QWL programs should be investigated and started as well as to evaluate how well the QWL programs are working. Attitude surveys have been central to most of the work in planned or organizational change, particularly in conjunction with the action-research model discussed in Chapter 7. Of course, the history of computer-based attitude surveys, or survey-based feedback, is lengthy. Most of the early applications were, of course, mainframe-based and stand-alone systems. Today, there are a large number of microcomputer applications, even some that allow the employees to enter their responses to attitude questions interactively.

Since the literature on attitude surveys and survey-guided feedback in organizational change is voluminous, specific reports are not covered in this chapter.[13] Further, since the QWL subfunction is still emerging and being defined, no other specific applications are examined in detail. Remember, though, that this is currently a very important area and it will remain so in the future.

## Summary

This chapter has been a continuation of Chapter 8. Three more subfunctions—compensation and benefits, performance management, and quality of work life (QWL)—were covered. The applications in compensation and performance management show the value of having an HRIS, both for the individual employee and management. In fact, acquiring and using an HRIS may be a positive QWL change.

## Discussion Questions

1. What kinds of reports from the compensation management application would be of interest to line managers? Why?
2. Why might the annual benefits report for each employee be designed as a turnaround document for employees to sign and return?

3. Describe in broad outlines one way compensation data, both wages and benefits, could be used in a DSS for future planning and staffing levels.

4. Using the information for each application in the performance management sub-function, specify an ad hoc report you would want as an HR professional. Now, do the same assuming you are a line manager.

5. How would you create a new report that examined the linkages between individual performance appraisal, attendance, and disciplinary actions?

6. What do you consider the most important emerging area in QWL that needs an HRIS application? Why?

7. Describe how a manager could use reports from both the QWL and performance management subfunctions to improve employee morale. Do the same assuming you are an HR professional.

# Notes

1. R. Frantzreb, *The Personnel Software Census* (Roseville, CA: Advanced Personnel Systems, 1988).

2. For more information on compensation and benefits, see R. M. McCaffery, *Employee Benefit Programs: A Total Compensation Perspective* (Boston: PWS-KENT, 1988), 250; M. J. Wallace and C. H. Fay, *Compensation Theory and Practice* (Boston: PWS-KENT, 1988), 423; R. Henderson, *Compensation Management*, 5th ed. (Englewood Cliffs, NJ: Prentice-Hall, 1989), 578; G. T. Milkovich and J. M. Newman, *Compensation*, 2nd ed. (Planto, TX: Business Publications, 1987), 655; D. W. Belcher and T. J. Atchison, *Compensation Administration*, 2nd ed. (Englewood Cliffs, NJ: Prentice-Hall, 1987), 464.

3. For complete treatments of this topic, see H. J. Bernardin and R. W. Beatty, *Performance Appraisal: Assessing Human Behavior at Work* (Boston: PWS-KENT, 1984); M. J. Kavanagh, "Evaluating Performance," in K. M. Rowland and G. R. Ferris, eds., *Personnel Management* (Boston: Allyn and Bacon, 1982); M. J. Kavanagh, W. C. Borman, J. W. Hedge, and R. B. Gould, *Job Performance Measurement in the Military: A Classification Scheme, Literature Review, and Directions for Research* (Brooks Air Force Base, TX: AFHRL-TR-87-15, Air Force Human Resources Laboratory, 1987).

4. For example, see J. S. Kane, "Measure for Measure in Performance Appraisal," *Computers in Personnel* 2 (Fall 1987): 31–39; D. C. Martin, "Automated Appraisals," *Computers in Personnel* 1 (Winter 1987): 30–34; T. Cannon, J. Debenham, and G. Smith, "Developing a Computer-Assisted Evaluation System," *Personnel Administrator* 28 (September 1983): 43–47.

5. For a review of unit productivity criteria and demonstration of a new method for its measurement, see R. D. Pritchard, S. D. Jones, P. L. Roth, K. K. Stuebing, and S. E. Ekeberg, "Effects of Group Feedback, Goal Setting, and Incentives on Organizational Productivity," *Journal of Applied Psychology Monograph* 73 (1988): 337–358.

6. Kane, "Measure for Measure."

7. For costing absenteeism, see W. F. Cascio, *Costing Human Resources: The Financial Impact of Behavior in Organizations*, 2nd ed. (Boston: PWS-KENT, 1987). For computer-based attendance tracking, see E. J. Drumm, "Stolen Moments Recaptured by Attendance Tracking," *Computers in Personnel* 3 (Fall 1988): 14–17.

8. For a good discussion of these areas, particularly in terms of their costs to the firm, see W. F. Cascio, *Managing Human Resources: Productivity, Quality of Work Life, Profits*, 2nd ed. (New York: McGraw-Hill 1989).

9. D. W. Myers, "Comshare's Profiles/PC," *Personnel Administrator* 32 (May 1987): 87–89.

10. For varying ideas on QWL, see W. F. Cascio, *Managing Human Resources*, or V. G. Scarpello and J. Ledvinka, *Personnel/Human Resource Management: Environment and Functions* (Boston: PWS-KENT, 1988).

11. J. M. Rosow, "QWL Issues for the 1980s," *Training and Development Journal* 35 (1981): 33–52.

12. C. D. Bower and J. J. Hallet, "Issues Management at ASPA," *Personnel Administrator* 34 (January 1989): 40–43.

# 10

# Applications III—
# Payroll Systems
# and HRISs

$\mathbf{P}$ ayroll systems exist in every company. For the most part, they only receive attention when something goes wrong (e.g., when the checks are late). In the past, payroll has often been viewed as an unglamorous area filled with "bean counters" and financial control staff. Today, however, payroll is becoming a much more visible function in the organization. As discussed in Chapter 3, new legislation and changing demands for compensation and benefits options have brought payroll out of the back room and into the realm of corporate strategy and planning. In Chapter 9, a variety of compensation and benefits applications were discussed. This chapter examines potentially the most complicated HRIS application—payroll.

First, the development of payroll systems is reviewed and the reasons why payroll and HRIS are often separate functions are discussed. Second, the functions of a payroll system are examined to provide a review of the payroll process. The third section deals with the differing objectives and work demands of payroll and human resources departments. Fourth, the ways in which payroll systems and HRISs are linked are covered. Finally, some of the key design issues in evaluating payroll/HRIS packages are discussed.

## The Evolution of Payroll Systems

Traditionally, payroll systems and HRISs have not been integrated. That is, if both systems existed, they were usually completely independent. Today, only approximately 30 percent of organizations use combined HRIS/payroll systems.[1] This separation occurred for a variety of reasons, including the timing of systems development, the nature of work demands on each system, and differing ownership within the organization. These issues are discussed below.

As noted in Chapter 1, payroll was one of the first business functions to be automated. Payroll tasks were cyclical, repetitive, dealt mostly with numerical data, and could be completely described in a computer program. Early commercial computers were designed for just such structured tasks. Gathering payroll information, computing pay amount, and issuing checks were jobs that fit with batch-oriented computers. Computer time was limited and expensive and "canned" software programs were available. The processing was standardized, transaction oriented, and fit well with the capabilities of early mainframe computers. Payroll processing was a visible area where cost savings were fairly easy to document, which helped justify the purchase of early mainframe computer systems.

Most medium to large businesses have used an automated payroll system since the 1950s. Since the payroll process was viewed largely as a financial processing task impacting the firm's general ledger, ownership of payroll fell to the organization's financial control function. Other than deducting taxes and a few benefit charges, the demands on the system were limited. Federal regulations were few, payroll was done the same way each pay period, and the only reports required of the system were financial. As discussed in Chapter 1, the human resources department dealt mainly with employee relations at this time. Thus, payroll and HR usually had an arm's-length relationship and interacted only when a pay rate for an employee changed or someone was fired or hired.

In the late 1960s and early 1970s a new information system was introduced into organizations—the HRIS. HRISs developed as a response to new and proposed federal legislation (e.g., Civil Rights Act of 1964, EEO laws) as well as a recognition by organizations that improved management of employee information could lead to increased organizational efficiency. Unlike payroll systems, the type of information kept in HRISs was mostly text. HRISs were primarily concerned with generating compliance reports, facilitating ad hoc inquiries, and enhancing managerial decision making. Although 10 to 20 percent information overlap between the systems was common (e.g., name, address, Social Security number, benefit codes), the systems were independent. Payroll systems and HRISs had little need to communicate.

Today, the trend is toward integrating payroll/HRIS. This is particularly true for companies adopting computer-based systems for the first time. At a minimum, the HRIS and payroll system must interact closely. They must share data, use common inputs, and interface with external systems (e.g., benefits vendors, general ledger). In order to comply with state and federal laws and manage compensation and benefits, information must be extracted and matched from both systems. For example, to process health benefits, information on the employee, his or her insurance elections, number and age of dependents, and so on may need to be output from the HRIS to the payroll system to accurately calculate deductions. More and more, payroll systems and HRISs are being merged into a common system. Later in this chapter the ways in which payroll and HRIS can be linked or integrated and the advantages and disadvantages of tying payroll and HRIS together are discussed.

The increased complexity of payroll administration, systems, and legal requirements has given rise to demands for greater degrees of training for the payroll personnel. A professional organization, the American Payroll Association, provides a series of seminars leading to certification as a payroll specialist. The association also sponsors conferences and publishes educational materials of interest to professionals in the payroll area. Readers wishing more information on payroll administration may wish to contact this organization.[2]

## The Payroll Process

To organizations, the payroll function is an integral component of business operations. It provides information on the cost of personnel in the production of goods or services.

Payroll processing and management has several functions in the organization:

Ensuring the timely payment of employees

Providing appropriate financial controls over the largest single organizational expense (i.e., personnel costs)

Complying with state and federal regulations

Making accurate deductions of shared-cost benefits [e.g., 401(k) plans, health insurance]

Providing accurate data to the general ledger of the firm

Documenting payroll deductions for tax purposes

Generating reports necessary to the efficient operation of the organization

To most employees, "payroll" means receiving a check. They do not realize the effort and processing necessary to ensure that checks are correct and issued on time. They view the process as a fairly simple one:

Count up my hours

Multiply by my hourly rate

Take out the taxes

Cut a check

As all payroll managers know, it is not that simple. Exhibit 10.1 illustrates a generic payroll process. Several tasks or activities that occur at each stage of the process are described on the following pages.

**Exhibit 10.1**  The Payroll Cycle

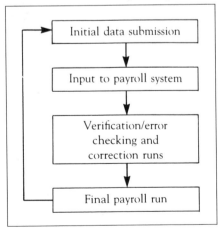

## Initial Data Submission

This phase begins the payroll process. Most of the payroll documents (i.e., time cards, sales reports, overtime and premium time forms) for payroll processing are submitted at this time. This information typically includes the type and number of hours worked by each employee, employee change information (e.g., salary changes, benefit changes, separations, hires), commission information, and corrections from the last pay period. Data are submitted in written or electronic form to the payroll office. In larger organizations, information may be collected at a variety of locations and transmitted to the central data processing center for processing. For example, one regional bank with branches from Maine to Alaska collects individual payroll information at each branch and submits it to regional DP centers, which then transmit payroll data by satellite to the central DP facility in Maine. At the end of the payroll process, the Maine center transmits payroll amounts and deductions to the regional sites, which cut the checks and send them to individual branches for distribution.

## Input to the Payroll System

Payroll data are usually input by payroll staff. In some organizations this process is automated (e.g., a machine reads the time cards and transfers the information to the payroll system). If paper records are used for input, they are now archived, microfilmed, or in some other way stored for later reference.

The system is also updated with new or corrected reference information. This could include updated benefit cost tables, revised tax tables, or new pay rate schedules. The payroll system will need to interface with systems and modules that may include the general ledger, external benefits suppliers, the compensation module, a flexible benefits package (if used), an incentive compensation data base, profit-sharing information, and so on. Preliminary error checking is also done at this time. This often takes the form of rule-based input qualification. For example, the system might indicate an error if the number of premium hours reported exceeds the number available.

## Verification/Error Checking and Correction Runs

In this step, initial payroll processing occurs and the output received is examined for accuracy. This checking is done by payroll staff. Errors are identified by comparing payroll output to historical records and normative data by the rules established in the system. For example, any very large changes in gross pay for an employee as compared with the prior pay period would be checked for correctness. Corrections are made through verifications of input documents or contacts with line departments. Corrected data are input to the system and a new batch run is completed. This process continues until the payroll is reasonably correct. That is, all major errors have been eliminated and the payroll manager is ready to "sign-off" on the payroll run. It typically takes several cycles to reach an acceptable payroll run.

### Final Payroll Run

The last step in the payroll cycle is the final payroll run. This run results in the generation of checks or electronic transfers, the transfer of final data to the general ledger, the creation of reports, and updates to external systems (e.g., benefits vendors). At this time it may also be necessary to issue a small number of manually authorized checks if late information is received or serious errors are identified (e.g., the profit-sharing bonus is missing from the CEO's check).

Problems or errors in this run are noted so that corrective action may be taken in the next cycle. At the conclusion of this step the process starts again for the next payroll period.

### Other Cyclic Payroll Processes

Whether payroll is done weekly, biweekly, semimonthly, or monthly, additional processing activities must be done on a regular basis. These vary by organization but include activities such as generating quarterly income and deduction summarizations for tax purposes, quarterly benefit deduction reconciliations with vendor systems, yearly summaries for payroll to budget, variance reports for individual units (e.g., hours paid to budgeted hours), and W-2 forms. Timeliness and accuracy are critical for these reports, especially those that are tax-related. Late or incorrect reports to state or federal agencies can lead to substantial penalties.

## Payroll Versus Human Resources: Differing Perspectives

When considering a new payroll system or combined HRIS/payroll, the questions of where payroll belongs often arises. That is, Is payroll an accounting or a human resources subfunction? Traditionally, payroll has been viewed as an accounting activity, usually reporting to the controller of the organization. A recent survey of payroll administrators indicated that 81 percent of payroll groups reported to the financial function of the organization, 15 percent reported to HR, and the remainder reported elsewhere.[3]

No matter where payroll resides in the organization, it is important to keep in mind the differing perspectives of payroll and HR groups. These differences in viewpoint will impact the working relationship of payroll and HR staffs as well as the manner in which the payroll system and HRIS are interfaced. In addition, these differences are likely to influence the selection of new systems and may determine if an integrated HRIS/payroll system is feasible in the organization.

Payroll is a control-oriented function—it is concerned with monitoring and controlling the "people costs" in the organization. Thus, payroll is concerned with verification of hours worked, accuracy of tax calculations and other deductions, monitoring of payroll budgets, authenticity of requests for pay changes, timely filing of state and federal reports, and monitoring of compliance with company policies concerning pay and benefits. Work is done according to a rigid schedule. Consistency is desirable, efficiency is high, and changes in operating procedures are uncommon. Payroll departments are held accountable for timely, low-cost, and accurate performance.

Human resources is primarily a service-oriented function. HR groups often develop client relationships with line management and provide a variety of services ranging from employee recruiting to outplacement services. The goal of the HR group is to enhance organizational effectiveness through programs designed to attract, train, and retain qualified employees. HR groups deal as much with exceptions as they do regular tasks. While some tasks are cyclic (e.g., monthly head count reports), many activities are conducted on demand (e.g., recruiting, compensation surveys, ad hoc reports on individuals or groups of employees). Change is constant. Few activities are done the same way, on the same time schedule, and with the same priority year after year.

Payroll and HR groups approach work differently, with somewhat inconsistent objectives, methods of operation, and goals. The information systems they use reflect these differences. Consequently, when organizations consider combining HRIS and payroll systems it is often difficult to develop or purchase a system that both groups find acceptable. Vendors tend to offer systems that are primarily either payroll or HRIS oriented, but "also" support the other function. This often results in payroll and HR groups favoring different systems. Each tends to focus on those systems designed primarily on its function. Fortunately, more true hybrid or integrated HRIS/payroll systems are being developed.

The evolution in technology, together with increased information demands, is leading both groups to begin working together more closely. The following section presents an overview of the types of payroll systems and how they work with the HRIS.

# Payroll Systems and the HRIS Link

Payroll systems and HRISs can be linked in a variety of ways. The options range from maintaining completely independent systems that do not interact or share data to fully integrated systems utilizing a common data base and query language. Payroll or payroll/HRISs can be grouped into four types: (1) service bureau–based systems, (2) independent systems, (3) interfaced systems, and (4) integrated systems. Each approach has advantages and disadvantages for the organization. Each option may be the "best" solution for a given organization. Determining the best solution will depend on a thorough needs analysis as described in Chapter 5.

## *Service Bureau–Based Systems*

Many corporations do not process their own payroll. Rather, they contract with independent service organizations specializing in payroll processing. Approximately 35 percent of organizations use this approach.[4] The payroll service bureau receives basic payroll information from the organization and completes all the processing. The client organization receives the checks for distribution, reports, and a bill for the service bureau's work.

In terms of the HRIS link, service bureau–based systems usually operate independently from the organization's information systems. However, the bureau may be able to exchange data with the organization's HRIS. Whether this is feasible depends on the specific systems used by each organization. The service bureau may also provide basic HRIS services, since a number of data elements included in the payroll system (e.g., salary history data, job code, work location, name and address) have HRIS uses. This may be accomplished through written requests to the service bureau or by a terminal at the organization linked to the vendor's system. Service bureaus produce a number of standard HR reports, but these are not typically customized to the needs of each subscribing firm.

There are several advantages of service bureau–based systems:

The cost and maintenance of software (and potentially hardware) is avoided. Start-up costs are also low.

The service bureau usually provides technical support in designing the payroll system and may be able to devise a more efficient paper flow for the organization.

Additional staff is unnecessary. If payroll had previously been done in-house, staff may be reduced.

Service bureau–based systems may do a better job complying with the myriad of state and federal laws than in-house systems. Since payroll is their primary business, they can devote the resources to ensuring that the system is up-to-date.

Cost per check issued is usually fixed, and more accurate budgeting is possible. Service bureaus typically charge about $2.00 per paycheck issued.

Additional applications packages are often available from the service bureau.

Service bureaus often provide backup facilities in the event of a catastrophic event (e.g., fire, flood).

The disadvantages of service bureaus include the following:

The organization has less control over payroll data. Security becomes a concern since the data are physically at another organization's facility.

If HRIS services are available from the bureau, variable costs can be difficult to control. That is, each request for a report incurs a charge. "Interesting" reports can often exhaust the payroll budget.

Standard HRIS reports produced by the service are not tied to the specific needs of the organization and are consequently not of great utility. Since HRIS reports are a low priority for the service, their timeliness and accuracy are often poor. This typically results in low satisfaction with the HRIS capabilities of the system.

The HRIS services provided are usually limited. HRIS is a sideline for these firms and is often not well supported. Remember, their systems are payroll-oriented, stressing efficiency, accounting, and cyclic operations—not flexibility, ad hoc inquiry, and what-if analyses.

Turnaround time on HRIS-type inquiries may be slow, especially if the request is made during a high payroll demand period (e.g., near the end of a biweekly payroll period or the end of a quarter).

If the organization has an HRIS, the feasibility of interfacing the in-house system with the service bureau may be low. This is especially true if different hardware and operating systems are used by each system. Because of security and operational reasons, some bureaus may not be receptive to the company's HRIS tying into the payroll data base.

## Independent Systems

Another option for linking payroll and HRIS is not to link them. In most companies (70 percent), this is the current state of affairs. Typically the payroll system is older, mainframe-based, reports to the accounting/controller department, and has been in place and operating satisfactorily for a number of years. The HRIS system, on the other hand, is probably recent, may be microcomputer-based, and is located in the HR function. While a few reports may be traded back and forth, the systems are completely independent. Since the old adage of "don't fix it if it isn't broken" applies, many companies deliberately keep payroll independent when adding an HRIS.

Although there is a trend toward greater integration of payroll and the HRIS, a case may be made for retaining separate systems in some situations. Maintaining separate systems may be the best option when the following conditions exist:

Budget does not allow purchase or conversion to an integrated system. Limited resources may be better spent purchasing either a sophisticated HRIS or an improved payroll system.

It is unlikely that the HR and payroll departments will be able to agree on a single package.

The payroll system is operating efficiently and is able to support changes in tax regulations and benefits.

The payroll system is user friendly when it comes to generating reports and providing output to the HR group.

The organization wishes to separate payroll from HR and the HRIS for financial control or security reasons.

## Interfaced Systems

Interfaced systems are those that provide a regular link between the systems. This is usually a specific electronic link or interface that allows some data to flow between the separate systems. Such an interface allows inquiries and reports to be generated that may not be possible using either system alone. The systems are still separate, using independent data bases and potentially different computer and operating systems.

Some of the advantages of interfaced systems include the following:

Data redundancy may be reduced. For example, home and work addresses need to be kept only in one file in one system.

Existing systems (either payroll or HRIS) may be retained and interfaced with the new package. This is not an option in all circumstances due to differences in technology, operating systems, or software. However, where feasible, this option can result in significant cost savings.

Security of payroll data can be maintained since the HRIS and payroll system are separate.

Ownership of each system can reside with the group most concerned with its "care and feeding."

Interfaced systems have several disadvantages:

Data integrity can become a problem if care is not taken to ensure that the same field names, data definitions, and data maintenance proce-dures are used in both systems. Guidelines need to be established to ensure that any editing or changes to the data are known by each system. One method of enhancing data integrity is to run a regular batch update of one system based on the information in the other system.

The systems typically interface only in a few areas (e.g., benefits elections). Consequently the interfaced system may not be able to support a broad range of reports that require data from both systems.

Users who need to use data and information from both systems will need to learn two systems, increasing training costs.

A separate software package may be required to facilitate the transfer of information between the payroll system and the HRIS. This inter-facing software is a third package to be purchased and maintained. There are now two links: (1) HRIS to interface software, and (2) interface software to payroll. This makes total systems management more complicated and potentially more costly. When communica-tion glitches occur in the transfer of data, it is more difficult to diagnose the problem since three software packages are involved.

The organization is still supporting and maintaining two or three systems. When problems occur between the systems, it typically falls to the organization rather than the vendors to resolve the problem.

## Integrated Systems

Integrated systems incorporate both payroll and HRIS functions in a sin-gle system. These products most commonly rely on a relational data base to support both payroll and HRIS activities. Since they serve two major functions, these systems are very sophisticated and complex.

The advantages of integrated systems include the following:

Streamlining of functions is possible. HR and payroll may be combined, potentially resulting in staff reductions.

Cost savings can be realized since only one software package needs to be purchased and maintained.

Data quality and integrity can be improved since all input is into one system. There is only one set of procedures, one definition, and one interpretation of a data item.

Communication between the HR and payroll departments is enhanced since a common system is in use. There may be possibilities for cross-training HR and payroll personnel.

Both functional areas are better able to respond to ad hoc requests for information and to develop more sophisticated applications.

The combined data base allows quicker response to changes in legal requirements. For example, benefits discrimination testing requires information traditionally kept partially in the HRIS and partially in the payroll system. An integrated system is best able to respond to new and unique requests for information and reports.

The disadvantages of integrated systems include the following:

Combining systems may lead to friction between groups who have traditionally operated independently. As previously noted, HR and payroll departments operate differently and have differing objectives. This friction may be short term. However, the project team selecting and implementing the system should be aware of these potential problems and seek to remedy them.

Implementation can take longer and be more involved since two major systems are involved.

The overall risk involved in the system selection is greater. If a poor decision is made, its impact will be felt throughout the organization.

Security concerns can be greater since payroll and employee data are in one system. Maintaining system security and catastrophe planning (e.g., developing contingency plans so that operations may continue after a major system failure such as fire, flood, etc.) become absolutely critical.

Vendor support can be a problem if the vendor is primarily either a payroll or an HRIS company. The vendor may provide only limited expertise and support in the other area.

The trend in companies is clearly toward integrated systems. As reporting requirements grow and organizations seek to streamline operations, more integrated systems will be implemented. Many payroll systems, designed in a less demanding business and regulatory environment, will be unable to meet the information needs of organizations in the 1990s. A recent report indicated that 64 percent of the companies surveyed had undertaken major changes or revisions in their payroll system in the past three years.[5] As organizations update and upgrade systems, HR and payroll groups are becoming more closely associated than ever before.

The next section examines the key feature and design considerations in purchasing or designing an integrated payroll/HRIS.

## Key Features and Design Considerations in HRIS/Payroll Systems

Selecting a payroll or HRIS/payroll system is a critical undertaking for any organization. As with HRISs, a needs analysis is the first step in the process. The techniques and procedures covered in Chapters 5 and 6 apply to the selection and design of payroll as well as integrated HRIS/payroll systems.

There are, however, a number of key features essential to the success of a payroll or integrated system that deserve specific attention.

## Information Security

Security is an important issue for HRISs; it is a *critical* issue for payroll systems. Security in this context is more than ensuring that information is kept confidential. It also includes the physical safety of the system. Provisions need to be made for backing up and archiving payroll data off-site and providing alternative processing capacity. Security management is an ongoing task, as new threats to information systems continue to develop. An example will make this clear.

Recently a major organization suffered the loss of all of its payroll records. It seems that a disgruntled employee with access to the payroll system became suspicious that he was going to be fired. In order to retaliate against his employer, he planted a computer virus in the system. Several days after leaving the company, all 120,000 payroll records mysteriously disappeared. Although the former employee was caught, fined, and sent to prison, the organization was left with a serious problem. Not only were employees inconvenienced by late paychecks, but an enormous amount of manual labor had to be done to reconstruct the payroll history of all employees in order to comply with tax-reporting regulations. Many organizations appoint a security director for the system. This individual is charged with developing security procedures, monitoring compliance with those procedures, and developing techniques to counter new threats as they develop.

## Interfaces with Other Systems

As with the HRIS, the payroll system is required to interface with a variety of other systems, both internal and external to the organization. The needs analysis for a payroll system must pay specific attention to the interface or communication requirements of these other systems. Questions dealing with system interfaces should be a formal part of the needs analysis. These questions should address the technical aspects of interfacing with each additional system:

What type of operating system does the system use?

Does the system use a specific package to facilitate communication or interchange of data? If so, does that package have any specific format or operational requirements the project team should know about?

Are there any major changes, revisions, or enhancements planned in the system you are planning to interface with? When? If there are, how will that impact the interface? Would a new interface be delayed? Will the new or revised system work differently?

Does the system have the capacity (e.g., storage, processing time available) to work with the proposed payroll/HRIS? If the system is currently overloaded, interfacing may not be feasible.

How often and in what volume will the systems need to transfer information? Will a hard-wire connection be required? Is enough storage (temporary or otherwise) available to accommodate the transfers?

The potential interfaces with the payroll system include the following:

*HRIS.* Whether independent, interfaced, or integrated, the payroll system will need to communicate with the HRIS in some way. As previously discussed, this can range from a paper output to a fully integrated system.

*Pension and retirement accounting.* The system should work with the various retirement and/or savings plans of the organization. Most retirement plans are based on hours worked or amount earned and must get this information from the payroll system. For example, most employers credit an employee with a year toward pension vesting based on a certain number of hours (usually a minimum of 1,000) being completed in a one-year period. This information is typically drawn from the payroll system. In addition, some pension and retirement systems are managed by external vendors (e.g., insurance companies), and the payroll system must interface their system(s).

*External benefits vendors.* Organizations purchase benefits ranging from health insurance to day care from outside vendors. For example, a medical insurance carrier may wish to interface with the payroll data base to determine the coverage option chosen, verify copayment amounts, verify coverage status, and so on.

*Financial institutions.* Payroll systems are required to handle electronic transfers to various financial institutions. For example, many employers offer direct deposit of employee checks. In addition, the system may need to provide transfers to federal, state, and local taxing agencies. The system may also be required to support payroll account balancing.

*General ledger.* The general ledger interface will be of key interest to the financial control staff of the organization. Overall, this is probably the most important interface. Any new system must be examined for fit with the organization's general ledger and other financial information systems.

*Information input systems.* Data will be input into the system in one or more ways. This may include keyed input, input transferred from another system, automated input, or input from some other source. The payroll system may need to accommodate input from a variety of sources.

The quality and ease of use of various interfaces is very important to the overall success of the system. Unfortunately, many vendors claim the ability to interface effectively with other systems but are often unable to deliver a usable link. Too often the user is left in the middle, with each software vendor (the payroll vendor and vendor of the other system) blaming the other for the inability of the systems to work together. If you are told that a particular system will interface with another, demand proof. If the systems do not work together in a sales demonstration, they probably will not work any better on the job. Ask for a list of users of interfaced systems and verify the vendor's claims with them.

## Design Features Unique to Payroll Systems

A number of design issues do not fit neatly into design categories. These issues are critical to the success of payroll or payroll/HRIS and deserve mention. The following list presents some of these questions:

How flexible is the payroll system in dealing with new regulations? Changes in the tax code? Who will be responsible for updating the system to meet these changes? According to a recent survey, the number-one concern of payroll managers was tax law changes and their system's ability to comply with them.[6] For example, a 1988 change in the New York State (NYS) tax code caused serious problems for many businesses. Until 1988, the number of exemptions an employee claimed for tax calculation purposes was the same for state and federal taxes. Beginning in 1988, NYS allows one *less* exemption than the federal government. This change caused enormous difficulties for payroll managers, because most systems were designed to accommodate only one exemption field. Systems must now track exemptions differentially based on the state in which the employee works and modify calculations accordingly. In one tax law change, NYS made thousands of payroll systems obsolete.

What does it cost to issue a payroll check? Costs typically range from $1.00 to $5.00 per check, with the average approximately $2.35 per check.

How many employees can the system handle with reasonable speed and turnaround time?

Can the system deal with any unique payroll problems that your organization has? For example, can it pay contract labor? Commission sales personnel? Temporary employees?

Does the vendor provide updates to tax tables? For all states? What about foreign tax compliance? Expatriate compensation?

If a service bureau–based system is contemplated, how will your organization communicate with the service bureau? On-site terminals? Paper only?

If your organization supports a flex-benefits system, can the new system accommodate it? How easily can changes in the benefits options be accommodated by the system? Can in-house staff make such changes or will programming by the vendor be required?

Will the new system meet the requirements of the financial group in the organization? Of the internal and/or external auditors? Will they be willing to sign off on reports generated by the system? Does it provide an adequate audit trail? Are any built-in computations in compliance with GAAP (Generally Accepted Accounting Principles) standards? Who will make sure that changes in GAAP are updated in the system?

How much customization will the vendor package require to fit the requirements of the organization? Even though payroll processing is a fairly well defined task and similar across organizations, approximately 80 percent of all packages require some degree of customization.[7]

## Summary

Today, payroll systems and HRISs are more closely related than ever. Many organizations have learned that these systems must share data in order to deal with increasing information and reporting demands. In this chapter payroll systems and their relationship to HRISs were examined. First, the evolution of payroll systems was reviewed. Second, the payroll cycle was discussed to provide a context for discussing payroll systems. Third, the ways in which HRISs and payroll systems can be linked were covered. Finally, critical design issues for payroll and combined payroll/HRIS were reviewed.

## Discussion Questions

1. Describe the payroll process. What steps are usually included? What are the key tasks in each step?
2. How do payroll and human resources departments differ in terms of orientation and mission?
3. Describe the advantages and disadvantages of service bureau–based systems, independent systems, interfaced systems, and integrated systems.
4. What types of other systems are payroll systems typically interfaced with?
5. How would the needs analysis differ between one targeted at selecting an HRIS and one targeted at selecting a combined system?
6. How are financially oriented staff of the organization likely to view the payroll/ HRIS? What would they be likely to emphasize in selecting a system?

## Notes

1. B. Rumac, L. Holter, and S. Livacz. *A Summary Report on an Executive Survey of Payroll and Human Resource Issues* (Roseland, NJ: Automatic Data Processing, 1988), 41.
2. The American Payroll Association, P.O. Box 2344, Grand Central Station, New York, NY 10163. (212)661-9145.
3. D. J. Salam and L. K. Price. *Principles of Payroll Administration* (Paramus, NJ: Prentice-Hall Information Services, 1988), 2051.
4. Rumac, Holter, and Livacz, *A Summary Report.*
5. Ibid.
6. Ibid.
7. G. Berleth, K. Reilly, and D. Risteau. *The American Payroll Association's 1988 Basic Guide to Payroll* (Englewood Cliffs, NJ: Prentice-Hall Professional Newsletters, 1988), 350.

# IV
## Future of HRISs

# 11

# Future Directions

The field of human resource management is rapidly changing and will continue to change in the future. As noted in Chapter 3, the human resources management (HRM) system, of which the HRIS is a part, is extremely sensitive to influence from the external environment. Evolving business demands, increasing regulation, changing labor demographics, and an increasingly competitive marketplace all influence the HR department.[1] Advancing technology both fosters and supports this change. In this chapter, how HRISs will both influence and be influenced by the future environment is examined. Some ongoing trends are highlighted and some speculations on what may happen in the future are offered.

## Perspective: The Systems Model of Organizational Functioning

Before speculating about future changes, a perspective for this chapter must be established. To do this, refer to Exhibit 1.4—the systems model of organizational functioning. A few features of this model reflect our perspective.

First, the organization operates within a changing external environment. Second, the strategic management system must respond to changes in the environment to enable the organization to attain its goals. Third, the strategic management system interacts with the HRM system. While the HRM system often responds to company strategy, it can and should influence company strategy in some cases. Fourth, the HRIS is part of the larger HRM system and interacts with all the other HR subfunctions. Together, these elements contribute to the success of the organization, with goal attainment (or lack thereof) serving as a feedback mechanism to company management.

When the organization is considered within this systems model, several points become clear. It is the role of the HRM system to support and occasionally guide company strategy. This contributes to organizational success. An effective HRIS can be a valuable resource for managing the HR function and can allow the HR department to better serve its clients. And as changes occur in the environment, the business strategy, or the HRM system, the HRIS must respond if it is to continue to be a valuable tool. The HRIS does not manage either the business or the HR function—people do. This is the perspective that guides our contemplation of the future.

Given this perspective, some of the expected changes that are likely to involve the HRIS are discussed. Specifically, changes in technology, HR practice, the skill requirements and career patterns of HR personnel, and organization and structure are examined. The applied research that is needed to support these changes in the HRIS field is also considered.

Predicting the future is always tricky. It is not the point of this chapter to try to provide a comprehensive view of the future of human resources. Rather, the chapter offers a taste of the possibilities. Only time will tell which predictions are hits and which are misses.

## Technology

Technological changes are discussed first because they will influence or even make possible some of the other changes.

According to our definition, an HRIS is not simply a computer system. It also incorporates an extensive human element. The role of people has been emphasized throughout this book. However, HRISs are to a certain extent technology bound. Although user needs or demands can ultimately influence technological advances, HRISs are in many ways a reflection of the existing technology. Changes in computer hardware, software, user interfaces, and communication links will influence the capabilities of future HRISs.

## Hardware

Computing power, speed, and storage capacity have been increasing both absolutely and relative to cost. The capabilities of yesterday's mainframe computer are rivaled by today's **laptop microcomputer.** The physical space needed to maintain personnel data bases has continued to decline. Organizations are starting to use microcomputers and minicomputers more extensively than in the past. The distinction between mainframes, minis, and micros is blurring. Computer hardware should continue to improve, becoming more powerful at lower costs.

The continuing improvements in computer hardware will allow for changes in HRIS capabilities and organizational strategies. Increased computing speed and power will allow more complex HRIS applications, including more sophisticated decision support systems (DSSs). Improved microcomputing capabilities will allow organizations to pursue a decentralized information strategy if they want to. And smaller businesses that previously could not afford a system are starting to find the technology within their reach. These issues are addressed further later in the chapter. The key point here is that hardware improvements will at least allow for, if not require, changes in the HRM and strategic management systems.

## Software

HRIS software also continues to improve. HRIS software vendors are responding to user needs and gradually improving their products. Data base management software and spreadsheet packages have become easier to use, allowing HR functional specialists to develop some of their own applications. Data base management systems are becoming more powerful (e.g., they have greater relational capabilities), allowing for a greater integration of information. These trends will continue.

Two software applications that may become a part of HR's future are expert systems and desktop publishing. These are discussed briefly below and on the following pages.

**Expert Systems**    In the future more sophisticated software applications will be used. DSSs will become more common and *expert systems* may be applied to HRM problems. Expert systems incorporate the reasoning of human experts and existing research evidence to solve problems. They suggest solutions to problems by applying the same rules of thumb that human experts use to narrow the range of possible actions.[2] They are not simply number crunchers but instead use "fuzzier," human-like logic in attempting to support problem analysis.

For example, with the rapidly increasing complexity of employee benefits, benefits counseling has become a challenge. An expert system that incorporates the decision processes of benefits experts as well as actuarial data could be developed to advise employees regarding their benefits. Factors such as employee age, risk aversion, family status, retirement and health goals, and availability of other coverage could be provided by the employee during an interactive session. On the basis of the information the employee has provided, the expert system could suggest to the employee the optimal distribution of his or her benefit dollars within the company's flexible benefits options. As with all expert systems, the final decision is made by the user, in this case the employee; but the system could help focus the employee's alternatives, reflecting expert thought processes and complex analyses.

Because expert systems hold exciting potential for the HR field, they have recently begun to receive some attention in the HR literature. Thus far, expert systems have rarely been used for HR applications. Whether they will be effectively applied to the HR function remains to be seen.[3]

**Desktop Publishing**   Recent software and hardware improvements are creating a new industry—desktop publishing. Using desktop publishing software and improved laser printing capabilities, organizations and vendors can produce documents that have virtually typeset quality with greater ease and less expense than in the past. Reports and documents complete with integrated graphics, borders, columns, headlines, and other publication features can be developed.

Desktop publishing capabilities can be applied to support the HR function. Surveys, performance appraisal forms, training materials, and other forms and documents can be developed in-house. These materials will be updated and improved more often because changes will not be as expensive or time-consuming as in the past. Employee communication pieces, including benefits statements and newsletters, could also be developed in-house, providing better, more attractive, and more persuasive feedback. In general, desktop publishing may prove to be a valuable public relations tool. Instead of relying on outside firms or other departments in the company, some HR departments may establish their own desktop publishing capabilities.

## User Interfaces

Some of the most important changes in HRISs will be in their user interfaces—the parts of the system that the user sees and interacts with. As the user pool extends to the line and into upper management, the way users access the system must become simpler. Some of the necessary technology exists today, but its use should become universal in the future. Some of the innovations in user interfaces are discussed below.

**Front-Ends**    One way in which user access is improving is through the use of microcomputer front-ends to mainframe systems. Currently, it is easier to learn to use a microcomputer system than a mainframe system. Companies that need to maintain a mainframe system may link a microcomputer front-end to their system. This allows less sophisticated users to access the HRIS through the microcomputer without having to learn the nuances of the mainframe. Power users can continue to use the mainframe for their needs.

**Natural Language Interfaces**    All HRISs need to have report writing and ad hoc query capabilities. Over the years, query languages have improved, becoming easier to use. The trend is toward what can be called *natural language interfaces*. Eventually, requests for information will sound less like computer programming languages and more like the way we speak. This will both facilitate access to less sophisticated users and reduce the learning curve for power users.

**Other Ease-of-Use Features**    Future HRISs may incorporate other ease-of-use features. Rather than relying solely on the keyboard, some HRISs will incorporate alternative means of accessing the system. Touch screen technology allows users to touch a point on the screen (perhaps designated by an icon or a symbol) to invoke a command.

Some computer systems use a mouse to communicate with the system. A mouse is a device that when rolled on a desk moves a pointer across the computer screen. Clickers or buttons on the mouse are pressed when the pointer is in the desired spot to invoke a command.

These technologies exist today and will probably be incorporated into the HRISs of the future. In addition, as technology improves, systems that use voice activated interfaces, image capture boards that incorporate video camera images into the computer, or other exotic tools that will improve system usability may be used.[4]

*User Access Guidelines*    Recently IBM has put forth a concept they refer to as Systems Application Architecture (SAA).[5] Among other features, this concept suggests using "common user access" (CUA). CUA implies that all applications that are developed based on SAA guidelines will incorporate similar user access features (e.g., pressing function key F1 can always call up user help messages). The idea is that a user who moves from one application to another or from one computer to another would have a head start on using the new system. Time will tell whether IBM's SAA approach catches on. However, the idea of standard user features across systems may be a valuable one, at least within organizations if not for the entire computer industry.

## Communication Links

Communication links include a variety of system connections, including mainframe to microcomputer, data base to data base, IBM to Apple computers, and corporate headquarters to field sites. Currently, communication links remain an obstacle to maximizing HRISs' potential. Improving connectivity is a challenge to allowing smooth data integration and sharing across diverse users and locations.[6] During the next few years dramatic improvements in this area will impact the way HR information is used.

*LANs and WANs*    Local area networks (LANs) and wide area networks (WANs) that link computers together, allowing information sharing among users, are already being used.[7] Improvements will allow LANs and WANs to accommodate more users with greater speed and ease and fewer problems. Organizations will use multiple, interconnected LANs to facilitate information sharing. In the distant future, perhaps wireless LANs, in which information is shared between computers without the need for cables, will be possible.

*Upload, Download, and Data Base Connectivity*    Many organizations link their microcomputers to a centralized mainframe. They upload and download information between their mainframe and microcomputers. While this may sound simple, in practice it can be quite difficult.

In the future the upload/download process will be vastly simplified. Microcomputer front-ends will be able to send, receive, and process information with the mainframe smoothly, quickly, and efficiently. Simultaneous processing between microcomputers and mainframes will be possible. In addition, improved linkages between data bases will allow for greater information sharing among users.

*Remote Access*   Telecommunications to allow cross-country and cross-world information sharing will be used much more. The marketplace has become a global one, and many companies have offices around the world.[8] The ability to share HR information on a worldwide basis will become more critical.

Finally, more companies will use information kiosks (similar to automatic teller machines) and direct phone-to-computer linkups. With these, employees can check the accuracy of their personnel information, inquire about health insurance coverage, or check a pension balance. Remote access allows employees to share the advantages of a state-of-the-art HRIS without an increase in the Human Resources Information Center (HRIC) staff to personally answer every employee question. HR personnel will no longer need to be directly involved in addressing these time-consuming and common requests.

Together, these advances in communications will enable users in the field to immediately update a centralized data base and to access up-to-the-minute data from elsewhere in the organization. Information from different data bases will be able to be combined, and diverse geographic locations will be served. Restrictions will be based more on company policy, as they should be, and less on technical feasibility.

## Changes in HR Practice

HR practice will undergo rapid change in the next decade. There will be a continuing shift from a record-keeping focus to a more proactive decision-making and consulting role. This does not mean that the traditional information management role of HR will decrease in importance but rather that HR managers will shift to a greater emphasis on strategy, decision making, and the use of information to enhance the quality of business decisions. They will take a greater "customer" focus, providing services to support the business, and a more consulting role than in the past.

HR will still be the caretaker of the employees and, naturally, will remain sensitive to changing government regulations that affect the human resources of the firm. They will still need to be able to provide basic employment services effectively and cost-efficiently.

However, HR managers will be released from some of the paperwork requirements demanded by manual systems that dominated their time and fiscal resources. They will be able to shift their focus.

## Strategy and Decision Making

Many have argued that HR professionals need to take a more strategic approach,[9] and the literature cited in Chapters 1, 3, and 8 indicates this has already begun. Unfortunately, the demands of day-to-day HR management have often precluded giving adequate attention to strategic issues. The growing concern of top management regarding labor costs as well as the availability of information introduced through the HRIS means greater opportunities for HR managers to become involved in strategic planning activities. In the future, this trend will continue.

*Information to Support Strategy*    The ability to provide relevant information quickly and accurately will facilitate the HR group getting more involved in the strategic planning process. Better integration of information is one key. As a result of the predicted improvements in relational data base capabilities and communication linkages, greater integration of information within the HR function should occur. For example, many companies will establish tracking systems that will combine employee attitude data, cost information, payroll information, turnover data, and performance records to assess the HR effectiveness of various business units or functions. These will be used to assist organizational strategy (e.g., Is this unit ready for expansion?) and to target HR interventions.

In addition, companies will begin to integrate HR information along with information from other functions (e.g., marketing, finance, accounting) to provide executives with a clearer picture of overall functioning. The work underway in executive information systems (EISs) is the foundation for this advancement. Technological advances in data bases, communication links, and user interfaces will facilitate the development of future EISs. HR information will be an integral part of these systems, which will further necessitate HR involvement in a strategic role.

***DSSs and Other Relevant Applications***   In conjunction with this greater emphasis on strategic planning, HR will be more involved in developing and using DSSs and modeling techniques. As with the DSS examples in Chapters 8 and 9, the ability to ask (and receive answers to) what-if questions about decision alternatives will help foster a strategic orientation. The development of models based on known associations among HR variables will lead to a greater use of DSSs in the HR function. This modeling is also likely to lead to greater precision in HR decisions and to enhance HR's contribution to the bottom line as management starts using this tool to aid their decision-making process. This development of DSS capability will enhance the consulting role of the HR professional with management.

In addition, other strategic HR applications, including HR planning, labor negotiations, succession planning, international staffing, and all forms of cost analysis, will increase. As health-care costs continue to rise and organizations become more cost conscious, the cost-effectiveness and accountability of HR will be emphasized increasingly. Benefit analyses will surpass compensation analyses as the primary focus of some systems.

As more companies become involved in the international arena, effective international staffing will become essential to organizational success. International data bases will require some different data elements, analyses, and reports than their U.S. counterparts. Dealing with international data bases will become a critical HRIS function. Applications that can support international staffing, including recruitment, placement, and compensation, will become more prevalent.

HRISs will make cost and utility analyses considerably easier to accomplish. That is, HR will be able to monitor the costs and benefits of many of its programs and activities, and these figures will be used to justify budgetary planning. The role of HR practitioners has already begun to change in many firms, and the increased use of the HRIS is accelerating this change.

## *Customer Focus and Consulting Role*

A related change that will occur in HR practice is a move toward more of a customer focus and a consulting role.[10] That is, the HR group will focus on providing services to employees, line managers, and senior management, often by serving as an internal consultant. This will better enable the HR function to truly support the business.

The HRIS will help facilitate and accelerate this change. Many administrative tasks that previously required significant amounts of time (e.g., EEO reports) will be made much easier and less time-consuming by HRISs. Although it is unlikely that fewer HR staff members will be required, their time will be more productively spent supporting the business. Efficiencies in gathering information and generating reports will likely be offset by increases in the demand for information by government agencies, line and senior management, and employees. It is possible that companies will have more HR generalists in the field providing direct support to the business (i.e., closer to their customers) and fewer centralized administrative support personnel.

As HR departments become more proficient using their HRISs, line managers will expect more from the system and more from the HR function. They will get this support from the HRIC as well as from HR practitioners assigned to the field. In general, HR professionals will spend more time working with others, both managers and employees, providing content expertise (e.g., assistance with benefits, recruiting, outplacement) and information resource support. This should help enhance HR's image and status since they will more effectively serve their organizational clients.

## Smaller Businesses

HR practice will also change for smaller organizations. The advent of sophisticated microcomputer-based HRISs will give smaller organizations the ability to support HR activities that once were available only to larger organizations. For example, smaller organizations will be able to offer their employees cafeteria benefit plans and other sophisticated benefits. As government reporting and testing requirements grow, HRISs may offer virtually the only hope for complying. In the longer term, expert systems may provide HR managers in the small organization with advice typically available only to larger organizations with extensive staffs.

## Applied Research Activities

Finally, applied research activities in HR departments will increase as the HRIS is implemented. Applied research involves investigations that focus on practical HR or management problems that are seriously interfering with the operation of the firm (e.g., an abnormally high turnover rate). This is a specialized form of internal consulting.

Because time spent on paperwork requirements will decr[e]
professional can focus more on problem analysis. Given the
of the computer to compute mathematical and statistical analyses quickly,
more and more HR professionals will be spending their time analyzing rather
than simply reporting. They will be more capable of determining if their
ideas about problems are right or wrong. For example, the employment
manager may feel a turnover problem is due to a heavy reliance on one
source for new recruits. With the HRIS, he or she can easily check this
hypothesis by examining the tenure and job performance of all employees
hired from that source and comparing it with other sources. Improvements
in ad hoc query capabilities will further support this role. Naturally,
these changed roles for HR professionals mean changed needs in skills and
staffing.

## Changes in HR Skills and Staffing

Just as the demands on the HR department are changing, the skills and training of HR professionals will need to change. At one time it was sufficient to
be a competent administrator to manage the human resource function. And,
as the standard line went, to be an effective HR professional, all one needed
was to be "good with people." Today and in the future, however, the successful HR professional must be part HR generalist, part HR functional specialist, part consultant, part business manager, *and* must understand and be
comfortable using information systems.[11] The introduction of the HRIS into
modern HR departments has demanded that the HR professional develop a
new mix of skills to do his or her job effectively. This change in skill mix
will require different training and career patterns.

### Academic Programs

Traditional academic programs have targeted the HR content areas.
Undergraduate and graduate programs in business have provided a strong
foundation in management and the knowledge base of HR. Until very
recently, however, students interested in HR careers received little formal
training in the use of computers and HRISs. Several universities have begun
to include HRISs as part of their curriculum. For example, the Industrial and
Labor Relations School at Cornell University has integrated computers into

their undergraduate program, and Rutgers University includes HRIS education in a number of managerial training courses. The State University of New York at Albany has developed a specialization in HRISs in their Masters of Business Administration program. Organizations are beginning to demand computer competence in new HR hires. As a result, the trend to increased systems education in college programs is likely to continue.

## Professional Development

HR professionals currently in organizations are also going to need to update their HRIS skills. This can be accomplished in a variety of ways. Training programs, both internal and external, will focus more on the HRIS. Some of these programs and the professional organizations that provide them were mentioned in Chapter 3. These programs provide information about the use of HRIS technology and its management.

Job rotation programs in HR will begin to include HRIS assignments as critical components. It may be argued that the best place to start a career is in the HRIC. Experience with the HRIS allows HR professionals to get an overview of all areas of HR by understanding the type, flow, analysis, and use of data and information by each client of the HR department. Such rotation assignments also allow current employees in the HR department to understand the interrelationships between HR functions and the relation of the HR department to other departments in the organization.

It is also likely that HRIS assignments will be critical later in the careers of HR professionals. At this point, the focus will be on managing the system rather than operating it. As operators of the HRIS, HR professionals are becoming aware of the power and capabilities of the system. Managing the changes brought about by the HRIS is the next challenge for HR professionals. In addition to management and administrative skills, systems management skills are becoming a critical requirement for HR managers. It is hard to conceive of a senior HR professional in the year 2000 who has not had some HRIS experience.

## Changes in Organization and Structure

HR departments are going to experience significant changes and restructuring in the future as a function of the acquisition or reautomation of an HRIS. As discussed in Chapters 4 and 7, implementing a new HRIS is a major organizational change that affects a variety of stakeholders or users. Things will not be the same in the organization in terms of the management of its human resources. This change will manifest in a number of ways. For our purposes, two general and seemingly contradictory trends, decentralization and centralization, are the focus. In addition, the relationship between the HR department and the EDP/MIS group is addressed.

HR departments in the future are likely to experience both the decentralization of some functions and the centralization of others.

## Decentralization

It can be argued that there is a general trend toward decentralization in all areas of management. Layers of management are being eliminated and managerial responsibility is being pushed lower in the organization. The adoption of an HRIS has made decentralization of the HR function possible. New technologies and software make information more readily available. This allows HR departments to make information more accessible at all levels of the organization. New technologies ranging from LANs to WANs and information kiosks allow all types of users to access information. Improved communication links and user interfaces will allow the hands-on user pool to expand.

Line managers will be able to generate many of their own reports without relying on the HR or EDP group. Large organizations utilizing networks and distributed data bases will allow the "local" HR group to acquire, maintain, and manipulate information about "their" employees. The local HR group will generate reports and "own" their data. Thus, large corporate HR staffs become less necessary as decentralization progresses; local HR teams will support the business units.

## Continued Centralization

At the same time decentralization is occurring, some areas will maintain or increase their centralized focus. Subfunctions such as compensation planning and management, payroll, benefits, and government reporting are likely to remain centralized. Given the increased regulation in the area of compensation and benefits discrimination testing and the severity of penalties, it is unlikely that compliance in this area will ever be decentralized. Likewise, staff planning and interdivisional transfer programs are also likely to remain centralized. The corporate HR staff is likely to become smaller and more specialized as they deal with fewer but more technical topics. A strategic decision facing all larger companies will be to determine which activities are to remain centralized and which can be better served in the field. Although most companies have already grappled with this issue, changes in technology will force them to reevaluate their decisions.

As the HR department extends the HRIS to more and more of the HR subfunctions, the internal structure of the department will change. Some HR professionals will be specifically assigned roles as HRIS specialists, and in larger organizations an HRIC may be established. Where company size does not allow this expenditure, the control of the HRIS will be placed in a separate section. As indicated in Exhibit 1.4, the HRIS serves all the HR subfunctions. The HRIS section will emerge as an independent, service-oriented group.

### Relationship with EDP/MIS

Many organizations that have implemented an HRIS have witnessed friction between the HR and EDP/MIS groups. In part this is a function of miscommunication. Often, the EDP/MIS group did not understand the needs of the HR department, and the HR group lacked the computer sophistication to clearly express their HRIS needs. Hopefully, this will become less of a problem in the future.

As the HR department staff members become more computer sophisticated, they will be in a better position to talk with the EDP/MIS group. Many organizations are hiring HRIS specialists to serve as liaisons to the EDP/MIS group. While initially this raises the issue of turf infringement, it has been our experience that the EDP/MIS group eventually respects the HR department more, and the HR department is better able to express their needs when they have internal computer expertise. In addition, some companies are on their second, third, or fourth HRIS. It is becoming more common for the EDP/MIS group to have someone with HRIS project experience. This also facilitates the communication between the two groups.

Although there may always be some friction between the EDP/MIS groups and the HR department, their relations should improve in the future.

## Applied Research Needs

Applied research will be needed to support these projected changes in the HR function. Research is called for in the following areas: (1) instrumentation in needs analysis techniques and implementation; (2) development of DSSs, artificial intelligence, and expert systems in HR; (3) implementation and system effectiveness; and (4) the user learning curve.

The first of these topics deals with developing accurate and acceptable ways of evaluating the various phases of systems development and implementation. If possible, standardized surveys should be developed to assess employees' attitudes before, during, and after implementation of the HRIS. Likewise, a comprehensive methodology for needs analysis would be quite useful. This would include questionnaires, interview formats, and focus group protocols. Such research will lead to improved needs analysis techniques and, in turn, improved system effectiveness.

The development of DSSs and other expert systems in HR has already begun. However, the critical element in artificial intelligence, DSSs, or any expert system is the underlying mathematical model that defines the functional relationships among the HR variables, including cost information. Without these data regarding costs, it is exceedingly difficult to build and use a DSS in an organization since costs, whether in the public or private sector, are the bottom line. This process of model development is critical before further DSS development in HR can proceed.

Because implementation is so critical, researchers should also study how various implementation strategies relate to system effectiveness. Which factors are related to system effectiveness? What is system effectiveness? How can organizations best structure their implementation and support processes to encourage system use and effectiveness? As systems are implemented in other countries, how do cultural differences influence the implementation process? What should be done to facilitate international implementation efforts? Both case studies and cross-organizational empirical studies should prove helpful to future development efforts.

A related research issue deals with improving the learning curve. What can be done to facilitate user learning? How should user training be structured? How should user interfaces, screens, and reports be arranged? What forms of documentation are most effective? Research that improves our understanding of the user's learning curve will assist trainers and system designers in improving system use. It should reduce learning time and decrease user errors.

As a field, we should continue to conduct research regarding HRISs and should share the results of that research. This research sharing can help guide and advance the application of HRISs in the future.

# In Closing . . .

Because of regulatory, business, labor market, and technology pressures, human resources management is rapidly changing. Human resource information systems are becoming an integral part of HR practice. HRISs can help support a company's HRM system and, in turn, their strategic management system as well. Indeed, it is unlikely that organizations will be able to manage their human resources very effectively in the future without using an HRIS.

The HRIS is a tool to enhance HR management. As with any tool, it can be used effectively or ineffectively. In this book the critical issues associated with using an HRIS have been highlighted. A successful HRIS begins with an appreciation of what it is and of the environment in which it must function. Next, a project plan is developed and a formal needs analysis conducted. The importance of a thorough needs analysis cannot be emphasized enough. It is unlikely that you will be satisfied with a system if you do not really know what you want it to accomplish. The system is then designed and developed or purchased. Implementation is also a critical step, because a system is only as good as the willingness of the users to work with it. Finally, systems must be maintained and evaluated. Any system will cease to serve the needs of the organization if it is not maintained. HRIS management is an ongoing process, not a one-time event.

One final thought: an HRIS is only one part of the larger human resources system. HR professionals are first and foremost HR professionals, not computer operators. However, by better utilizing new technologies, HR professionals can become more effective and can contribute more effectively to organizational goals.

# Notes

1. Impending changes in the labor market led the American Society for Personnel Administration to convene a panel to identify major areas for change in the HR field of the future. The areas they identified are (1) education, training, and retraining; (2) demographics; (3) work and family relationships; (4) productivity and competitiveness; and (5) employer/employee rights and responsibilities. The results of this panel can be found in C. D. Bower and J. J. Hallet, "Issues Management at ASPA," *Personnel Administrator* 34 (January 1989): 40–43.
2. V. Krebs, "Can Expert Systems Make HR Decisions?" *Computers in Personnel* (Winter 1988): 4–8.

3. For more about expert systems, see M. M. Extejt and M. P. Lynn, "Expert Systems as Human Resource Management Decision Tools," *Journal of Systems Management* (November 1988): 10–15; M. Turner, *Expert Systems: A Management Guide* (Princeton, NJ: PA Computers and Telecommunications, 1987); R. G. Vedder, "Teaching Artificial Intelligence in the Business School," *Interface* 8(4) (1987): 19–22; C. Carr, "Expert Support Environments," *Personnel Journal* (April 1989): 117–126.

4. For more on video technology, see R. Nardoni, "Micro-based Video Applications in Human Resources," *HRSP Review* (Winter 1987): 5–8.

5. The SAA concept goes well beyond common user access and is quite technical. To read more about SAA, see the SAA issue of the *IBM Systems Journal* 27(3) (1988); and J. Tibbetts, "The SAA Pioneer: SAA Iconography," *SAA Age* 1(10) (1989): 16–19.

6. B. Radford, "The Connectivity Challenge in HRIS," *Personnel Administrator* (July 1988): 61–63 includes a case study of the connectivity issues within a company that has an IBM-PC–based local area network and a VAX 11-780 and uses a payroll vendor that has an IBM mainframe.

7. The LAN market is expected to demonstrate a compounded average growth rate of at least 45 percent over the next five years according to R. B. Fireworker and H. Stewart, "Guidelines for Success with LANs," *Journal of Systems Management* (May 1988): 36–39. For more information about LANs, see T. Liang, "Local Area Networks: Implementation of Considerations," *Journal of Systems Management* (January 1988): 6–12.

8. R. L. Totterdale, "The Global Reach of Distributed Processing," *Computers in Personnel* (Fall 1987): 4–10.

9. R. E. Miles and C. C. Snow, "Designing Strategic Human Resource Management Systems," *Organizational Dynamics* (1984): 36–52; R. Schuler and I. C. MacMillan, "Gaining Competitive Advantage Through Human Resource Management Practices," *Human Resource Management* 23 (1984): 241–255.

10. R. Schuler, "A Case Study of the HR Department at Swiss Bank Corporation: Customerization for Organizational Effectiveness," *Human Resource Planning* 11(4) (1988): 241–253; R. S. Schuler and S. E. Jackson, "Customerization: The Ticket to Better HR Business," *Personnel* (June 1988): 36–44.

11. According to one consulting firm that caters to Fortune 500 and Fortune 50 financial firms, "One out of three searches since 1982 has required of the candidate hands-on experience designing and/or implementing integrated planning and tracking systems . . .". This was cited in C. J. Despres and T. H. Rowley, "Desktop Computing and HRM: A Professional Challenge," *Personnel Administrator* (May 1986): 65.

# Appendix:
# Data Flow Diagrams

Data flow diagrams (DFDs) are the major tools of structured analysis, which is a way of usefully partitioning a broad area that needs specification, in this case, the HRIS. A DFD is a network representation of a system. According to DeMarco, with DFDs the system can be understood without a "monolithic Victorian novel" set of specifications.[1] The purpose of a DFD is to portray the system in terms of its component pieces, with all interfaces among the components indicated.

DFDs show, in graphic form, how data flow through and are transformed within a system. Thus, in an idealized HRIS derived during the needs analysis, data flows and transformations for all the programs within the HR function are shown. However, keep in mind that the major purpose of DFDs is to communicate. DFDs are meant to stimulate dialogue among users and designers, and through this dialogue to produce DFDs with more specific details to capture the HRIS in graphic form. As illustrated in Exhibit A.1, DFDs use four basic elements: (1) data flows, represented by straight lines or vectors that are named; (2) processes of the data, represented by circles or "bubbles"; (3) files or data stores, represented by open-ended polygons; and (4) data sources or destinations (sinks), represented by boxes.

**Exhibit A.1**   Data Flow Diagram Elements

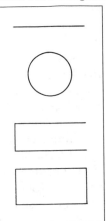

Exhibit A.2 contains a DFD for estimating personnel supply in a typical human resources planning (HRP) program in the HR department. The other part of the HRP program, the estimate of future demand of employees, is not shown since this would complicate this introductory example. In fact,

**Exhibit A.2**   Data Flow Diagram of HR Supply Forecasting

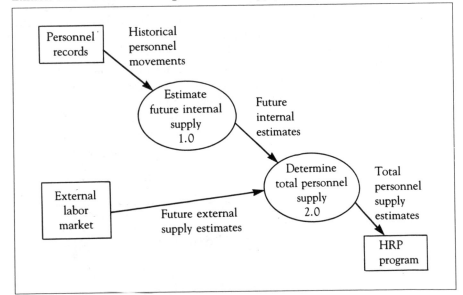

for better communications the user may want to keep the personnel demand forecasting in a separate DFD.

In Exhibit A.2, the data for internal estimates of available employees in the firm in the future come from the personnel records, indicated as a source on the left side of the DFD. The source for the data on the future external supply estimates is the external labor market. Since the data from the external labor market usually come in the form of estimates, there is no need to have a processing, or data transformation, bubble as there is in the case of internal supply estimates. Since the data from the personnel records are simply historical movements, both turnover and internal transfers, demotions, and promotions, there is a need for a processing bubble (1.0) to estimate future internal supply. This would be done through the typical statistical or mathematical techniques available. Notice that the name of the data flow changes after it passes through a processing bubble, thus indicating a transformation of the data. The final data flow, total personnel supply estimates, would then go to a sink, that is, the HRP program. There could easily be files in the DFD, for example, for any of the data flows. However, these were omitted to keep this example simple.

Several additional points about Exhibit A.2 are worth noting. First, all data flows must be named. Second, after it passes through a processing bubble, the data flow must change names. Third, data flows from files are not named, since it is assumed the system users know what is necessary to access from the file. Fourth, each bubble is numbered. This enables the system analyst to develop *layered* data flow diagrams. Each of the bubbles in Exhibit A.2 could be "exploded" to a new DFD that would show exactly what happens in the transformation of the data flow. For example, bubble 2.0 could be a new DFD showing how the two estimates, internal and external, are combined to form a total. This could vary in detail. The level of specificity of a layered DFD is primarily left to the discretion of the system analyst and the user or client—remember, the primary goal of DFDs is to communicate. Their value lies in the user's changes to the initial DFD. This iterative process in the development of DFDs between the system analyst and the user assures the final product will be as accurate as possible.

# Note

1. DeMarco, *Structured Analysis*.

# Glossary

**Action-research organizational development** An approach to planned change in organizations (organization development or OD) that involves an interaction between taking specific actions and collecting data, through research, to evaluate those actions.

**Ad hoc query or inquiry** Statements or commands given to a computer or data base system that cause information to be extracted from the data base. Ad hoc queries are not usually stored in the system and are not part of the regular reports available to users. Typically, they provide an "immediate" answer to a one-time question that a fixed or library report cannot address.

**Ad hoc report** Report that is not standard on the HRIS, which results from an ad hoc inquiry. Although this type of report is usually printed out in hard copy, it can usually be viewed on a terminal screen before printing.

**Adverse impact** A statistical decision that the organization has unfairly discriminated on the basis of a protected category under law (race, gender, age, handicapped, Vietnam veteran, etc.) in terms of an employment decision, for example, hiring, promotion, pay raise, or layoff.

**Age Discrimination in Employment Act (ADEA)**    Federal law of 1967, amended in 1986, that prohibits employers from discriminating on the basis of age against people over 40 years of age. It also eliminates mandatory retirement for most employees.

**Air Force Human Resources Laboratory (AFHRL)**    The military installation that does applied research on the human resources of the U.S. Air Force.

**American Payroll Association**    A professional organization interested in payroll and compensation issues. The organization provides training and certification of payroll personnel.

**American Society of Personnel Administration (ASPA)**    The national professional organization for anyone who works in the personnel/human resources field. In 1989, the name of this organization was changed to the Society for Human Resource Management (SHRM).

**Applicant-tracking system**    An information system that is used to keep track of people who apply for positions in a company. In computerized form, this is usually a software package that keeps track of new entries (employees) into an organization as well as those who were not selected.

**Application**    In the context of this book, this can be any HR subfunction that is transferred from a manual mode to a computer mode. For example, see Applicant-tracking system.

**Application generator**    A software program that assists users or programmers in creating other software programs or applications. These are most commonly found in association with data base products. For example, R:Base for DOS uses an application generator to query users about the basic functions of an application and then proceeds to write the program code to create the application.

**Backup system**    For any computer-based HR system, a backup copy of all files must be kept. Although this can be a manual backup in a file cabinet, it is usually better to have a backup record of your entire HRIS on floppy disk or magnetic tape.

**Batch system**    A computer system in which jobs can be submitted at any time but are only run in batches at a certain time, for example, Tuesday at 10:00 A.M. or every day at 4:00 P.M. This system is different than an online system, in which computer jobs can be run as received at any time.

**Bits**    The means by which most computers store information, usually in terms of 0's or 1's.

**Black box system**   A computer system or software program which is so poorly documented that the program structure or operating logic of the system is unknown to the users. "It works, but we're not sure why."

**Byte**   A single character (e.g., the letter "J") composed of 8 bits.

**Cafeteria benefit plan**   Employee benefits formerly were offered only as a predetermined package, that is, a certain pension and medical plan, holidays off, and so on. With the advent of dual-job families, many companies are offering flexible benefit programs, usually called cafeteria plans, in which the employee chooses to accept or refuse various benefit options.

**Cataloged or library report**   A report that, although not distributed on a standard basis, resides in a catalog or library and is available upon request.

**Changing**   The second phase of Lewin's three-stage model of planned organizational change. During this phase employees' values, attitudes, and behaviors are reshaped.

**Compensable factor**   A factor or characteristic of a job that an organization uses to determine its wage and salary structure. For example, the amount of skill required on a job is usually a compensable factor.

**Compiler**   A software program that converts English-like computer statements (e.g., GO TO) to binary code known as machine language.

**Comprehensive information inventory**   The third step in the DECIDE approach to needs analysis. It involves collecting the information used by the HR department.

**Comprehensive Omnibus Budget Reconciliation Act (COBRA)**   A piece of federal legislation that requires all group health plans (except for federal government and church plans) to offer health benefits to a variety of former employees (terminated or retired). This complex law is still being interpreted by the courts.

**Computer virus**   A computer program that often damages data or other software programs. Virus programs attach themselves to other programs and thereby gain entry to new computer systems when users share programs or data.

**Computer workstation**   The physical equipment necessary for a user to interact with a computer, either a microcomputer, minicomputer, or mainframe computer.

**Cost/benefit ratio**   This ratio involves comparing the costs and benefits of any new product or program, expressed in dollars. It is used to decide whether to purchase the item. In this book, for example, it could be an evaluation of whether or not to acquire an HRIS.

**CPM (Critical Path Method)**   A project management technique that identifies the most critical activities and their time milestones to monitor the progress of the entire project.

**Crash**   When the computer system stops functioning or breaks down unexpectedly.

**Customized software**   After a company has purchased a software package from a vendor, it is usually necessary to modify it to fit the specific environment. This results in customized software.

**Data base**   A collection of information arranged in order so it can be accessed by computer programs.

**Data base management system (DBMS)**   Software packages designed to facilitate the input, manipulation, and output of information. Popular products of this type include dBASE IV and R:Base for DOS.

**Data conversion**   The process of changing from an old system to a new one. It addresses the question, Will the new system run under real conditions?

**Data dumps or extracts**   Raw data that have been downloaded from one system, typically for entry into another system.

**Data element**   Also referred to as a field, a data element is composed of a series of bytes. Employee name, health coverage code, and salary are examples of data elements or data fields.

**Data flow diagram**   A graphic representation of how data flow to, from, and within a system as well as of the processes that transform the data and the places where the data are stored (see the Appendix for an example).

**Data integrity**   Refers to the maintenance of the accuracy and timeliness of information in the computer system. Also includes procedures to ensure that changes to data elements are made correctly and by users authorized to make those changes.

**Data processing (DP) department** *or* **DP/MIS department** *or* **MIS department**   The department within the organization that is responsible for computer operations.

**DECIDE**   The six-step needs analysis process described in this book.

**Decision Support System (DSS)**   A computer-based, interactive system of software and hardware used to aid decision makers. It allows decision makers to ask "what-if" questions regarding decision alternatives and to receive rapid answers, usually on a computer terminal.

**Distributed data base**   System in which the data base is maintained in discrete units at several locations. Requests for information from the data base may require data to be extracted from several locations.

**Distributed processing**   Data manipulation is done at a number of physically separate locations or computers. Often, each site conducts some of its own processing and uploads other tasks to other sites.

**Documentation**   Manuals and other written information about the operation, maintenance, or design of a computer system or software package.

**Download**   Passing information from a mainframe computer to another system or storage medium.

**Early information inventory (EII)**   A stage in the DECIDE approach to needs analysis. It involves preliminary familiarization with the range of information used by the HR department.

**Edit controls**   Management practices and standards that regulate the input and alteration of information in the HRIS. For example, only certain individuals may be authorized to change salary information.

**EEO** *or* **EEO/AA**   Acronyms for Equal Employment Opportunity and Affirmative Action, which refer to the program within the organization that is designed to meet the guidelines of various laws and regulations regarding fair employment opportunities for all people.

**EEO code**   Usually refers to numbers that indicate racial and gender information regarding employees.

**EEO-1 report**   An annual report required by regulatory agencies that is designed to show how well organizations are complying with fair employment laws and regulations.

**Electronic Data Processing (EDP)**   The automated processing of routine information like monthly reports of salaries paid.

**Employee assistance program**   HR programs concerned with providing help to employees who need it. Typically this involves drug and alcohol problem referrals and help with other personal problems.

**Employee master file**   File that contains all the relevant information needed by the organization about each employee. In a manual or computer system, this is the largest information file, and pieces of it are used for all individual applications.

**Employee Retirement Income Security Act (ERISA)**    Federal law passed to eliminate corrupt practices in retirement fund management and to protect the retirement benefits of employees.

**Executive information system (EIS)**    System designed to present data from several data bases in a manner that is usable and understandable to computer-naive executives.

**Exempt employees**    Employees who are exempt from coverage under the Fair Labor Standards Act (FSLA).

**Executive support systems (ESS)**    See Executive information systems.

**Field**    See Data element.

**File**    A computer file contains information on a specific topic or group. It is composed of many records that describe the people, jobs, or whatever is in the file. For example, the employee benefits file would contain data elements pertaining to employee benefits and would include that information for all employees.

**Flat file**    A data base design in which all data elements are retained in a single table.

**Flextime**    An organizational program that allows employees to vary the times they arrive and leave the workplace. It usually requires that each workday include certain core hours for everyone—for example, 9 A.M. to 3 P.M. daily.

**401(k) retirement plan**    Special retirement plan that permits employees to place more of their current earnings into their pension fund without being taxed. It is a way to avoid higher taxes on current earnings; the taxes are paid on the lower retirement income.

**Full time equivalents (FTE)**    An indication of the number of full time employees that it would take to work a given number of hours. For example, a 20-hour-a-week worker would equal .5 FTEs.

**Gantt chart**    A graphic representation of the time line and major objectives of a project to be used for project management.

**General ledger**    The accounting system used by an organization. All financial data pass through and are consolidated in the general ledger.

**Hardware**    The physical equipment in a computer system. Software runs on the hardware.

**Homegrown documentation**    The record of the special activities necessary to implement a part of or the entire HRIS in an organization. It is a historical record of how it was done.

**HR functional specialist**   A human resources professional who is trained in and assigned to a specific HR subfunction (e.g., compensation).

**HRIS strategy**   The long-term plan for acquiring and maintaining information and computer systems in the HR function.

**HR subfunctions**   The various programmatic efforts that constitute the HR function in the organization.

**Human Resource Information Center (HRIC)**   The people (or person) whose primary responsibilities are to support and administer the HRIS. This term refers to the function, not to any physical location.

**Human resource planning (HRP)**   A critical component of the HR function, HRP attempts to identify and implement appropriate activities to ensure that the HR function is supporting company direction. This is done through a process of data collection, analysis, and evaluation.

**Human Resource Systems Professionals (HRSP, Inc.)**   A professional organization that focuses on computer-based HR systems.

**Human resources information system (HRIS)**   A system used to acquire, store, manipulate, analyze, retrieve, and distribute pertinent information regarding an organization's human resources.

**Human resources management system**   The management system that integrates the HR subfunctions and the HRIS.

**Human Resources Planning Society (HRPS)**   A professional organization that focuses on strategic human resource management.

**Icon**   A symbol that stands for a word or idea. For example, a dollar sign might be substituted for the phrase "compensation module."

**Information evaluation**   A stage in the DECIDE approach to needs analysis. This stage involves analyzing the information collected in earlier stages.

**Integrated payroll systems**   Payroll processing information systems that are part of the HRIS rather than a separate system.

**Interactive systems**   Computer applications in which the computer's responses are dependent on the user's actions. Interactive systems work in real time; that is, they process the user's instructions as soon as they are received.

**Interfaced payroll systems**   Settings in which the payroll system and HRIS can exchange data. In some cases the systems may share some limited amount of data.

**Job analysis**   Techniques used to analyze jobs to determine the tasks, duties, knowledge, skills, and abilities necessary for a person to perform on the job.

**Job sharing**   A program that allows more than one person to share the same job within the organization. In a typical arrangement, two part-time employees would share one full-time job.

**Laptop microcomputer**   A small microcomputer that when closed can be easily transported. It takes up relatively little space but can have most of the capabilities of a full-size microcomputer.

**Laser printer**   Computer printer that generates reports more quickly and quietly than previous generations of printers. When used with the necessary software, it can produce reports and graphics that approach or match typeset quality.

**Mainframe computer**   A large freestanding computer that serves a large number of individual users. Processing and storage are done solely at the mainframe computer rather than the terminals attached to it.

**Management information system (MIS)**   The computer-based set of rules and directions that organize pieces of data meaningfully to create information for organizational use.

**Manual system**   An information storage and retrieval system that is not automated. In a manual HR system, employee files are maintained on paper in file cabinets.

**Markov procedures or analysis**   Complex mathematical procedures that can be used to project historical patterns of employee movements into the future.

**Microcomputer**   A personal computer typically small in size and used by one person at a time. Microcomputers may be linked in networks. They are based on single microprocessor chips.

**Minicomputer**   A small computer system that typically supports a number of terminals (as opposed to computers). Several users can use a minicomputer simultaneously.

**MIS department**   See Data processing department.

**Module**   A component of the HRIS that is directed to one specific function of human resources and that has its own input forms, screens, reports, and/or analyses.

**Multiple level password** *or* **password feature**   A characteristic of computer systems that provides security by restricting access. However, users have different accessibility to certain kinds or levels of information in the system's multiple levels.

**Needs analysis**   The process of identifying the information management requirements of an organization or computer application.

**Needs analysis plan**   The specific steps and procedures to be followed in conducting the needs analysis.

**Needs analysis evaluation**   The final step in the DECIDE approach to needs analysis. It involves a critical review of the needs analysis process.

**Network**   An interconnected set of computers that can share information.

**Occupational classification**   The classification of jobs within an organization into categories of similar jobs, commonly called job families. For example, clerical and mechanical are typical job families.

**Occupational Safety and Health Act (OSHA)**   Federal law designed to protect employees from unsafe working conditions.

**Omnibus Budget Reconciliation Act (OBRA)**   This act affected employee benefits in terms of pensions. Starting in 1988, pension accruals and participation are required for employees in company pension plans beyond a plan's normal retirement age (usually 65).

**Organization development (OD)**   The process of managing planned change in an organization. See Action-research organizational development.

**PERT charts**   PERT stands for Program Evaluation and Review Technique. It is a method for graphically showing the sequence of activities in a project. Major objectives are shown as well as a time line in order to manage the project effectively.

**Piggybacking**   The technique used during implementation of the HRIS to test the effective functioning of the new system. The new HRIS is run in parallel with the old HR system.

**Power users**   Technically sophisticated users, they use the system frequently and require greater computing capabilities from the system.

**Privacy Act of 1974**   Federal law that regulates the way in which federal agencies handle information on employees. It is designed to protect the rights of individuals regarding personal information.

**Production or fixed report**   A preprogrammed, unmodified report that is run and distributed on a predetermined time schedule.

**Project team**   In developing and implementing the HRIS, this is the group of people selected to manage the total project. The members are selected based on the importance of the HRIS to their function and are from a variety of departments within the organization.

**Protected classes**    Anyone who is protected by federal or state law from unfair employment discrimination.

**Prototyping**    A sample or shell version of a system's screens, reports, and so on. Prototypes are developed quickly and are used to determine user acceptability and programming feasibility.

**Quality circles**    Teams formed within an organization with the specific goal of increasing productivity quality through higher employee participation.

**Query language**    The syntax or language used to request ad hoc information from the HRIS. It is usually simpler to use than standard computer languages.

**R&D (research and development)**    The HR function within the organization that is responsible for applied research efforts.

**Reautomation**    Projects in which companies are expanding, revising, revamping, or replacing their current HRIS.

**Record**    Each record is made up of many fields or data elements. An employee's record is made up of all the data fields that pertain to an employee and contains only the data for that employee. A job record contains all the data fields used to describe that job.

**Refreezing**    The third phase of Lewin's three-stage model of planned organizational change. This phase involves the stabilization of new behaviors and attitudes consistent with the change that has taken place in the organization.

**Relational data base**    A type of data base design in which information is linked by certain common data elements or relational factors.

**Report**    Formatted information retrieved from a data base.

**Request for proposal (RFP)**    A statement of intent to purchase a particular product or service. It also includes specifications required in the product or service. Interested vendors then respond with proposals or bids on the product or service.

**Screen linking**    Programming a system so that the user will automatically advance to another screen when work on the current screen is completed.

**Service bureaus**    Vendors of computer services to other organizations. Service bureaus most often provide assistance with payroll and accounting tasks.

**Sociotechnical systems organizational development**  A type of organization development that focuses on the interdependence of the technical and social systems when introducing new changes, such as a new HRIS.

**Software**  Computer programs used to analyze data and produce reports.

**Software-hardware configuration**  The specific combination of computer hardware and software that is necessary to accomplish the system's objectives as defined in the needs analysis.

**Stakeholders**  People in the organization who have a vested interest (stake) in the development and implementation of a new HRIS.

**Stand-alone software**  Computer software that is developed for a specific application, such as applicant tracking, as opposed to integrated software for an entire HRIS.

**Status change document**  Form that originates from and is completed by a manager or employee to update the employee's record in the HRIS.

**Strategic management system**  The management system in the organization that generates the strategic plan.

**Survey-based feedback** *or* **survey-guided feedback**  A planned change or OD technique that involves collecting data from employees using surveys, analyzing the data, and then providing feedback from the survey to managers and employees in order to bring about change.

**System maintenance**  Keeping the system operational, including making modifications to correct bugs, dealing with emergencies, and dealing with new requirements.

**System specifications**  The desired outputs, inputs, and processing requirements of the system, and the potential errors and procedures to locate or prevent them.

**Tax Reform Act of 1986**  This act impacted employee benefits in terms of pensions. It attempted to make pension benefits equitable across employees regardless of pay level. Highly paid employees could not have a pension or tax-advantaged plan that was not available to lower paid employees. The Act is highly controversial and will likely be amended.

**Terminal emulation**  A microcomputer acting like or emulating a "dumb" computer terminal with no processing capabilities of its own.

**Testing**  Investigating the readiness of a system. Designed to answer the question, Does the system produce the results it should under specified conditions?

**Title VII of the Civil Rights Act of 1964** Federal regulation that prohibits unfair employment discrimination on the basis of race, color, national origin, religion, and gender.

**Transactions** Discrete actions taken by a computer that are common and repetitive. For example, payroll systems are often transaction based.

**Turnaround document** A form used to confirm the accuracy of data maintained in the HRIS. For example, a turnaround document containing personnel information may be sent to each employee. Each employee would be asked to verify his or her data, adding or correcting data as appropriate.

**Turnover rate** The rate at which employees leave the company. It is usually expressed in the form of a percentage and may be broken down into voluntary and involuntary turnover.

**Unfreezing** The first phase of Lewin's three-stage model of planned organizational change. This phase involves motivating employees to change their current attitudes and behaviors so the organization can be ready to adopt new change.

**Upload** Passing information from a microcomputer or minicomputer to a mainframe computer.

**User interface** The part of the computer system that the user sees and interacts with.

**Vendor** A person or firm who provides services or products for sale to other firms. In HRISs, the most common ones are software and hardware vendors.

**Vendor "demo" packages** Computer software, usually on a floppy disk, provided by a vendor, that demonstrates the capabilities of the total software package.

**Wage survey** A survey of the salaries of selected jobs in a variety of organizations used to determine the wage and salary structure of a single organization.

**Work force dynamics reporting** An examination of employee movements over a period of time including turnover, transfers, promotions, and demotions.

**Work force profile review** A "snapshot" or report of the current work force, including their relevant demographics, that is useful for HR planning purposes.

# Author Index

347

# Subject Index